STEPHEN J. RANDALL is a member of the Department of History at McGill University.

Drawing upon extensive research in the United States, Colombia, and Great Britain, *The Diplomacy of Modernization* examines the evolution of United States foreign policy in Colombia between the world wars, concentrating on the period of the Herbert Hoover and Franklin D. Roosevelt administrations, years generally associated with the formulation and implementation of the Good Neighbor Policy.

Historians of United States-Latin American policy have concentrated on the giants of the inter-war years – Mexico, Cuba, Brazil, and Argentina. Yet the second-ranking powers such as Colombia are particularly significant for an understanding of the factors which shaped inter-American relations, the objectives of U.S. policy, and the impact of a major industrialized nation on a developing society.

By the end of the first world war Colombia occupied an important, though clearly secondary, place in United States-Latin American policy. During the 1920s Colombia was the third- or fourth-ranking trading partner of the United States in South America. Her strategic proximity to the Panama Canal also made her adherence to a pro-United States position an important objective of Washington's policy, as did the promise of major petroleum reserves that were yet to be exploited. Conscious of these issues and concerned that the spark of nationalism generated by the Mexican revolution would inflame other developing nations in Latin America, United States officials in the 1920s and 1930s re-examined the methods of American diplomacy and gradually moved away from the cruder forms of military intervention, gunboat and dollar diplomacy.

In analysing the commercial, financial, and industrial presence of U.S. interests in Colombia and their diplomatic manifestations, this study suggests the extent to which the United States erected a policy designed to provide primacy for American interests rather than the equality of treatment implied in the terms 'good neighbor' and 'open door.'

STEPHEN J. RANDALL

The Diplomacy
of Modernization:
Colombian-American
Relations, 1920-1940

UNIVERSITY OF TORONTO PRESS
Toronto and Buffalo

Library of Congress Cataloging in Publication Data

Randall, Stephen J 1944-
  The diplomacy of modernization.

  Bibliography: p.
  Includes index.
  1. United States – Foreign relations – Colombia. 2. Colombia – Foreign
relations – United States. 3. United States – Foreign relations – 1923-1929.
4. United States – Foreign relations – 1929-1933. 5. United States – Foreign
relations – 1933-1945. I. Title.
  E 183.8.C7R 36   327.73'0861   77-4480
  ISBN 0-8020-5372-6

This book has been published during
the Sesquicentennial year of the University of Toronto

To my family

Contents

viii Contents

Preface

This study grew partly out of my all too brief involvement in Colombian society in 1967 and 1968, when I taught at the National University and Centro Colombo-Americano in Bogotá at the same time that my wife was a graduate student at the Instituto Caro y Cuervo. There are many Colombians who, each in his own way, contributed to this study but may remain unaware of and unthanked for their assistance.

The study also derives from my response as a Canadian to relations with the United States during the past generation. Any analogy between the Canadian and Colombian positions vis-à-vis the United States may be a weak one. Certainly few Colombians today or in the 1920s and 1930s would have identified Canada as an equal victim of American 'imperialism'; yet, weak as the analogy may be, there are similarities which might explain the fact that Canadian nationalists have looked to the Latin American and West Indian experience with a degree of empathy, and that within the Western Hemisphere Canada is identified by some Latin American nations as a potential counterweight against the United States, given Canadian concern for natural resource development and protection of offshore fisheries, and Canadian sensitivity to American investment. Almost identical in population, both Canada and Colombia have been until recently essentially producers of raw materials and semi-finished goods. Both have had export oriented economies and have traditionally provided convenient markets for American manufactured goods and capital investment, although 'modernization' has progressed more rapidly in the Canadian instance. Both countries have for some time been strong supporters of the United States in the international arena, particularly during the Cold War. In both there have been nationalistic stirrings at various times in this century; but in neither instance has nationalism effectively challenged the traditional relationship with the United States. In Colombia and Canada, the years between the two world wars were crucial for determining specific patterns of economic development. These were also the years when New York emerged as the world's financial capital, as the center of power shifted from Europe to the United States.

Although I do not develop the Canadian analogy in this study, it is one which, valid or not, has shaped my understanding of American foreign policy. The chapters which follow are especially concerned with the relationship between government and private enterprise, the factors which shaped policy-making in both the United States and Colombia, and the nature of the Colombian response to the American presence. By examining in detail United States policy in one area of Latin America, we may hope to understand more fully the nature of what became the Good Neighbor policy and why in the short term it appears to have achieved its objectives.

Some personalities accustomed to the limelight I have moved to the wings. This includes presidential figures of the 1920s and to a certain extent presidents Herbert Hoover and Franklin D. Roosevelt, as well as important administration officials such as Sumner Welles during the Roosevelt years. In doing so, I do not intend to negate their contributions to the development of United States foreign policy in Latin America. But one needs to examine more exhaustively other influences and other levels of policy-making in order to grasp the relationship between the articulation of principles in the executive office and their implementation by officials in the middle level bureaucracy and in the field.

My intellectual and personal debts are many. I am grateful to Kenneth McNaught of the University of Toronto for his constant interest, his perceptive insights into the dynamics of the American political economy, and his direction of the manuscript at several stages; and to William C. Berman, also at the University of Toronto, for his constructive criticism, unfailing wit and good humor, and constant friendship. Robert Accinelli's cautious and critical reading of the manuscript contributed to what I hope are important clarifications. Robert F. Smith of the University of Toledo has offered insightful suggestions on a number of occasions. I have benefited as well from conversations and suggestions from David Green, University of Saskatchewan; Sheldon Liss, University of Akron; Geoff Smith, Queen's University; William McGreevey, formerly at the University of California, Berkeley, and with the Smithsonian Institution at the time of writing; Miguel Urrutia Montoya, author of an outstanding work on the Colombian labor movement and a prominent member of the cabinet in the government of Alfonso López Michelsen; and Henry Berger, Washington University, St Louis. The members of the 1974 committee of the Frederick Jackson Turner competition, in which this manuscript was a finalist, provided exhaustive and penetrating critiques which made possible what I hope is a meaningful revision. My gratitude goes as well to those individuals who extended the courtesy of interviews.

For their constant expertise and frequently their individual interest in the project, I would like to thank the librarians and archivists of the following institutions: the National Archives; the Manuscript Division of the Library of Congress; the Columbus Memorial Library of the Pan American Union; the Herbert Hoover Library; the Franklin D. Roosevelt Presidential Library; the Houghton and Baker libraries at Harvard University; the Manuscript Division at Princeton University Library; the Sterling Memorial Library at Yale University for permission to consult and cite from the papers and diary of Henry L. Stimson; the Minnesota Historical Society; the Columbia University Oral History Project; the Biblioteca Nacional and the Biblioteca Luís Angel Arango in Bogotá. Material from the diary of William Phillips is published by permission of the Houghton Library, Harvard. I am grateful to the publishers of *The Journal of Interamerican Studies and World Affairs*, *The Americas*, and *The Canadian Journal of History* for permission to use material which has appeared in their journals.

To M. Jean Houston, Margaret Parker, and other staff of the University of Toronto Press goes my gratitude for providing the encouragement, constructive criticism, and expert guidance which made the tortuous path to publication somewhat smoother. I am especially grateful to G. Matthews of the Geography Department of the University of Toronto for applying his cartographic skills to the preparation of the maps which appear in this volume.

Finally, I should like to draw attention to the fact that this book has been published with the help of a grant from the Social Science Research Council of Canada using funds provided by the Canada Council and grants to University of Toronto Press from the Andrew W. Mellon Foundation and the University of Toronto, and with the additional assistance of the Faculty of Graduate Studies and Research at McGill University.

STEPHEN J. RANDALL
Montreal, August 1976

THE DIPLOMACY OF MODERNIZATION

Abbreviations

BFDC	United States Bureau of Foreign and Domestic Commerce
BPAU	*Bulletin of the Pan American Union*
CR	United States Congressional Record
DANE	Departamento Administrativa Nacional de Estadistica
EWK MSS	Edwin Walter Kemmerer papers
FO	British Foreign Office Files
HAHR	*Hispanic American Historical Review*
JABA	*Journal of the American Bankers Association*
OHC	Oral History Collection, Columbia University
PRO	British Public Record Office
RG	Record Group, National Archives, Washington, DC
SS	Secretary of State
SC	Secretary of Commerce
TWL MSS	Thomas W. Lamont papers

Introduction

There are few watersheds in history, and the more one examines American foreign policy in Latin America after the first world war, the more one is struck by the threads of continuity that run through the fabric of American diplomacy. Certainly there was a shift in international power – political, economic, and military – in favor of the United States after 1918, a fact which made more feasible the realization of policy objectives on the larger stage. In the case of United States-Latin American relations the shift in power was marked primarily by the erosion of British influence and the temporary setback experienced by Germany. In terms of American objectives in the Western Hamisphere, what little digression there was took place as much as a result of what might be referred to as the externalization of the progressive outlook, with its emphasis on order, stability, organization, and expertise, rather than as a consequence of altered power relationships.[1] American policy objectives in Latin America after the first world war continued to derive from traditional political, economic, and strategic considerations that had since the nineteenth century given Latin America a unique place in United States foreign relations. The years between the wars witnessed an evolution in policy, not an abrupt departure.

The attainment of objectives in Latin America did not come easily in spite of the enhanced international power of the United States.[2] In part because of the legacy of ill will among Latin Americans toward the imperial powers, and in part because of a growing belief in American official circles that American interests were not well served by an overtly aggressive diplomacy, American policy-makers in the 1920s began a reassessment of hemispheric relations. This was a gradual process, reflective of the on-going nature of policy-making as well as the fact that American officials continued to be dissatisfied with the position of the United States. These were not decades of complacency, but rather of questioning and groping for maturity. In the Latin American instance, the search for new guidelines was provoked by the Mexican revolution and what was perceived as a threat to American interests in Mexico and other societies which might emulate her example. It received impetus as well from the very negative response which swept Latin America when the United States landed marines once again in Nicaragua in 1927.[3]

The crash in 1929 and the subsequent depression created additional anxieties about American prosperity, as it derived from international trade, and intensified the effort to achieve predictability of markets and investments in Latin America. Out of the search for order came the policy of nonintervention. Military and old-style dollar diplomacy gave way to military missions and the services of experts in finance, transportation, industrial development, and communications as the ethos of liberal capitalist development gained ascendancy.[4]

The belief that military intervention in Latin America would not in itself bring stability but would rather perpetuate hostility and distrust and occasion retaliation against American interests was not a radical and new insight on the part of policy-makers in the 1920s. It represented a persistent but generally sublimated line of thought that can be traced back into the nineteenth century to such secretaries of state as James G. Blaine. Prior to the Hoover administration, two major secretaries, Elihu Root and Charles Evans Hughes, used the analogy of the good neighbor in reference to United States policy in the hemisphere, although Hughes in particular pursued a hard line in his relations with Latin America.[5] Until Herbert Hoover assumed the presidency, the Good Neighbor as a non-interventionist policy was far from a reality. It did gain strength late in the Coolidge administration, when Secretary of State Frank Kellogg urged the completion and publication of the departmental document by J. Reuben Clark on the Monroe Doctrine. Clark's *Memorandum on the Monroe Doctrine*, in part rejecting President Theodore Roosevelt's justification of military intervention in Latin America under the provisions of the doctrine, did not come to public attention until 1930, contrary to Kellogg's original intent. Secretary Kellogg at no time, however, relinquished his support for the inviolability of American property in Latin America. He continued hostile to the Mexican revolution and earlier as senator had opposed any treaty with Colombia which would imply that the United States had acted improperly at the time of the Panamanian revolt against Colombia.[6]

The ambiguous response of State Department officials to the final publication of the memorandum underlines the absence (at that juncture) of a clearly defined policy toward the question of interventionism; but it is apparent from the evidence that there was not only considerable reluctance to endorse Clark's position but also doubt as to the efficacy of raising the tangled and emotional question at all. President Hoover and the Department of State may have been distracted from Latin American affairs at this time by the Senate debate over the London Naval

Treaty, but Hoover imparted the distinct impression that he wanted the issue buried, not clarified.[7]

In other areas Hoover's contribution to the improvement of inter-American relations was more positive. As chairman of the International High Commission and as secretary of commerce, he worked persistently to make the American presence, especially its economic presence, in Latin America a meaningful one. He sought more effective controls over private American loans and urged concentration upon productive loans which would bring positive benefits to the host nation as well as the creditors. Perhaps atypical of his government contemporaries in his plea for loan control, Hoover was nevertheless highly representative of a prevailing sentiment in this period emphasizing international cooperation in the areas of industrial and financial development.[8] He made this position explicit in an address before the Gridiron Club in Washington shortly after his Latin American tour: 'It never has been and ought not to be the policy of the United States to intervene by force to secure or maintain contracts between our citizens and foreign states or their citizens. Confidence in that attitude,' he concluded, 'is the only basis upon which the economic co-operation of our citizens can be welcomed abroad.'[9]

President Hoover and subsequently Roosevelt, responding to the obstacles confronting their policies in Latin America, came to enunciate the principles of the Good Neighbor. The movement toward official nonintervention took place gradually between the Havana Conference of American States early in 1928, Cordell Hull's signing of the Convention on Rights and Duties of States at the Montevideo Conference in 1933, and the refinement of the latter document at the 1936 Buenos Aires Conference. Renunciation of intervention may have done no more than add a new veneer to an old structure, apply new tools to a familiar task; yet the Hoover and Roosevelt administrations supplemented their rhetorical adherence to the policy by withdrawing troops from Haiti and Nicaragua and refraining from using them in Latin American crises throughout the 1930s. The new orientation was a significant contribution to inter-American harmony. It has too frequently, however, been viewed as a selfless, disinterested abandonment of gunboat diplomacy which sprang from a fundamental change of heart as well as policy, rather than as a tactical shift necessitated by developments in Latin America and by the needs of an expansionist, capitalist society. As N. Gordon Levin has argued in *Woodrow Wilson and World Politics*, Wilson as president consolidated one of the basic premises of modern America foreign policy – the search for a path that not only avoided but tempered socialism and revolutionary nationalism. Wilson sought to do so in such a fashion as to enable the United States to defend its national self-interest while simultaneously articulating the principle of internationalism.[10]

Both Herbert Hoover and Franklin Roosevelt, and especially the latter, were heirs to the progressive tradition and to Wilsonian internationalism, although the Republican president and his secretary of state, Henry Stimson, may have imposed a more pragmatic stamp upon the legacy than did their successors.[11] Both men, and many of their closest associates, sought to encourage Latin American countries, including Colombia, to adhere to a non-nationalistic, non-socialistic approach toward economic development. American policy-makers actively encouraged the establishment of governments committed to private enterprise capitalism and sympathetic to foreign investment as a vehicle for economic modernization. As Carl Parrini has demonstrated for the years during and immediately following the first world war, the United States was unsympathetic to the idea of state capitalism at home and combatted it in Latin America on the assumption that it would undermine American investment abroad and reduce the effectiveness of American diplomacy.[12] In key strategic areas such as aviation and the exploitation of petroleum reserves the United States modified any adherence to the principle of free competition and encouraged a select number of American-based firms to acquire semi-monopolistic control, partially out of concern that otherwise the state-supported enterprises of Germany, Britain, and Japan would attain predominance.

The structures established to implement American policy did undergo some transformation between the wars, and it is in this respect that the Roosevelt administration made its strongest institutional contribution to the formation of the Good Neighbor policy. In the decade of the 1920s and during the Hoover presidency the relationship between government and private enterprise in the area of foreign policy was highly positive, even though institutionally rather informal. Certainly, as secretary of commerce, Hoover substantially expanded the functions of his department as well as the Bureau of Foreign and Domestic Commerce. As Robert Seidel has demonstrated, the Republican administrations of the 1920s also made extensive use of what was a progressive emphasis upon the importance of 'experts' in establishing policy and serving abroad as missionaries of American ideas. Yet the Reciprocal Trade Agreements program, the Export-Import Bank, and the Foreign Bondholders' Protective Council, among others, had to await the election of Franklin Roosevelt, even though something comparable may have been envisaged by Hoover. Such organizations were established on the basis of an assumption or philosophy pervasive in the progressive era that government and quasi-government agencies designed to deal with the business community were most effective when the business community exercised a major influence in their operations, with government providing a forum and establishing the guidelines.[13]

The Good Neighbor policy, then, represented in part the application to foreign policy of some of the ideas concerning business-government relations that were current in the progressive period. In its application to Latin America, the policy was also part of a larger debate over alternative routes to economic modernization. A fundamental question which confronted American policy-makers was the manner in which Latin American nations would seek to develop their economies, whether through continued reliance on the traditional extractive-export sector, including agriculture, or through economic diversification and industrialization under state initiative and control. Although the context was clearly distinct from the period of decolonialization that followed the second world war, the essence of the Good Neighbor period and its diplomacy was an embryonic conflict, now blossomed, between the industrialized and the developing nations.

The broader historical developments characteristic of the 1920s and 1930s have tended to receive less than their due in the extant historiography on the Good Neighbor policy. The traditional historiography has inclined to emphasize the movement away from military intervention as an end in itself rather than as a mechanism designed to achieve the larger objectives of American policy; these included international and domestic stability and prosperity, foreign political structures conducive to American trade and investment, ideologies compatible with American political ideals, and American supremacy in Latin America over her traditional European and recent Asian rivals. Alexander DeConde, for example, in his excellent account of Herbert Hoover's Latin American policy, concludes that 'Hoover's foreign policy was predicated essentially on a desire to maintain peace and had as one of its main objectives the creation of a policy of good will and neighborly understanding towards the Southern Americas.'[14] Similarly, Bryce Wood in *The Making of the Good Neighbor Policy* accurately identifies three major policy objectives in this period: the protection of American property and lives abroad; the advancement of democracy; and the defense of strategic areas. He does not, however, explain why these objectives were identified by American policy-makers, nor does he explore their ramifications within the broader context of the American political economy. Wood also detects a sharp dividing line between the Hoover and Roosevelt administrations and their conception of the Good Neighbor. To argue that the Roosevelt administration arrived independently at the idea of nonintervention as a basic premise of its Latin American policy during the 1933 Cuban revolution is perhaps to ignore the clear lines of continuity which run through the period. This is not to imply that the policies were identical, but merely to suggest that President Roosevelt was not an especially original thinker in either his domestic or foreign policies.[15] Recent analyses of Cuban policy, even those which tend to be sympathetic to the Roosevelt administration, suggest the extent to which policy altered more in tactics than in objectives where Cuba was concerned, and that the United States not surprisingly expected a policy of nonintervention to yield very pragmatic returns. It is difficult to perceive the

Good Neighbor even prior to 1939 as 'characterized by the practices of mutual respect and restraint.'[16]

The one work which provides a conceptual framework for its analysis of the Good Neighbor is David Green's *The Containment of Latin America; A History of the Myths and Realities of the Good Neighbor Policy*, which concentrates upon the mature years of the policy, the late 1930s and 1940s. The most appealing aspect of this analysis is the contention that one of the basic factors shaping United States-Latin American relations in the 1930s was the emergence of 'depression nationalism' in Latin America and the concomitant anxiety which it produced in the United States. Some historians might quarrel with the application of the term *nationalism* to Latin American societies like Colombia, which were highly fragmented socially, economically, and politically in the interwar years. Whether the upsurge of protectionism, a heightened awareness of the American presence, and challenges to foreign domination of industry and natural resources were manifestations of nationalism or xenophobia, there is little question that American policymakers perceived events in terms of an emergent nationalism and responded to them as such. With Latin America struggling in the depression decade not simply for a larger share of hemispheric wealth but for more effective control over economic growth and economic diversification, the United States responded with institutions such as the Export-Import Bank, the Reciprocal Trade Agreements program, the Inter-American Bank, and the Inter-American Financial and Economic Advisory Committee, which were designed to strengthen the traditional economic ties binding Latin America to the United States rather than to promote economic development along self-determined lines. *The Containment of Latin America* documents very thoroughly the manner in which the Roosevelt administration fostered economic and political integration within the hemisphere to combat nationalism and to militate against the threat (real or imaginary) to hemispheric security from fascism on the right and socialism on the left. The Good Neighbor ultimately failed to achieve the long-range effects anticipated by Latin America because it was only a defensive maneuver against nationalism abroad and against economic stagnation at home.[17]

The record suggests that this concern with the deterioration of the international economy and the emergence of what was viewed as a more radical situation in Latin America contributed substantially to the new veneer which was applied to United States-Latin American policy, and that the facelift began before Franklin Roosevelt took office. Herbert Hoover's secretary of state, Henry L. Stimson, placed the economic dimension in perspective in an address before the Union League Club of Philadelphia on 1 October 1932, well into the depression and on the eve of the presidential election. The secretary emphasized on that occasion:

Our foreign trade has now become an indispensable cog in the economic machinery of the country ... The prosperity of the American people and the standard of living of our workers is now closely related to the development and maintenance of this trade structure.

The principles which should guide the foreign policy of such a nation stand out in clear relief. She should cultivate the good will and confidence of the other peoples throughout the world with whom she must trade. She should promote those conditions of world peace upon which economic and political stability everywhere must rest ... [18]

As the following analysis of Colombia suggests, the expansion of United States-based corporations into Latin America added a dimension to foreign policy in this period. Imbued with pervasive economic and often political power, American subsidiaries operating in Latin America embodied both the means and objectives of American policy. Their frequent domination of a major export sector of a local economy gave companies considerable influence and responsibility. At the same time the expansion of multinationals enabled the State Department as well as other government agencies and departments to plan resource policies with greater predictability, particularly where petroleum was concerned, and to expand foreign markets. The general assumption on the part of American officials that such investments and trade were mutually beneficial to host and donor nation as well as strategically important made the maintenance of a stable environment for American subsidiaries abroad a major objective of United States policy. [19] American officials viewed the multinational corporation as an agent of modernization and as a contribution to the Latin American struggle for development.

A case study can be a particularly useful historical tool for testing general hypotheses. The existence of several major general studies of the Latin American diplomacy of Presidents Hoover and Roosevelt suggests the need for a more concentrated examination of the articulation and implementation of that diplomacy. Colombia is well suited for such an analysis. [20]

Colombia in the interwar years was both a variegated and closely knit society. Controlled politically and economically by a small white minority (in a population of approximately eight million) concentrated in the highlands, the country was highly fragmented socially and geographically. Three mountain spurs of the Andes running in a north-south direction and the jungle areas of the lowlands presented depressing obstacles to the communication of ideas, as well as the transport of people and goods. The radio, telephone, and airplane as well as improved maritime transport made it possible for Colombia to move out of its isolation in these decades. But it was a slow and sometimes painful experience for the majority of the population, for whom a rural community had been the world, and where the Church had been at once the main contact with the outside and a shield against the intellectual and social currents of the twentieth century. There were in addition another quarter of a million native Indians, from the Putumayo regions in the south to the Guajira Peninsula in the north, who remained entirely outside the Colombian mainstream until the missionary, the trader, and the oil pipeline broke into their world.

It was a paradoxical society that had a generally sophisticated, internationally educated elite, but was nevertheless 49% illiterate in the 1930s; it was a predominantly agricultural society where only 2% of students enrolled in institutions of higher learning were involved in agricultural programs; cities such as Bogotá, with its finely appointed homes of Chapinero, also attracted burgeoning hillside slums, where the absence of sanitary facilities meant that in heavy rains refuse washed through the residential streets exposing the 'better' classes to typhoid and dysentery. In 1929 almost 3,000 Colombians died of typhoid and another 3,000 died of dysentery and enteritis; 42% of all deaths were of undetermined causes because of the absence of an attending physician. [21]

Developing nation though it was, Colombia was nevertheless of considerable importance to the United States in terms of inter-American relations. Proximity to the Panama Canal above all else made her adherence to a pro-American policy vital to American security. In addition, the promise of untapped petroleum resources necessitated the watchful concern and occasional interference of the State Department to ensure the exploitation of the reserves by interests responsible to the United States.

In the 1920s and 1930s Colombian trade with the United States was significant in terms of American trade with the rest of Latin America. Taking South America alone (thus excluding the trade of Mexico and Cuba), Colombia customarily ranked third or fourth in the value of its exports to the United States and third in imports behind Argentina and Brazil. By 1932 Colombia was second in South America in terms of the total value of its trade with the United States. [22]

Altered trade patterns during the first world war increased inter-American trade, but in the case of Colombia it was a change of degree rather than orientation. Both before and after 1914 the United States was the principal market for Colombian exports and the main supplier of finished products. In 1926 the American market absorbed 85.9% of Colombian exports of coffee, gold, and bananas. After 1926 there was a slight decline in the percentage of Colombian exports which went directly to the United States; yet the statistics in themselves are misleading. The initiation of petroleum exports in 1926 by Standard Oil's subsidiary meant that a portion of Colombia's second largest export in value went initially to the Dutch West Indies for refining and then was re-exported to the United

States. Imports from the United States demonstrated a similar decline. Shut off from Europe during the first world war, in 1919 Colombia had turned to the United States for 72.4% of its imports; in 1933 that figure fell to 33.8% as the result of European competition and the growing attraction of protectionism in Colombia.[23] The American reaction to this early depression decline in exports to Colombia (and to Latin America in general) forms the core of the initial chapters in this study and serves as a springboard for the broader aspects of Colombian-American relations between the wars.

A marked increase in American investment in Colombia in the 1920s, particularly in government bonds issued to finance a series of poorly administered public works projects, drew the Colombian economy deeper into the American circle of influence. American investors injected capital into oil, public utilities, coffee, fruit, sugar plantations, cattle ranching, mining, manufacturing, and marketing enterprises, and along with the capital came technicians, management personnel, and government advisers, who made their own mark on the nation. By the end of 1930 Americans held almost $172,000,000 in Colombian government bonds and had placed another $130,000,000 into direct investments, in contrast with the decline in British investment to $42,000,000 from $55,000,000 seven years earlier.[24]

The expansion of the American presence did not take place without provoking reaction. The interwar period in Colombian-American relations in fact witnessed a major debate over the role which American capital, technology, and entrepreneurship should assume in the economic development of the country. Colombian opinion in the period covered a broad spectrum, from those who welcomed American capital and expertise to those who questioned its impact on Colombian society. Critics tended to be weak in influence and few in number among Colombian elites, although the gradual emergence of a middle class that was not tied to the traditional agricultural sector, especially coffee, suggested an impending fragmentation of political and economic power. As the awareness grew of the extent to which it had mortgaged its future in order to finance the expansion of the 1920s, the nation passed through a phase of introspection which witnessed the evolution of an indigenous labor movement and a more concerted attempt to control the exploitation of natural resources.[25] This process of change in Colombian society in the 1920s and 1930s requires substantially more critical scholarship. Until Colombian historians have thoroughly examined the political and economic structures of the society for this period as they have for the earlier nineteenth century, it will remain difficult to evaluate the impact of the American presence.

The following chapters examine thematically the primary areas of contact between the United States and Colombia between the wars. My concern in the first two chapters is the evolution of commercial relations after the first world war, with particular emphasis upon the Colombian and American shift toward protectionism following the crash in 1929 and the negotiations leading to the conclusion of a trade agreement in the 1930s. In the following two chapters I trace the convoluted paths of United States indirect investment, American assistance in establishing and then reorganizing a central banking system, and efforts to recover lost investments following a depression-induced default on foreign bond issues. The focus of the narrative and analysis then shifts to the diplomatic, political, and strategic ramifications of American direct investment in the petroleum, banana, and aviation industries, each of which was a major aspect of Colombian development as well as a prominent feature of inter-American diplomacy in these years. Topical as the structure of the book is, the focus remains the nature of Good Neighbor diplomacy and the relationship between that policy and the modernization of Colombia. The basic issues in Colombian-American relations involved concrete questions pertaining to Colombian development and the role which American capital, technology, and expertise would play in that development, whether in the area of extractive industries, agriculture, transportation, or finance, although emotions and abstract ideals often obfuscated the pragmatic dimension of the issues.

Colombian-American relations between 1920 and 1940 divide into several readily distinguishable periods. In 1922, the ratification of the Thomson-Urrutia Treaty between the two nations brought to an end, at least diplomatically, a generation of Colombian bitterness over American action at the time of Panama's secession from Colombia.[26] The apparent willingness of the United States to assume some of the responsibility for the diplomacy of the Republican administration of Theodore Roosevelt, the treaty's provision for an indemnity payment of $25 million, and the generally favorable international environment after the first world war ushered in five years of economic boom and apparent prosperity which has earned the deserved epithet 'the dance of the millions.'

By 1927 some of the optimism was wearing thin, in both the United States and Colombia, as it became increasingly apparent to even the most skeptical observer that Colombian governments at all levels, from city to nation, had overextended their indebtedness in borrowing abroad in order to finance ambitious public works projects. At the same time, political opponents of the dominant Conservative party, which held office throughout the decade, began to question the efficacy of what some portrayed as a growing overdependence upon the United States. For the remaining three years of the presidency of Miguel Abadía Méndez (1926–30) a reinvigorated anti-Americanism began to set in, reflected in part in the sympathetic response evoked by the minister of industries, José Antonio Montalvo, when he sought to revise existing petroleum laws and to revoke the Barco petroleum concession held by a subsidiary of Gulf Oil.[27]

A major, bloody, and prolonged strike against the United Fruit Company on the Atlantic coast in late 1928 also occasioned increasing polarization over the activities of American enterprise in the country, and especially the privileged status of the banana company in the agricultural sector. As the petroleum and banana industries emerged as divisive factors in Colombian-American relations in the late 1920s, aviation began to assume larger proportions in hemispheric affairs. Colombia's well-established and pioneering commercial airline, SCADTA (Sociedad Colombo-Alemena de Transportes Aéreos), established by German nationals following the first world war, competed vigorously within Colombia, in the Caribbean, and on the west coast of South America with Pan American Airways, competition which was not effectively resolved in favor of the American firm until after the outbreak of war in Europe in 1939.[28]

The onset of depression conditions after 1929 served as a catalyst in bringing a sense of urgency to the need for a resolution of these conflicts and added a further commercial dimension to the issues which absorbed Colombian-American relations in the interwar years. A coincidence of factors – the petroleum debate, the competition between SCADTA and Pan American, the United Fruit Company strike, and the deterioration of the international financial and commercial situation – created a context in which the political reversal suffered by the Conservative party in the 1930 presidential elections was not surprising. In the elections of that spring Liberals and dissident Conservatives succeeded in placing in the Presidential Palace Enrique Olaya Herrera. His inauguration in August 1930 initiated a four-year period of strong official support for American objectives in Colombia during which a number of outstanding disputes inherited from the presidencies of Pedro Nel Ospina and Miguel Abadía Méndez were resolved.

It was ironic that Olaya should ride into office in the aftermath of inflamed anti-Americanism and that at least some of his support came from those who had objected to the government's vigorous suppression of the strike against the United Fruit Company in 1928. By the time he assumed the presidency, Olaya had enjoyed a distinguished public career as a journalist-publisher, diplomat, and senator and possessed substantial influence among Conservatives in spite of his expressed liberal preferences. Nothing in his previous political record suggested that he might exploit anti-American sentiment or pursue policies hostile to United States interests, and there was convincing evidence to the contrary. As a senator in the early 1920s and briefly as minister of foreign affairs under President Jorge Holguin, Olaya was instrumental in attaining the passage through the Colombian Congress of the Thomson-Urrutia Treaty with the United States. In part as recognition for his contribution to the treaty debate and in part because of his recognized statesmanship, Olaya was appointed minister to Washington in the spring of 1922, where he remained until the 1930 presidential campaign. Throughout his term in Washington he worked energetically to establish Colombian-American relations on a stable and non-divisive basis and sought to attract American capital to develop the industrial potential of Colombia. His enthusiasm in this regard was undiminished when he moved into the Presidential Palace, and his presidency subsequently witnessed four of the most significant years in Colombian-American relations in the interwar period, although he was rightly criticized for his almost naive faith in the omnipotence and benevolence of the United States.[29]

Under Olaya's leftish-Liberal successor, Alfonso López (1934–8), relations between the two countries were more strained. Alfonso López Pumarejo, twice president of Colombia, his brother, Miguel, who was a prominent figure in Colombian coffee circles, and his son, Alfonso López Michelsen, president at the time of writing, are among the most significant political figures in twentieth-century Colombian political history. Alfonso López was a slight man with finely drawn, almost youthful features and an air of Realpolitik and intellectual vigor about him that nevertheless failed to stifle his charm and popularity. Although his paternal grandfather had been a tailor and active in establishing an artisans' association in the mid-nineteenth century,[30] by the time he reached maturity his family was established in national banking. Following service in the lower house of Congress, López participated in the establishment of what proved to be the short-lived American Mercantile Bank of Colombia, an affiliate of the Mercantile Bank of the Americas, earlier formed by Brown Brothers & Co., J. & W. Seligman & Co., and the Guaranty Trust Co., three financial houses which played a prominent role in Colombian investment during the 1920s. Although López appears to have continued to believe that American financial institutions were important to Colombian development, his resignation as a director of the Mercantile Bank of Colombia following an extended dispute with Seligman & Co. and the failure of his family's banking interests in the postwar recession rather soured his view of foreign capitalism, and he remained more cautious in his relations with the United States than was his predecessor.[31]

López presided over a Liberal Party which had undergone an important transition since the first world war. Conflicts with the Conservatives over religion were temporarily sublimated as the Liberals found themselves confronted with a challenge from the Socialist and Communist left, which began to make serious inroads into both Liberal and Conservative support. The formation of Socialist and Communist parties compelled the Liberals to confront more directly the difficulty of incorporating within a single party an essentially bourgeois leadership and base with increasingly vocal and politicized urban and rural workers, a segment of the population to which Alfonso López was more sensitive than any of his predecessors. During the 1920s, and especially during López's presidency, the Liberals experienced considerable success in eroding the embryonic strength of the Socialist left, with the result that after 1925 even a leading Socialist figure such as Jorge

Eliécer Gaitán argued that the Liberal party was the most appropriate vehicle for political and economic reform.[32]

As López drew one wing of the Liberals to the left, Olaya and Eduardo Santos (Olaya's political heir following the former's premature death, and editor of *El Tiempo*) occupied the center right of the party, the Moderate Liberals. During López's first term, from 1934 to 1938, his wing gradually gave ground to his more cautious critics within the party. As president, López did little, nevertheless, to lend substance to Conservative and American anxieties prior to his election concerning the extremism of his political leanings. López's interest in international relations and international finance was keen. He had served at both the London Economic Conference and the Inter-American Conference at Montevideo in 1933. But the primary focus of his ideology and energies during his years in office was on domestic reform, where he made substantial advances in the direction of resource controls, and agricultural, tax, and constitutional reform. His domestic program, La Revolución en Marcha, was inspired to some extent by López's reading of the New Deal in the United States and Lázaro Cárdenas's revival of the momentum of the Mexican revolution.[33] Yet the reforms of the López years failed to confront successfully the question of national control and mastery over economic development. The principle of private enterprise and the fact of the American presence, which had seemed to some threatened by López's election, were passed virtually unscathed to Eduardo Santos in 1938, in part because of the success of American diplomacy and pro-American elements in Colombia, but to a great extent as a result of the failure of López to consolidate the power of the left.

On the eve of the second world war, then, the United States had weathered successfully more than a decade of challenge to its interests – political, economic, and strategic – in Colombia. In defending those interests, American officials insisted that they sought only an open door, equal access for trade and investment, and defense of the principle of hemispheric security; yet an examination of Colombian-American relations strongly suggests the exclusiveness of the open door policy and the Good Neighbor as they applied to Latin America. Claiming that they sought equality rather than privilege in Colombia, American officials nevertheless attempted to exclude foreign competitors from key sectors of the economy, especially petroleum and aviation, but even to some extent in a non strategic sector such as the banana industry, which remained dominated by the United Fruit Company. To what extent there were alternatives to the course of action followed by both Colombia and the United States and to what extent Colombian elites perceived other routes to modernization as either desirable or practicable certainly are subjects that deserve more careful analysis by Colombian historians. But, to return to a hypothesis I suggested earlier in the introduction, the contention is that in the interwar years in Colombian-American relations, years which witnessed the evolution of the Good Neighbor and the expansion of American involvement in Colombia, the fundamental issue was whether Colombia would pursue a road to development independent of the United States. That it did not do so was in part a consequence of the realities of international power, in part the result of very successful diplomacy by the United States, and in part the effect of the lack of commitment to such a course among members of the Colombian political sector.

1

The United States and the Colombian marketplace 1920-33

The financial and commercial rupture which accompanied the crash of 1929 represents something of a watershed in Colombian-American commercial relations in the interwar years. Prior to the crash, the 1920s were a period essentially of commercial and financial expansion, with most of the capital investment coming from the United States. During the decade international coffee prices were strong, allowing Colombia to enjoy considerable prosperity derived from its main source of international revenue.[1] After the 1929 crash, coffee prices declined, with the anticipated impact upon the economy. Even prior to the onset of depression, American credit for Colombian development was becoming more difficult to obtain as concern arose over the stability of existing investments. By 1930 sources of American credit had been virtually exhausted. Credit restrictions and a steady decline in coffee prices pushed the Colombian economy toward a phase of retrenchment which strained Colombian-American relations for several years during the administrations of Abadía Méndez, Olaya Herrera, and López. The general decline of international trade and the apparent threat to American prosperity presented by nations such as Colombia which turned to protectionist commercial policies intensified the desire of American officials to achieve relatively liberal international trade policies. They sought as well to secure an open door against protectionism in Latin America and against competition from European trading rivals. In practice, the open door in Latin America was designed to ensure American hegemony rather than equal access to the markets of the region.

During the depression, the expansion of trade was one of the ways in which policy-makers attempted to promote domestic economic recovery. There was, of course, no unanimity either among businessmen or in government circles in these years over the relative utility of trade expansion as opposed to other mechanisms for lifting the United States and other nations out of the economic slump. There was no clear division between those who sought solutions abroad and those who identified the domestic situation as the primary cause of the economic malaise. Those who looked for the answer in retrenchment and protectionism won the early rounds in the debate. The protectionist levels of the Smoot-Hawley Tariff of 1930, which evoked such a negative response abroad; the decision of the Roosevelt administration in 1933 to depart from the gold standard in order to protect the dollar; the absence of a meaningful effort on the part of the United States to make the 1933 London Economic Conference a significant international attempt to find a solution to the monetary crisis; and the fact that President Roosevelt devoted little attention to foreign policy in 1933 and to the desire of the State Department for the passage of general commercial legislation all suggest the inability of the internationalists to prevail over other persuasions. Yet the tensions between advocates of expansion and those of retraction were there; and the failure of the internationalists to determine policy on several occasions should not divert attention from their significance in shaping overall American policy. An examination of the Colombian experience serves to highlight certain dimensions of American commercial objectives in Latin America as a whole, and to place them in their proper perspective in relationship to other aspects of American foreign policy.

As a market in South America, Colombia, as noted earlier, occupied a relatively important position. The possibility of expanding that market and developing the nation's petroleum resources was a consideration early in the 1920s in bringing final Senate acceptance of the Thomson-Urrutia Treaty, which settled the long-standing dispute between the countries over the role of the United States in the Panamanian revolt a generation earlier.[2] Even during the first unsuccessful attempt by the Wilson administration to obtain Senate approval in 1914, considerable support was mustered from advocates of commercial expansion.

In a 1915 submission to the Senate Foreign Relations Committee, a former minister to Colombia and director general of the Pan American Union, John Barrett, stressed the necessity to reinvigorate trade with Colombia. 'It is my sincere belief,' he noted,

that none of [the Latin American Republics] has greater undeveloped material and commercial potentialities than Colombia ...

It is also the one country of South America which naturally with the opening of the Panama Canal will be most easily reached by the commercial interests of the United States.[3]

John H. Hammond, chairman of the Executive Committee of the Foreign Bond and Share Corporation, subsequently expressed similar support of the treaty, when he urged Frank Kellogg to do whatever possible to improve relations with the nations of South America. 'American trade must be developed,' he wrote, 'and I believe that a favorable settlement with Colombia would greatly assist.'[4]

Following ratification of the Thomson-Urrutia Treaty in April 1921 American businessmen rallied to the potential of Colombian-American commerce. Little more than a month after ratification, a group of prominent individuals engaged in commerce with Latin America gathered for a luncheon at the Hotel Astor in New York. Sponsored by the Pan American Advertising Association, the meeting featured three speakers involved in the development of Latin American trade: Abel Camacho, a Colombian counselor for the Carib Syndicate, one of the more active petroleum interests in Colombia; Julius Klein, at that time professor of Latin American history and economic sat Harvard and later head of the Bureau of Foreign and Domestic Commerce; and Earl Harding, chairman of the Colombian Commercial Corporation.[5] The consensus was that the utilization of the financial energy generated in Colombia by the American indemnity payment of $25 million under the provisions of the treaty should be used to stimulate an effective transportation network. Harding claimed that, if it could be reached, Colombia offered United States manufacturers 'not only an enlarged market but the early prospect of an absolutely new market' for a wide variety of products, with a potential purchasing power exceeding that of Cuba. An American commercial attaché in Bogotá, Walter Donnelly, several years later echoed Harding's assessment. 'It is important,' Donnelly advised the head of the Bureau of Foreign and Domestic Commerce, 'that our manufacturers become well entrenched at present even if they do not secure much [immediate] business.'[6]

One potential area of friction between the two countries was the persistence of high tariff legislation during the Republican 1920s. American protectionism had long been the source of anti-American sentiment in Latin America, and later in the decade the southern republics were apprehensive that Herbert Hoover would continue the policy of his predecessors.[7] His evident adherence to protectionist principles[8] and the tariff legislation before Congress in 1928 and 1929 did little to relieve Latin American skepticism.

Hoover nevertheless attempted to justify the tariff on the basis of its flexible provisions. On 24 September 1929, the president issued a public statement in which he argued that 'the flexible tariff provision is one of the most progressive steps taken in tariff making in all our history.' Thomas Marvin, chairman of the United States Tariff Commission and a noted protectionist, was in full accord with the president's assessment. The day after Hoover's public statement he wrote the president: 'The effort to liberalize our tariff methods has never received stronger impetus than the statement you issued yesterday on the need of maintaining a flexible tariff.'[9] Unfortunately, since the flexible provisions were never systematically utilized, this was more rhetoric than substance.

When Hoover ultimately signed the Smoot-Hawley Tariff bill in June 1930, he claimed that, as compared with earlier legislation, its rates were not unreasonable and that the increased power of the Tariff Commission would alleviate the danger of injustices in the tariff schedules. Many of Hoover's personal justifications, however, appeared after the fact, and he signed the measure following receipt of a memorandum from Henry L. Stimson indicating Latin American opposition to increased protectionism. Hoover allowed domestic political considerations to subvert his better inclinations and ignored repeated warnings against high duties.[10]

Opposition to continued excessive protectionism in the United States indicated the growing concern in some circles that Latin American nations would direct their trade elsewhere unless there were positive signs of reciprocity in the American market. At the 1929 Baltimore convention of the National Foreign Trade Council, John Barrett criticized Lawrence Downs, president of the Illinois Central Railroad, for his unqualified optimism that Latin America would remain a major market for the agricultural products of the Mississippi Valley. Barrett accused Downs and other agricultural interests of responsibility for creating Latin American anxiety over United States commercial aggression and warned that unless the United States provided greater reciprocity it faced the prospect of losing those markets.[11]

Secretary of Commerce Robert Lamont echoed Barrett's sentiments in an address before the council two years later. He called for the lowering of tariff barriers and the adoption of a more reciprocal approach to commercial relations. His criticism of the Smoot-Hawley tariff received strong support from the Argentine ambassador to the United States as well as from prominent American businessmen, including Thomas W. Lamont, a partner in J.P. Morgan & Co.; John Lonsdale, president of the American Bankers' Association; Edward Pratt, former chief of the BFDC; and Peter Fletcher, president of the National Council of Importers and Traders. Underlining the absence of official unanimity, however, Assistant Secretary of Commerce Julius Klein the same week defended American tariff policies at a meeting of the Export Managers Club.[12]

When prominent members of the Hoover administration spoke in favor of protection, however, they tended to view it in conjunction with market expansion. One of the most articulate representatives of this view was Under Secretary of State William R. Castle Jr. Castle combined a missionary heritage and its accompanying religious orientation with a career in business and diplomacy. His correspondence, speeches, and radio addresses during the Hoover and Roosevelt years reveal him to have been a strong protectionist and an occasional apologist for American armed intervention abroad. In a radio address over WJL in New York City on the evening of 15 January 1932, Castle suggested that the distribution of production was 'perhaps the outstanding feature in foreign relations.' Later, sniping at the Roosevelt administration, he contended that the only way to alter Latin American trade was to give the area a sound economic reason for increasing its purchases from the United States.[13]

Whether or not Hoover was justified in his assumption that the international movement toward protection preceded the passage of the Smoot-Hawley Act, the fact remains that there was a pronounced movement in Latin America to protect domestic agriculture and industry and to discourage imports in order to stabilize a balance of payments in the first years of the depression. This movement was not directed solely against the United States, although, as the 1930 Stimson report to Hoover indicated, there was intense agitation in Argentina, Cuba, and Uruguay during congressional consideration of the tariff.

The Colombian response was milder than that of other Latin American nations, which is not surprising in the light of Colombia's favorable balance of trade with the United States.[14] Press opinion in 1930 reflected a degree of confidence in the Colombian position. A typical editorial comment following the enactment of the Smoot-Hawley Act was that of the Conservative *El Nuevo Tiempo* on 21 June 1930. Lamenting the failure of the United States to assume more responsible leadership of international trade, the paper warned that 'although the new tariff law of the United States does not directly threaten any of our most important industries, it is impossible for us to neglect its international significance.'

The same day the Liberal *El Tiempo* carried a sharply anti-American, antiprotectionism editorial. Expressing some concern that hides had been removed from the free list in the new tariff schedules, the editorial nevertheless concluded:

It would be absurd for us to imprison ourselves behind a China wall and not admit foreign goods when so many products from abroad are imperative to our existence. On the other hand, it is no less absurd to open our doors to all foreign material and to have our populace without work ... We must defend national employment and the exploitation of our natural resources.[15]

That Colombia did not voice an official protest against the Smoot-Hawley Act was due largely to the continuance of coffee on the free list; yet even the pro-American Liberal administration of Enrique Olaya Herrera gave warm support to a protectionist sentiment which had gained ground during the 1920s as a result of the growth of both the manufacturing and agricultural sectors. Olaya does not appear to have become ideologically committed to protectionism. But a number of the emergency measures implemented by the Colombian government to meet the demands of a depressed market had the effect of whetting protectionist appetites and led to the subsequent institutionalization of these emergency measures.[16]

An important factor in the development of Colombian protectionism through-out its history has been the regional nature of the support given to the policy. The lack of an effective transportation network in Colombia contributed to the extreme economic and cultural regionalism yet evident in Colombian society. During the twenties and thirties the coastal areas of the country sought readily available foreign products. The interior, particularly Bogotá and Medellín, where it was impossible to produce goods to compete with foreign imports in coastal cities, demanded government measures to curtail importation of less expensive commodities, primarily textiles and foodstuffs.

A Colombian commission headed by a Swiss economist, M.H. Haussermann, in 1925 recommended a moderate upward revision of the entire Colombian customs tariff, but it was not until 1930 that the government moved to implement the proposals. Once initiated, however, the movement toward higher protection gathered momentum. By August of 1930 the American minister in Colombia, Jefferson Caffery, reported 'intense agitation around the country for protection,' especially generated by the recently organized National Federation of Manufacturers and Producers. Warning the State Department that under the circumstances some revision of rates was inevitable, Caffery unsuccessfully lobbied major Colombian parties on behalf of American interests.[17]

By mid-October suggested rates had in some cases moved beyond those of the Haussermann project. In an effort to slow the trend, left-wing Liberal representative Alberto Lleras Camargo sponsored a bill enabling the Executive to put the entire Haussermann plan into effect. The Chamber passed a modified bill of that nature in November. Senate opposition necessitated further alterations, and it was not until January of the following year that the completed bill went to the president. On 8 January President Olaya decreed an increase in duties on a wide range of foodstuffs, including flour, wheat, refined sugar, and lard.[18]

The majority of these increases were to the detriment of American agricultural exports. But some American-financed enterprises in Colombia profited from the increased protection. This was certainly true of the sugar industry in the prosperous Cauca Valley, where more than two million dollars in American capital had been invested.[19]

With protectionists having the upper hand, Caffery approached Olaya in an effort to moderate increases. He found the president in a sensitive position, as he had already committed himself to attempting a settlement of the Barco oil concession and was reluctant to complicate that issue. Olaya nevertheless assured Caffery of his good intentions and promised to protect American interests.[20]

In the weeks following Caffery's conferences with the president, Olaya proceeded to veto thirty-one of the proposed articles in the tariff bill; but he was reluctant to press Congress too hard. 'It is clear,' Caffery reported on 25 April, 'that the Colombian Congress is taking advantage of the fact that they have already voted a favorable oil law ... and ... that we want the Catatumbo contract approved, to play domestic politics with the tariff.'[21]

In September the Colombian Congress delegated extraordinary powers to the Executive for one year, allowing it to impose restrictions on a comprehensive list of imports, particularly luxury items, nonessential agricultural commodities, and articles which could readily be produced by Colombian industry. At the same time Congress prohibited the president from increasing duties on agricultural machinery, a Colombian import in which the United States was especially interested.[22]

Olaya moved immediately to implement the September legislation; on the 27th he issued a decree prohibiting the import of a number of luxury items and doubling the duty on certain other agricultural and finished products. On still other commodities the Executive raised tariffs one-quarter to one-half above their former levels. Congress did not relax the emergency provisions until the end of the year.[23]

As table 1 suggests, Colombian efforts to revise its commercial relations were directed to its generally unfavorable balance of trade, especially with Europe, rather than against the United States. This reflected the Colombian desire to use protectionism to stimulate economic diversification, not to close its doors against American products. Nevertheless, the protectionism of this period did contribute to a decline in imports from the United States and led to an intense debate over economic development.[24]

The deterioration of commerce following 1929 was increased incentive for the revision of relations with the United States. The pressure for a new treaty was of several years' standing. Prior to the depression, Conservative President Miguel Abadía Méndez recommended the initiation of talks leading to a new commercial agreement. Abadía viewed it as both a diplomatic and commercial venture. 'While it will not erase the memory in Colombia of the events and circumstances that led to the separation of Panama,' he commented, '[it] should contribute to a better understanding.'[25]

In 1929 the American government temporarily suspended all negotiations leading to commercial treaties.[26] This did not mean, however, that the efforts to improve the status of the Colombian market ceased altogether. In fact, the renegotiation of a series of commercial agreements in the 1930s was made possible by the persistent belief within influential circles in the United States that full recovery was dependent on rational interchange in the world markets, and that such interchange could take place only if the United States revised its trade policies to give greater encouragement to foreign exporters.

Throughout these years the Colombian-American Chamber of Commerce in New York was active in the encouragement of intercourse between the two na-

TABLE 1
Summary of foreign commodity trade 1923-38

Year	Imports		Exports	
	Value in gold pesos	% in relation to 1930 (=100)	Value in gold pesos	% in relation to 1930 (=100)
1923	65,722,434	94	54,756,757	53
1924	63,427,776	91	85,840,102	83
1925	98,223,632	141	84,088,100	81
1926	125,399,200	180	111,462,769	108
1927	139,680,438	200	108,020,294	105
1928	162,981,499	234	132,992,392	129
1929	140,408,526	201	120,703,823	117
1930	69,776,527	100	103,328,635	100
1931	45,612,544	65	79,822,085	77
1932	33,602,790	48	65,692,729	64
1933	38,432,356	55	46,695,385	45
1934	37,255,430	53	47,066,255	46
1935	41,049,055	59	42,395,444	41
1936	46,651,130	67	47,485,024	46
1937	58,370,759	84	52,345,985	51
1938	54,148,002	74	49,111,775	48

SOURCE: DANE *Anuario de Comercio Exterior, 1938* 3

tions, and the National Federation of Coffee Growers continued its efforts to secure the American market for Colombian coffee. With coffee prices severely reduced in the 1930s, the Colombian producers were dependent on the continuation of substantial exports to maintain a viable industry. Even more serious would have been the effect of the loss of the American coffee market on Colombian international credit. As one economist has suggested, in 1925 coffee exports represented 18% of Gross Domestic Product and 80% of total goods exports. In 1940, although there had been some decline in its relative importance, coffee still represented 16% of Gross Domestic Product and 59% of total goods exports.[27]

In 1931 a group of concerned American and Colombian officials and businessmen formed a Colombian-American Chamber of Commerce in Bogotá with a prominent Bogotano, Joaquín Samper, as president, and the American commercial attaché, Walter Donnelly, as vice-president. The new Chamber of Commerce was designed to 'create a bond ... between the commercial and industrial classes of both countries.' Simultaneously, President Olaya announced that five American experts in public administration and finance, headed by Edwin W. Kemmerer, the Princeton economist who had drafted a central banking system for Colombia in 1923, would be brought to Bogotá to suggest remedies for Colombia's financial ills.[28]

Confronted with major economic problems, President Olaya continued to look to the United States for succor. At the height of the dispute with Peru over control of the Amazon port of Leticia and the concern of coffee growers over American tariff intentions, Olaya's foreign minister, Roberto Urdaneta Arbeláez, instructed Fabio Lozano, the Colombian minister in Washington, to express the administration's desire to cooperate with the United States delegation at the London Economic Conference and to follow the American lead in economic policy. This was particularly significant in the light of the severe restrictions that exchange controls placed on Colombian exports and imports. It was not until April of 1933 that Olaya, by presidential decree, allowed the export of products other than coffee, platinum, petroleum, bananas, gold, cattle, and hides without any obligation to exporters to sell to the Bank of the Republic all foreign exchange realized from the transactions; under the provisions of the decree the Exchange Control Board was to permit the export of products only when exporters guaranteed the utilization of receipts in Colombia.[29]

The concern of American interests over their declining share of the Latin American market paralleled Colombian fears for the security of its own trade position.[30] Although the Roosevelt administration notified Congress, shortly after assuming office, of its intention to negotiate trade agreements, some eleven months elapsed before it took any definite action, partly because of the primacy of domestic considerations and partly because Roosevelt himself did not possess a clearly formulated policy. More the political pragmatist than his predecessor, Roosevelt nevertheless brought to the White House fundamental convictions that he shared with Hoover. In fact, as one analysis of the New Deal suggests, 'the evidence indicates that the New Deal's approach to foreign policy was as much shaped by older principles and traditions as by any initiated by Franklin Roosevelt, who, after all, had also grown up believing in such ... policies as that of the Asian Open Door.'[31] Still, differences there were – some substantive, such as the trade agreements program itself, others merely rhetorical. Both Roosevelt and his secretary of state had been nurtured in the progressive tradition, and the Roosevelt administration resorted with frequency to the Wilsonian rhetoric of internationalism; hence the references Roosevelt made in 1928 to the recovery of America's 'moral' leadership in Latin America and Cordell Hull's frequent equation of commercial and political instability with moral decrepitude.[32]

Hull spoke in less moralistic terms in a speech before the Good Neighbor League at the Hotel Commodore on 15 September 1936, but his appeal for an essential harmony between domestic and international policies was no less explicit:

The trade policy this country is pursuing fits well into our domestic economic situation and policies ... Certainly ... it should be clear, even to those engaged in industries that have been most direct beneficiaries of excessive tariffs, that this alone will not bring them prosperity ... They can thrive only when other branches of production thrive, including those industries that habitually dispose of a large part of their products in foreign markets.[33]

Two years earlier the secretary of state had informed the audience at the National Foreign Trade Council: 'The objectives of the United States which we are all ... concerned to reach ... are stable and permanent business recovery, and experience teaches that this requires both a domestic and an international program.' 'The purpose,' he concluded, 'is to promote the maximum amount of production that can be consumed at home and abroad.'[34]

Hull's personal preference was for some form of reciprocal trade arrangement; this led to his determination early in 1933 to use trade treaties with select Latin American states as a two-edged sword. On the one hand, sincere expressions on the part of the United States of its desire to improve trade relations would cut through some of the hostility toward the United States prior to the meeting of Inter-American states in Montevideo that December. On the other hand, a series of bilateral trade treaties would improve the trade picture until a more comprehensive plan could be instituted.

Colombia was one of the first countries approached. From preliminary discussions it was apparent that Olaya and his foreign minister, Urdaneta Arbeláez, were interested but tended to be skeptical about American reciprocity. Olaya was also concerned about the political repercussions of a commercial agreement with the United States and was thus reluctant to submit to Congress for ratification any agreement concluded with his northern neighbor.[35]

The U.S. Department of Commerce was equally interested in rectifying what it considered to be discriminations against American products in Colombian tariff schedules. The Bureau of Foreign and Domestic Commerce prepared a lengthy report, *Factors Affecting United States-Colombian Trade*, which strongly supported the negotiation of a treaty and recommended that any negotiations should seek to remedy the Colombian failure to distinguish among 'common,' 'medium,' and 'fine' grades of goods in its tariff, a practice that had worked against American products.[36]

A National Foreign Trade Council report, *The Financial and Trade Problems of Colombia in Their Relation to the United States*, prepared in collaboration with the Council on Inter-American Relations, the Colombian-American Chamber of Commerce, and the Committee on Inter-American Commerce, indicated the extent to which Colombia's instability was the result of her over dependence on four money staples – coffee, petroleum, platinum, and bananas – almost 98% of which went to the United States.[37] The National Foreign Trade Council was especially concerned by the marked decline of American exports to Colombia. In 1929 the value of American exports to Colombia was 60% of the value of its purchases. In 1930, 1931, and 1932, however, the south-bound flow of goods fell to 31%, 21%, and 17% respectively in terms of the value of American imports from Colombia. The council's analysis clearly indicated the margin for improvement in Colombian-American trade and the basis for the conclusion of a trade treaty. 'The primary problem,' according to the report, 'is the immediate creation of new sources of foreign exchange for Colombia, which in turn would be used for a larger consumption of American exports and the future expansion of the prosperity' of Colombia.[38]

The council was in the forefront of the more energetic leaders of commercial expansion. Eugene Thomas, president of the NFTC, supported Secretary of State Cordell Hull's efforts to have Congress expand presidential control over tariff rates. The NFTC worked actively to keep its members abreast of developments in foreign trade and to apprise the departments of State and Commerce of the consensus of its members.[39]

James D. Mooney of the General Motors Export Company, a member of the Latin American Committee of the NFTC, expressed ideas strongly in accord with the embryonic Reciprocal Trade Agreements program. Stressing the necessity for the stimulation of maximum two-way trade, he argued that the American search for markets could be fruitful 'only by making it possible for foreign nations to ship their goods to this nation in heavier volume' and that this necessitated broadening the free list. Only in this way could the United States ensure an outlet for the production of its most 'self-reliant and efficient industries: cotton, wheat, petroleum, automobiles, agricultural machinery.' The advantages of international trade, he maintained,

for the opportunities it provides to any nation to dispose of its productive surpluses in mutually beneficial exchange for the surpluses of other nations, is so clearly demonstrable as an economic premise that it gives one a feeling almost of futility to realize that selfish ... individual impulses so often stand stubbornly in the way of realization.

Mooney enthusiastically supported the use of the unconditional most-favored-nation principle and urged 'that the ultimate objective of America's commercial ... policy should look to equality of treatment.'[40]

Some exporters were less sympathetic to Latin American problems. Walter S. Brewster, president of the Textile Export Association of the United States, complained that in spite of Colombia's favorable balance of trade with the United States, American exporters had been experiencing increasing difficulty in obtaining dollar remittances for merchandise shipped to Colombia. Brewster viewed the situation as 'a gross injustice to United States shippers, since it is perfectly clear that Colombia has ample funds in U.S. dollars to make these remittances ... Colombia should be one of our best natural markets in Latin America.'[41] This combination of an apparent ignorance of the instability of the Colombian financial position with interest in the Colombian market was common in some circles during preliminary consideration of a treaty.

In the summer of 1933 both Colombia and Argentina accepted the American initiative to negotiate treaties. In Washington, observers interpreted the administration's efforts to conclude new agreements as an 'indirect reply to the apparent failure of the London Economic Conference to effect trade agreements for the immediate future.' Raymond Moley, assistant secretary of state, expressed the conviction that the State Department's move was directly in line with American objectives at the London Economic Conference, specifically the reduction of trade barriers and the avoidance of restrictive currency agreements.[42]

Private industry was enthusiastic about commercial prospects. A group of forty prominent manufacturers, led by W.R. Grace & Company, cabled the president:

The foreign and domestic traders of this country in support of your efforts to restore normal conditions are vitally concerned that Congress should grant you adequate authority to negotiate reciprocal trade agreements ... The lack of such authority has resulted in serious ineffectiveness in our tariff system in view of present world conditions resulting from tariff warfare and systems of imperial preferences.[43]

The State Department initiated talks with Colombian officials in late July 1933. William Phillips and Jefferson Caffery headed the American delegation, the latter because of his recent experience in Colombia as the American minister and his close relationship with President Olaya. The third member of the American team was Wallace McClure, chairman of the Latin American section of the Committee for Reciprocity Information, an intergovernmental entity.[44]

From the outset, the Colombian government experienced difficulties in selecting negotiators able to command political confidence in Bogotá. The discussions were barely underway when the Colombian delegation requested suspension pending the arrival of Arturo Hernández and Francisco Restrepo Plata, two Colombian tariff experts Olaya had appointed under pressure from industrial protectionists. With Miguel López Pumarejo, a brother of the future president and the representative of the National Federation of Coffee Growers in New York, the delegation appeared soundly representative of the Colombian economy.[45] Restrepo Plata was the president of the Supreme Customs Tribunal, whose support would be essential were it necessary to obtain congressional approval for the treaty; his personal prestige as one of Colombia's elder statesmen was considerable. A strong Conservative, Restrepo Plata had served as minister of finance under Carlos E. Restrepo in 1919. Hernández was also a Conservative and a member of the Customs Tribunal. Because of his deep protectionist sympathies Hernández had received support for his appointment as a delegate from the National Federation of Industrialists. The American legation in Bogotá was not sympathetic to his appointment. The minister, William Dawson, viewed him as 'a minor politician'; he had briefly been minister of public works in the Abadía Méndez administration, and was the leader of the very unpopular 'Rosca,' a powerful clique which controlled Bogotá politics from 1926 to 1930. Evidently it was Hernández's protectionist sentiments that most concerned Dawson.[46]

Colombian reaction to the projected trade talks was predictably mixed; support or opposition depended largely on the socioeconomic and political standing of the spokesman. What little initial commentary there was tended to be favorable. El Espectador, a Liberal daily that occasionally adopted an anti-American position, expressed on 18 July what was certainly the official and the dominant public sentiment – that any nation which purchased such a large percentage of Colombian exports was entitled to preferential treatment in Colombian trade relations.

El Espectador soon qualified its support for a commercial treaty with the United States. It portrayed the American initiative as an effort to prevent the forthcoming Montevideo Conference from turning into a miniature world economic conference and to calm the fears of American producers faced with increased competition from European exports and domestic Latin American producers. Colombia had been selected, the editorial contended, because Colombian exports did not threaten United States producers. El Espectador was skeptical, firstly because the Colombian agreement had been described as a model agreement for Latin America, and secondly because any agreement concluded prior to the Montevideo Conference would of necessity be signed in haste. The editorial cautioned that it would be preferable to insist on a temporary agreement.[47]

The absence of early press agitation did not indicate an inactive public opinion in Colombia. Protectionists had already pressed successfully for the nomination of Hernández to the Colombian delegation, and by the first weeks in August manufacturing interests were increasing the tempo of their campaign. The National Federation of Industrialists sent a petition to Olaya to impress on him the necessity of protecting local manufacturers, particularly the textile mills in Antioquia, against an influx of goods from the United States. Luis Vélez Marulanda, director-secretary of the federation, warned that the proposed commercial agreements were simply an effort on the part of the developed nations to conquer lost markets.[48]

The influence of the industrialists could not be discounted. The industrial class in Colombia was a comparatively small one but influential beyond its numbers 'by reason of comparative wealth.' By the end of 1940 there were only twenty-nine firms with a fixed capital investment in excess of one million pesos, and the overwhelming majority of manufacturing enterprises had less than 50,000 pesos in fixed capital investment. Dawson doubted that this small but influential faction could determine Colombian commercial policy if there was any threat to the coffee industry. The high percentage of the population that was dependent on coffee growing and export determined the outcome of any confrontation between the coffee federation and industry. Not only were coffee growers more highly organized and influential within the Colombian political and socioeconomic structure, but they also possessed the support of the American legation. A leading coffee grower informed Dawson that the industrialists' cause was futile and stressed that much depended on the American attitude. If the United States imposed a tariff on Colombian coffee, then the entire Colombian economic structure would be placed in jeopardy, as would American exports to that country, since they were purchased largely with coffee profits.[49]

The validity of the coffee growers' argument is difficult to refute, but their narrow-minded approach to Colombian economic development is equally evident. Certainly Colombia stood to benefit in the short run from exports of coffee to the United States, but continued concern over coffee exports diverted attention from long-range diversification of the Colombian economy. More significantly, it would appear that the coffee growers were anxious to ensure a market that was not in fact threatened – at least by a coffee tax in the United States – and the industrialists were quick to point this out.

Moreover, it is important to realize, since the coffee lobby played an important role in the negotiations, that it was not Colombian interests alone which were involved in the Colombian coffee industry. When coffee became a major world export commodity shortly after the first world war, American bankers in Colombia began to assume the leadership in handling exports to the United States. In addition, by the mid-1920s a few American companies had come to dominate the export of Colombian coffee. W.R. Grace & Company, which had been active in the market since 1924, became the second largest exporter of Colombian coffee in the thirties, and it was closely followed by the Great Atlantic and Pacific Tea Company's (A & P) Colombian subsidiary, the American Coffee Company.[50] The parent company became the largest distributor of Colombian coffee in the United States.

The domination of the export end of the coffee industry by American interests led worried coffee growers to seek security in the formation of the National Federation of Coffee Growers in 1928. Although the federation brought greater stability to the industry, it did not have a significant impact on the control exercised by American exporters. Consequently, in 1930 the federation agreed to cooperate with the A & P Company for the marketing of coffee in the United States, with A & P absorbing the advertising costs in return for a guarantee of coffee purity.[51] The struggle between the coffee interests and the industrialists over the trade treaty was, therefore, not simply a quarrel between two Colombian groups.

In mid-August Colombian press agitation increased in intensity, led by the Liberal *El Tiempo*, which on 15 August berated the Colombian public in general for its apathetic attitude toward a crucial development in Colombian-American relations and urged greater attention to the Washington talks. While *El Tiempo* was openly hostile, *El Espectador* vacillated, suggesting on 22 August that many of the nationalists' fears were unfounded and that any treaty negotiated with the United States would not be uniformly unfavorable to Colombian interests. *El Tiempo* claimed there was no honor in being the first Latin American nation with which the United States wished to conclude a commercial treaty, especially when the cost of military preparations for the conflict with Peru had weakened the Colombian bargaining position; it conceded, however, that the importance of the United States to Colombian exporters would be the ultimate deciding factor.[52]

Two prominent Liberal representatives, Julio C. Gaitán and Baldomero Sanín Cano, analyzed the projected commercial treaty for *El Tiempo* readers during the week of 22-29 August. Both men adopted flexible nationalist postures. Gaitán stressed the need for the continued protection of Colombian agriculture and praised the success of the Olaya administration in reducing imports of foodstuffs from twenty million pesos in 1928 to two million in 1932 although he was still not satisfied. On the 22nd he concluded: 'It would be impossible to deny that this country has the capacity to produce in sufficient quantity to satisfy the domestic need ... As far as commodities of primary necessity are concerned, we have demonstrated our capacity by the fact that in spite of the decline in imports ... those goods are not scarce nor have prices risen on the open market.' Referring to increased American efforts to improve cultural relations with Colombia, Gaitán warned that such efforts were solely to improve the atmosphere for trade.

One of the best indications of the trend in official Colombian opinion was a memo prepared by the minister to Washington. Fabio Lozano praised Roosevelt's foreign policy but expressed reservations about American commercial objectives. 'I consider it indispensable,' he suggested to the Department of State, 'that there should be no attempt at this time ... to accomplish ... something of immediate and strict advantage to the men of business of this country, but to lay extensive plans for future interchange.' To Lozano it was vital that Colombia defend certain domestic manufacturing interests. In spite of the fact that the United States imported the bulk of Colombian coffee, he noted, the greater portion of the profit on Colombian exports went to American enterprise; the same was true with respect to petroleum, bananas, and platinum.[53]

To dispel growing opposition to the proposed treaty in congressional circles, Urdaneta Arbeláez defended the government's position before the Senate. The episode was indicative of the depth of the concern over the negotiations, and diplomatically Olaya and his foreign minister both expressed the opinion that the Americans were trying to drive too hard a bargain.[54] American officials concentrated on the purely commercial dimension, although there was also lobbying by bondholders' groups, which viewed the treaty as an opportunity to force the Colombian government to meet its financial obligations.[55] There was only slight sympathy within the State Department for the plight of the bondholders at this juncture. Economic adviser Herbert Feis suggested that the commercial negotiations afforded an opportunity to impress on the Colombians that 'we expect them to exert themselves to make sacrifices to meet obligations held by American citizens.'[56] But for the moment the department went no further in this direction.

Major export associations such as the Institute of American Meat Packers, the Houston Foreign Trade Club, the Textile Export Association, and the American Manufacturers' Export Association made representations to the department in an effort to have the negotiators press for a lowering of the Colombian duties on lard, wheat, flour, rice, and cotton goods, and to emphasize the extent of foreign competition. O.J. Abell, the vice-president of the American Manufacturers' Export Association, asserted that 'the reaction of exporters to the Colombian status reflects an unwillingness to concede that the internal economy of Colombia ... justifies ... the prohibitive level to which its tariffs generally have been raised.'[57]

Jefferson Caffery, in a memorandum to Fabio Lozano, pointed out that the American draft of the treaty requested Colombia to reduce tariffs on some 31.7% (in value) of American products exported there in 1931. In 1932 exports from the United States to Colombia were more than 10.5 million dollars, of which 16.9% represented products on which the American government was seeking concessions. Caffery indicated that 99.2% of American imports from Colombia in 1931 were to remain on the free list in the American proposal.[58]

Lozano crisply replied that Caffery had selected misleading statistics and used them out of context, giving them even greater distortion. Admitting that the United States had an unfavorable balance of trade with Colombia, he argued in terms similar to those of Hoover and the business internationalists that the purpose in seeking a reciprocal trade treaty was to foster mutual economic development; it would be difficult for an agricultural nation such as Colombia to consider substantial reductions on foodstuffs, regardless of the importance of the United States to Colombian coffee exports. 'Any customs measure that would permit the economic weakening of the country by the ruin of her agriculture or of her industries will,' Lozano emphasized, 'injure American commerce, because it will end by reducing appreciably her consumptive capacity, and her purchases abroad will ... be reduced proportionately.' Playing on the American desire to achieve a settlement in the area of defaulted Colombian bonds, Lozano provocatively suggested that the country would be unable to resume service on her foreign debt without new investment.[59]

Throughout September the discussions lagged while each party considered the draft proposals. In the meantime some Colombian business interests were distressed more by exchange controls than by any threat from American commerce. The Chamber of Commerce of Barranquilla cabled to Olaya and his minister of finance, Esteban Jaramillo, that any further increases in the exchange rate would ruin Colombian importers on the Atlantic coast and have serious repercussions on the general economy. Similar criticism of government interference with trade came from the Federation of Commerce in Medellín.[60]

Pressure for liberalizing economic controls inspired a modification of the regulations. In early September the board of directors of the Bank of the Republic and the advisory board of the Office of Exchange and Export, with the support of the government, permitted the purchase of foreign exchange on application to the Control Office.[61]

In Washington the treaty negotiators were prepared by the end of October to resume discussions on a new Colombian proposal. The most emphatic Colombian reservations pertained to agricultural duties, the guarantee that no internal duties be imposed on roasted coffee by the United States, the necessity for Colombian municipalities to retain the right to levy taxes on imported goods, and their preference for a conditional most-favored-nation clause. The evidence suggests that only the American threat to end the negotiations enabled the Colombians to justify the concessions on agricultural products.[62]

Colombia subsequently raised the question of American petroleum imports in relation to the commercial treaty. When Fabio Lozano approached William Phillips about the possibility of obtaining higher quotas on Colombian petroleum exports to the United States, Phillips suspected (correctly as it turned out) that American oil interests in Colombia had initiated the enquiry. Phillips indicated that the secretary of the interior's 28 September order to restrict foreign crude oil imports to the average daily import levels for the second half of 1932 applied equally to all countries, although the companies could determine how they balanced foreign production.[63]

While the Colombian delegation in Washington does not appear to have seriously entertained the suggestion from petroleum interests, it was still under pressure from opponents of the treaty. In Bogotá, opposition intensified in certain business circles. Building on its earlier campaign, the National Federation of Industrialists appointed a committee to present to the minister of finance its protest against what it considered a wholesale reduction of duties;[64] support for the federation's campaign continued to come from Medellín's Conservative daily *El Diario Nacional*, with somewhat less enthusiastic backing from *El Tiempo*.[65]

On 7 December, *El Tiempo* devoted a full page to a survey of press opposition to the treaty, which typified the measured tone of the Colombian position. On the 5th, *Mundo al Día*, for example, suggested that 'without losing sight of the importance of coffee production in the national economy and the necessity of protecting that production as much as possible, we believe that it would be preferable for the United States to tax its importation ... in exchange for conserving our absolute political and commercial independence.'

'Calibán' (Enrique Santos) suggested in his regular column in *El Tiempo* on 8 December that even the present level of protection was not adequate for the defense of Colombian agriculture: 'The dilemma is this: either we demand complete protection or we will face ruin. As far as our manufacturing industries are concerned, we must evaluate the amount of capital invested in them to determine if they have sufficient strength to compete against the influx of foreign products under lower duties.'

Despite the opposition, the two delegations signed the treaty on 15 December, and in the weeks that followed public agitation diminished appreciably. The full-page anti-treaty advertisements which had earlier appeared every two days now disappeared. The American chargé, Sheldon Whitehouse, attributed much of the renewed calm to the moderate tone the highly influential 'Calibán' adopted very likely as a result of the close connection between Olaya and Eduardo Santos, Enrique's brother and heir-apparent to the leadership of the moderate Liberals. Perhaps more indicative of the Colombian business response, however, was an almost immediate decline in new investment in some industries.[66]

While the treaty was no total victory for the American negotiators, little sacrifice was involved in the maintenance of nine major Colombian exports on the free list, since, with the exception of petroleum, they did not compete with domestically produced goods. On the other hand Colombia conceded reductions on approximately 150 tariff items, largely manufactured goods, but also some agricultural products, such as lard, on which the American government had been most insistent.[67]

The Americans failed to obtain a reduction in the Colombian duty on wheat. American wheat producers and shippers indicated during the negotiations that the high duty of 1931 had resulted in a decline in American exports and an increase in the quantity of Canadian wheat that American shippers delivered to Colombian ports. The origin of the wheat was immaterial to the shippers, whose major concern was the activity of Colombian flour mills, 90% of which were controlled by American shipping interests. The State Department, however, was convinced that a Colombian tariff concession would have permitted American wheat to compete in the market.

Herbert Feis forwarded a memorandum, marked 'Urgent,' to the treaty division of the department expressing regret at the failure of the negotiators to obtain the desired reduction. 'I wonder,' he wrote, 'whether we might not let the Department of Agriculture know whether the treaty included provision for lowering the tariff on wheat ... Even outside of the treaty, do you think it would be possible to persuade the Colombian Government to facilitate sales of Pacific North-west wheat into Colombia at the present time? That is a problem with which ... the Department is especially concerned at the present moment.' [68]

Neither government ratified the treaty; yet the negotiations indicated the intensity of American disquiet over the state of the Latin American market and the changes taking place in the Colombian political economy. This was the only bilateral trade treaty negotiated by the Roosevelt administration, as it moved immediately in 1934 to the consideration of more comprehensive commercial legislation. Nevertheless, the American initiative in concluding the treaty appears to have achieved in part its design to mitigate the poor commercial image of the United States in Latin America before the Montevideo Conference.

At Montevideo in December 1933, Cordell Hull worked for the adoption of a resolution designed to counteract Latin American protectionism and to dispel the Latin American contention that the United States departure from the gold standard in April of that year gave Americans a competitive edge in trade. Accordingly on 12 December in the ninth committee, Hull proposed that

at the earliest practicable date ... the subscribing governments ... will simultaneously initiate between and among themselves negotiations for the conclusion of bilateral or multilateral agreements for the removal of prohibitions and restrictions and for the reduction of tariff rates to a moderate level ... The subscribing governments declare further that the most-favored-nation principle enjoins upon states making use of the quotas system or other system for limiting imports, the application of these systems in such a way as to dislocate as little as possible the relative competitive positions naturally enjoyed by the various countries in supplying the articles affected. [69]

Alfonso López, head of the Colombian delegation, presented the major response to Hull's proposals; he was enthusiastic but cautious. 'The United States,' he suggested, 'are beginning to follow an economic and political orientation more in conformity with the desires and more to the advantage of all the peoples of America,' particularly when contrasted with the European attitude which López encountered earlier at the London Economic Conference. He suggested, however, that Hull's objectives were too significant and comprehensive to be accepted by the conference 'without deliberate study,' and until 'we consult our Governments.' López concluded with a further critical reservation: 'My country ... was ... in principle ready to second the initiatives of Delegate Hull in favor of a general tariff reduction ... However, I have always had a great doubt whether ... the advantages of that course [for our countries] are analogous to those of the industrial countries.' When on 15 December the conference called for a vote on the Hull resolution, López answered in the affirmative, but added his reservations.[70]

Consequently, although López stimulated enthusiasm for Hull's resolution, he shared the hesitations of other Latin American delegations. As a personality Hull had taken Montevideo by storm; but the southern neighbors of the United States had often heard such professions of good intentions from Washington, and Latin American adoption of the American resolution on trade practices was largely a gesture of solidarity rather than acceptance of a practicable program. In short, one would find it difficult to share the unbounded enthusiasm Hull showed in writing to the American Manufacturers' Export Association to the effect that 'the adoption of these proposals ... marks the beginning of a new era in the commercial ... relationships between the American states.'[71] The United States had traditionally looked to Latin America as a source for raw materials, a market for American surpluses, and an area of strategic support; that approach to inter-American relations was inherent in both the Colombian treaty and the Montevideo proposals.

2

The United States and
the Colombian marketplace
1934-40

A number of factors prevented the 1933 bilateral trade treaty with Colombia from proceeding to ratification. The initiation of bilateral treaties was a stopgap measure by an administrator in search of a program, and the State Department preferred more comprehensive tariff legislation. Disappointed that President Roosevelt had not acted on his original announced intention to include tariff reform in his 1933 legislation, the department pressed vigorously for action in 1934 and held back the Colombian treaty pending the outcome of its efforts.

In the Roosevelt years the Department of State regained some of the initiative in foreign economic affairs that it had lost to the Department of Commerce in the Hoover ascendancy. But the conflict of bureaucracies over the control of foreign trade was not confined within interdepartmental parameters. The department also found itself in conflict with George Peek, adviser to the president on trade policy and subsequently head of the Export-Import Bank. Peek felt the inherent antipathy of a Midwesterner toward the eastern industrialist and interpreted the State Department's desire to utilize the unconditional most-favored-nation principle as a further sacrifice the American farmer would be required to make for the sake of the manufacturers.[1]

In Cordell Hull's absence from Washington during the Montevideo Conference in December of 1933 and early 1934, Peek experienced considerable success in urging on Roosevelt the merits of barter agreements and agricultural dumping practices. Roosevelt responded by designating Peek to chair a temporary interdepartmental committee with power to recommend 'permanent machinery to coordinate government relations to American foreign trade.' The fact that a committee with similar functions was already in existence (an Executive Committee on Commercial Policy was created in November with Francis Sayre as chairman) made Peek's influence appear even more startling.[2]

Late 1933, however, was very likely the nadir of State Department momentum.

From the Montevideo Conference through the introduction and implementation of the Trade Agreements Act, Hull's approach gained strength. While Roosevelt's opportunism in the political and economic arena determined that both Peek and Hull would be at least temporarily able to command support within the administration, Hull's increasing prestige, the support of such long-standing economic advisers as Charles Taussig, and the continuing depression contributed to Roosevelt's ultimate acceptance of Hull's guidelines.[3]

At the same time that it endeavoured to thwart Peek's influence, the Department of State pressed its own alternative. As chairman of the Executive Committee on Commercial Policy, Francis Sayre informed Roosevelt on 9 January: 'It is the Committee's hope that in the course of the next few months a tariff bill will be enacted giving the Executive power to modify duties and to establish foreign trade relations.'[4] Sayre sought to impress upon the president the impossibility of carrying through a tariff bargaining policy 'without some tariff bargaining legislation,' because 'to secure real concessions, the United States must similarly grant them, and the grant of substantial concessions ... will be almost sure to create sufficient opposition to prevent the ratification of the treaties by Congress.' Sayre was convinced that a practicable program of treaty bargaining required 'power by the President without reference back to Congress.'[5]

Influenced by pressure from the departments of State, Commerce, and Agriculture, on 2 March Roosevelt sent a message to Congress in which he spoke of the urgent need for new tariff measures. In outlining the requirements of new legislation, the president stressed the importance of trade to the American people. 'Idle hands, still machines, ships tied to their docks, despairing farm households, and hungry industrial families' were the conditions a stagnant foreign trade had imposed on American communities.[6] The Trade Agreements bill, introduced in the House the same day, was designed to give the president authority to negotiate executive trade agreements to alleviate the problem of surplus production.

The introduction of the Trade Agreements bill aroused immediate debate. Throughout the discussion of the bill in Congress, opposition centered on what many viewed as the surrender of congressional authority and on political opposition to a lowering of tariff schedules.[7] Because the State Department had not yet published the provisions of the Colombian treaty, uncertainty concerning its contents led to its consideration in the course of the general debate.

The Democrats carried the entire burden of the bill in Congress, yet outside the legislature there appears to have been considerable support for the measure from key business associations. Both the American Manufacturers' Association and the Cotton Shippers' Association, for example, expressed enthusiastic approval of the trade agreements program[8] – a position that was hardly surprising in the light of the United States's declining share of world trade in the early years of the depression.[9]

Following victory in the House by a margin of 274 to 111, the Trade Agreements bill went to the Senate.[10] In the finance committee on 26 April opponents drew a connection between the proposed legislation and the 1933 Colombian treaty; at that time the committee was satisfied by Assistant Secretary Sayre's explanation that the terms of the Colombian treaty had not been released simply because the treaty had not yet been submitted to the Colombian Congress.[11] There was sufficient bipartisan concern over the decline in international trade for the finance committee to report favorably on the bill.[12]

The brief reference to the Colombian treaty in the finance committee hearings aroused further controversy when the tariff legislation reached the Senate floor. On 22 May Republican Senator Henry D. Hatfield of West Virginia introduced a resolution requesting that the State Department furnish a copy of the Colombian treaty for Senate examination.[13] Hatfield was well known for his protectionist outlook, and just a few weeks earlier he had attacked Henry Stimson's free-trade leanings and internationalist sympathies. His comments revealed the extent to which both protectionists and internationalists in this period identified trade competition from Europe and Japan as a serious threat. Only their solutions differed. Hatfield concluded: 'If we revolutionize our industrial fabric it must be done in the interest of the American producer and American consumer, and not having upper-most in mind those who live in other parts of the world, where food products, due to favorable natural environments, are largely developed ... with little mental or physical effort on the part of those who ... ship them into competition in our home market.' On 23 May, in an exchange with Senator L.J. Dickinson of Iowa, Hatfield stressed that Colombian products were basically in competition with American agricultural goods; even industrially, where petroleum was a major export, the country had little to offer the United States.[14]

Senator Huey Long of Louisiana shared Hatfield's annoyance over the apparent reluctance of the State Department to make the Colombian treaty public. The department's rejection of the Senate request to see the treaty confirmed his suspicion that the terms of the Colombian treaty were of no particular benefit to American business; the attitude of the department was indicative, Long warned, of the disdain with which Congress could expect to be treated in commercial policy formulation should it abdicate its powers.[15]

To draw attention away from the Colombian treaty and gain support for the administration's tariff legislation, Senator Bryon Harrison of Mississippi, with Roosevelt's approval, sponsored an amendment to the bill providing for public hearings at which private individuals and groups could present briefs during the negotiation of trade agreements. Harrison's amendment, which became section 4 of the finished bill, was the only modification the administration required to win Senate approval on 4 June. Thomas Lamont of J.P. Morgan & Co. called the act 'the first constructive measure to remedy' the general decline in trade.[16]

The Trade Agreements Act was by no means a totally new departure in American tariff policy; it combined a number of features which had been present in earlier legislation. The delegation of authority to the president to raise or lower rates up to 50% for reciprocating nations was essentially the flexible tariff clause present in both the Fordney-McCumber Act of 1922 and the Smoot-Hawley Act of 1930. The concept of reciprocity had been part of the McKinley Tariff of 1890, generally identified with high protectionism; nor was the unconditional most-favored-nation provision unique to the Roosevelt period, having been present in the legislation of the 1920s as well. The significance of the Roosevelt legislation, however, was the increased emphasis on reciprocity and the willingness to transcend the voluntarism of the business-government relationship before 1932. This shift toward a modified form of state capitalism appears to have received support from internationalist business and banking interests in this period largely because of their realization that economic competitors in areas such as Latin America were receiving substantial assistance from their governments in the search for markets and strategic influence.[17]

The introduction of the Trade Agreements bill aggravated the conflict between the State Department and Peek's office. Armed with Roosevelt's delegation of power to head a committee to study weaknesses in American commercial relations, Peek threw himself enthusiastically into the project. In his subsequent report, Peek urged the adoption of a 'balance sheet' approach to foreign trade, in which bilateralism would be the basic format.[18]

Hull turned to Herbert Feis to provide material for rebuttal and to support more general tariff revision. In a report of 14 June, Feis countered Peek's contention that the establishment of private enterprise abroad operated to reduce the foreign demand for American goods. 'The creation of some of these enterprises,' Feis asserted, 'may have had as an immediate effect the curtailment of international trade, but the general experience has been that the development of other countries in time leads to the growth of trade with us.' Feis thought Peek justified in recommending that the American government keep more accurate statistical records on its financial and commercial relations with foreign countries. He flatly rejected, on the other hand, 'any tendency to regard the course of foreign investment as unnatural and completely out of accord with the situation in the U.S.'[19] Peek's recommendations had little effect at a time when the administration had thrown its full weight behind the Trade Agreements bill, but Peek would renew his attack in the fall of 1934 when the Colombian negotiations returned to public view.[20]

Throughout the late spring and summer of 1934 both Colombian and American officials assumed that a renegotiated treaty would contain few, if any, alterations. Still, some pressure groups in the United States remained discontented with

Colombian trade relations with the U.S. Following the passage of the Trade Agreements Act, the Luckett-Wake Tobacco Company of Louisville, Kentucky, complained that Colombian duties had severely curtailed American exports of leaf tobacco, from 185,678 pounds in 1928 to 35,475 pounds in 1933. Another group which had demonstrated perennial interest in the Colombian financial picture were the holders of Colombian bonds represented by Lawrence E. de S. Hoover.[21]

In late August, on the same day that a trade agreement was concluded with Cuba, the Department of State instructed the American chargé in Colombia, S. Walter Washington, to open the question of the commercial agreement with the Colombian government, mentioning that it was 'not anticipated that any important changes of substance ... would be proposed by the Government ... However, it would not be consistent with the purposes of Section 4 of the [Trade Agreements Act] to give any definite assurance to this effect.' Phillips, revealing the confidence in a prompt settlement that was characteristic of the department's attitude that summer, told Washington that the administration wanted to conclude a Colombian and Brazilian agreement simultaneously. 'It is therefore important that legislative action be taken on the new agreement with Colombia before the end of this year.'[22] In spite of the confidence expressed on both sides, final settlement was prolonged until May of 1936.

Following the announcement of negotiations with Colombia and Haiti, pressure from American exporters began to mount. There was evident dissatisfaction with the terms of the Cuban agreement as it affected textile exports, and such groups were determined to gain preferable concessions in the Colombian agreement.

On 12 September, Muñoz & Co., an exporting firm, enquired about the hearings on the Colombian agreement before the Committee for Reciprocity Information. Sharing the widespread concern of many American textile interests over the threat of Japanese trade, the company warned that 'in order to do anything worthwhile for the United States' export trade with Colombia ... something radical and dramatic [must] be attempted, as otherwise the treaty as far as textiles are concerned, will be meaningless.'[23]

Two essential problems confronted the American textile industry in the fall of 1934. Japanese competition was cutting into American foreign sales, and, in the aftermath of textile strikes in September, the industry also found itself faced with slow demand and declining prices for cotton and gray cotton cloth.[24]

Responding to his constituents in the 26th District of New York, Republican Congressman Hamilton Fish Jr subsequently claimed that some facts of the textile industry were not given sufficient consideration by the State Department during the Colombian hearings. Fish was especially concerned by the fact that in 1933 Japanese textile sales to Colombia had increased 50% although Japan purchased little from Colombia.[25] This imbalance in commercial relations with Japan disturbed the Colombian government as much as it did American textile interests.

The hearings on the Colombian agreement before the Committee on Reciprocity Information afforded Peek another opportunity to challenge the State Department by arguing that the terms of the agreement offered such minimal concessions to American interests that they would endanger subsequent negotiations.[26] He stressed that the agreement's failure to resolve the problems of blocked exchange and defaulted debts meant that the main issues had been avoided, and that the agreement did not in his opinion comply with the stated objective of the Reciprocal Trade Agreements Act – to 'expand foreign markets for American products.'[27]

Hull responded that the most-favored-nation clause would enable the United States to remain commercially competitive in areas where its exports were in considerable excess of its purchases. Sayre objected strenuously to Peek's contention that the department's program would result in the dumping of foreign products on the American market. 'Those in charge of the trade agreement program,' Sayre assured Roosevelt, 'are ... carefully [restricting] the concessions ... to each country to those commodities of which each country is the chief or at least an important source of supply.'[28]

The Department of Commerce was not as enthusiastic as the State Department. Although it opposed Peek's 'effort ... to divert the reciprocal trade program into a device for discriminatory two-way advantages,'[29] there were some misgivings concerning the ultimate impact of the trade program on commercial relations with Latin America. Henry Chalmers of the tariff division suggested that the benefits to agriculture might not be as considerable as many anticipated. In spite of considerable talk about offering effective reciprocity to foreign countries the concessions granted in the Colombian treaty had been minimal: 'We might have been able to get substantial concessions on a larger number of agricultural products from Colombia if we were giving her any important concessions that meant larger markets in the U.S. for her producers.' Chalmers asserted 'that continued duty free admission [of Colombian coffee] does not increase the purchasing power of the other country.'[30]

The business community does not seem to have shared the hesitation of the Department of Commerce. American exporters prepared extensive advertising and sales promotion campaigns in Latin America during the Colombian negotiations. The *New York Times* reported that anticipation of 25 to 50% increases in sales had stimulated a campaign more enthusiastic than that which followed the first world war, a contention substantiated by business correspondence with the State Department.[31]

James Edwards tried without success to have Peek's position on blocked exchange and defaulted debts accepted at the final meeting of the Trade Agreements Committee. The closest the Peek forces came to a modest triumph was the committee's decision to include a provision that when the trade agreement with Colombia was promulgated Colombia would endeavor to implement equitable treatment in its exchange controls,[32] an effort to undermine German trade.

The Department of State was also concerned about the exchange control situation, but it thought Peek's method and timing inopportune. In fact, Feis thought it unwise to conclude any exchange agreement with Colombia based on the Trade Agreements Committee resolution because it was milder than the agreement the department hoped to conclude with Brazil. He opposed any specific reference to the demands of American bondholders in the Colombian agreement because 'should events in Colombia necessitate 'special measures' ... it would be better ... to have complete liberty of action.'[33]

While Hull and his associates were defending the Trade Agreements Program against Peek broadsides, the negotiations with Colombia moved forward. By December of 1934 much of the optimism looking toward a rapid conclusion of the agreement dissipated with the realization that the political necessity for open debate in Colombia would inevitably prolong consideration.[34] Because of the primacy of the debate on the Leticia settlement, it is probable that rapid passage would not have been likely in any case given the climate of opinion in Colombia.[35]

The newly drafted agreement contained several important changes resulting from the successful lobbying by American interests during the Washington hearings. Significant revisions pertained to department and municipal taxation on foreign imports; the inclusion of a new article 10 providing for the control of the export and sale of arms and munitions to foreign countries; and a clause covering the question of foreign exchange control. The State Department revised the old article 4 to include provision for most-favored-nation treatment with respect to national, departmental, and municipal taxation; as revised, article 4 applied to all articles of import, whether included in the schedules or not, for national taxation, and to only those articles included in the schedules for departmental and municipal taxes. In return the United States offered to add three minor Colombian export commodities to the list of reduced duties: tolu balsam, ipecac, and castor beans.[36]

The official Colombian reaction was not favorable. The Foreign Ministry argued that article 10 could be used by the United States to discriminate against Colombia in a time of war with a third power. Secondly, the new article 4 would require a major financial reorganization of a number of departments, as Colombia's provinces were called, something that was impractical under the current economic circumstances. From the American perspective, of course, if the Colombian departments and municipalities could be forced to reorganize their financial operations, then not only American exporters but holders of Colombian bonds stood to gain from any increased economic stability which ensued.[37]

The American government countered the Colombian dissent by suggesting that article 4 contained the only major change in the agreement. Anxious to bring the Colombian agreement into effect simultaneously with the Brazilian, the State Department also considered yielding on article 4 if it proved to be a stumbling block.[38]

Arturo Hernández, the head of the Customs Tribunal and a cosigner of the 1933 agreement, pointed out that there were in fact a number of changes in the agreement. He objected to elimination of the anti-dumping clause, the alteration of the wording of article 2 which seemed to make it possible for the U.S. to impose additional taxes on Colombian goods, the revision of the old article 4 dealing with internal taxes, and the inclusion of article 10. He submitted these reservations to the minister of finance in a report which made a considerable impact on the López administration.[39]

The finance minister suggested that the American proposals disregarded 'many matters which were discussed thoroughly and agreed upon by the Colombian and American delegates when they negotiated the [original] treaty.' Since the American government had made fundamental alterations in the 1933 treaty, the minister, believed the treaty should be renegotiated.

The American chargé now found himself confronted with a more hostile attitude. Alfredo Michelsen, the secretary of the minister for foreign affairs and a customary confidant of the American legation, became cool. He informed the American chargé that he agreed fully with the Hernández report, and that President López would certainly be confronted with major political opposition should he submit such an agreement. The Senate Foreign Relations Committee had already approved the 1933 treaty and had agreed to a new agreement only on the understanding that any changes would be minor. Michelsen told Washington that Colombian officials believed the United States had taken advantage of its economic strength to press Colombia into a disadvantageous agreement. Washington felt out of touch and grew increasingly concerned. He informed the department that President López had an intense dislike for diplomatic conversations at the best of times and under the circumstances would probably not grant him an interview.[40]

The Department of State replied immediately to Washington's anxious despatch of the 23rd; Hull urged Washington to see the minister of finance as soon as possible to impress upon him the need for haste and to express American willingness to send an expert to explain the changes in the agreement proposed by the United States.[41]

In the meantime Olaya, formerly president and now foreign minister, attempted to counteract opposition in political circles to the new commercial proposals. Opposition from Hernández was still a major consideration, however. In spite of the considerable control which Olaya and López together exercised on the Liberal party, they feared that the Senate might not act against Hernández.[42]

To maximize his support, President López in February appointed his brother, Miguel, minister to the United States. In spite of the family connection, the appointment was not interpreted as an act of nepotism, since Miguel commanded significant political support in the capital. He was most closely identified with the National Federation of Coffee Growers, whose interests he had represented in New York for several years. His association with the powerful coffee federation and the fact that he had been one of the Colombian delegates to negotiate the 1933 treaty made his selection a logical one.[43]

Miguel López's connection with the coffee federation was particularly important in view of the conclusion of a Brazilian-American trade agreement on 2 February; Colombian coffee interests naturally wished to examine the Brazilian agreement to rectify any disadvantages in the Colombian-American pact. The appointment of López to the Washington post was, therefore, an effort to assure the federation that it would have an effective voice in the final agreement.[44]

The constant delay in considering the American pact during May resulted from the diversion of Colombian elections and the continued fear of the coffee interests that the American agreement did not provide sufficient security for Colombian coffee exports. Olaya was in no position to press his opinions at this juncture because he was ill, and his normal replacement at such times, the minister of finance, was occupied with the preparation of the budget.[45] In Olaya's absence, the Colombian government requested the minister in Washington to present its objections to the American proposals. On 27 May, when Donald Heath of the State Department spoke with Miguel López, the latter affirmed that his government wanted assurances that any anti-dumping clause would not be used to discriminate against Colombian coffee and was dissatisfied with the provisions of article 4.[46]

To assist in dispelling political opposition to the agreement, Miguel López returned to Bogotá from the Washington mission.[47] In part under his influence, the Colombian government modified its position somewhat. By the time the agreement was signed in July, pending approval by the Colombian Congress, Colombian negotiators had accepted the United States's position on the retention of an anti-dumping clause in the agreement. The State Department, on the other hand, decided not to press for a provision on the question of exchange control, at least in part from a desire to ensure acceptance of the agreement. As Assistant Secretary of State Sumner Welles observed at the time: 'So much controversy has been provoked in Bogotá and so much misunderstanding has resulted on account of our new requests that I don't think any trade agreement negotiations would have been concluded if the Colombian Minister had not himself gone to Bogotá.'[48]

Throughout August 1935 the Colombian press devoted little space to the trade agreement. It was not until late in the month that a protectionist Cali paper, *El Heraldo Industrial*, presented the trade agreement as one which adhered to the spirit of reciprocity. Pointing out that even the Federation of Industrialists had now inclined toward the treaty, the editorial expressed the hope that ratification of the agreement would stimulate the import of flour from the United States. As a reflection of intense Colombian regionalism, *El Heraldo Industrial* claimed that only the import of flour from the United States could break the monopoly of the Sabana of Bogotá's 'wheat trust,' which had made prices for flour prohibitively high in western Colombia. Past experience had demonstrated that the import of wheat was not the answer; what was essential was the availability of cheaper, higher-quality American flour. Certainly American imports would cut into the profits of the Colombian milling industry, but because of the highly mechanized nature of the industry this would do little to increase unemployment.[49]

When the State Department released the terms of the Colombian agreement in October, the *New York Times* reported an enthusiastic reception among American exporters. On 10 October the *Times* praised the Secretary of State for his conclusion of the reciprocal trade agreement and presented the pact as highly favorable to American commercial interests, granting concessions on 50% of imports from the United States.[50]

The Colombian reception of the agreement was less enthusiastic but on the whole positive. Many Colombian businessmen were optimistic about the prospects for improved trade relations, an optimism that was probably mirrored in the upward turn taken by the Bogotá Stock Exchange. Yet the National Federation of Industrialists continued to dissent following the signing of the agreement. The dominant Liberal press of Bogotá, *El Espectador* and *El Tiempo*, smothered the opposition by disclaiming any agreement with the anti-treaty coverage it published. *El Espectador* portrayed the agreement as recognition of the fact that Latin America and the United States were natural markets for each other's products and described the pact as the 'birth of a new orientation in commercial relations,' much the same phrase Cordell Hull had used two years earlier in Montevideo.[51]

What opposition there was came from the Conservative party press, motivated by both political pragmatism and economic conviction. The Medellín correspondent for *El País* on 13 October reported the dissatisfaction among manufacturers in the Antioqueño capital. He quoted the director of the National Association of Colombian Industry, Marco Tulio Pérez, to the effect that the treaty would make it virtually impossible for some domestic industries to survive. On the same day Guillermo Camacho Montoya, a prominent Conservative journalist, asserted in *El*

País that Colombian acceptance of the trade agreement would make the nation no more than a 'subsidiary of the United States.'

One of Barranquilla's major Conservative papers, *La Prensa*, was mildly opposed to the agreement. An article by Ramón Emiliano Veléz on 1 November attempted to draw a connection between the Colombian-American commercial agreement and domestic social unrest. He suggested that the adoption of a protectionist commercial policy had brought industrial progress to the country, with an improving standard of living for the Colombian worker. Acceptance of the agreement, he wrote, would result in the decline of production, increased unemployment, and social unrest that would erase the gains of recent years.[52]

The leading Conservative paper of Medellín, *El Colombiano*, took up the gauntlet against the agreement in an editorial of 5 November. Writing the lead editorial, the prominent Conservative Silvio Villegas argued that Colombian industrialists were completely justified in their alarmed reaction to the commercial pact. The partisan nature of the Conservative attack was apparent in the critique of the López administration. While many Conservatives, Villegas among them, could be classed as ideologically anti-American, most of the Conservative anti-trade agreement propaganda was directed toward regaining lost political power. Even in Villegas's editorial denouncing the commercial agreement, he devoted much of his space to a scathing attack on the Liberals' proposed labor reforms.[53]

Conservative opposition to the commercial agreement proved totally ineffective. With the party out of power, and with few prominent figures other than Laureano Gómez able to lead the opposition to President López's policies, the Liberal government was able to move forward briskly in 1935 and 1936 with its legislative program. Although the Conservatives opposed the conclusion of the trade agreement, party members were inconsistent in their approach to the issue, tended to place greater emphasis upon the dangers of López's domestic legislation, and appeared incapable of uniting with other anti-treaty factions. A striking example of this was furnished when the largely Conservative Bogotá City Council defeated a motion calling on Congress to reject the agreement. Council appears to have defeated the motion primarily because it was introduced by a Communist member, Gilberto Vieira.[54]

Vieira's motion in the council was indicative of the trend in the reaction of labor elements to the agreement. On 7 November, textile workers from the heavily industrialized Medellín area protested to Congress against the excessive protection of agriculture at the expense of the textile industry. The petition for the rejection of the agreement carried seven hundred signatures, but it seems to have been dismissed without any meaningful debate.[55]

The very heated six-month congressional debate over ratification of the Colombian-American agreement obscured the actual weakness of the opposition forces.

The 1935 Congress was composed almost exclusively of members of the Liberal party, where opposition to the agreement tended to be of an obstructionist nature led initially in both houses by a bloc of Antioqueño Liberals. As had been the case with the debate over the Reciprocal Trade Agreements bill in the United States, the Colombian Congress was jealous of its prerogatives and objected to what it viewed as excessive pressure from the president for a prompt acceptance of the commercial agreement without amendments.[56]

Given the apparent lack of sustained ideological opposition in Congress, representatives and senators gradually tired of obstructionist tactics. In February, the Chamber voted for ratification by a 69 to 5 margin, and early in April the Senate followed suit.[57] In one of the final speeches on 6 April, Senator Héctor José Vargas, Boyacá, spoke briefly about his reasons for supporting the treaty. His explanation was highly indicative of the official Colombian attitude at that moment toward relations with the United States:

I have voted for the treaty ... with the United States because I consider that, in accepting the point of view of their new commercial policy, granting them important concessions without having obtained anything except a confirmation of our present status, we give them the best evidence of our sincere desire to cooperate ... toward the re-establishment of the balance and rhythm of our commercial interchange.[58]

The effect of the reciprocal trade agreement on Colombian-American trade should be viewed largely in terms of the objectives with which the United States pressed for agreements in Latin America. American officials hoped to obtain more than short-term increases in the export of surplus commodities to the other republics. The Trade Agreements program was clearly both a strategic and a trade weapon designed to combat European and Japanese competition for the markets of South America.[59] In the process of stabilizing the market in Colombia, the trade agreement of 1936 not inadvertently accomplished a second and closely related purpose – drawing that nation more fully into the American sphere of influence.

American concern with competition from Europe and Japan was particularly significant in view of the relatively short period during which the United States had been dominant in the Colombian market. The disruption of the nineteenth-century patterns of trade during the first world war and the simultaneous rise of coffee as a major world export had led to a decline in the importance of British trade for Colombia and the advance of the United States. At the outbreak of war in Europe in 1914 Colombia sent 50% of her exports to the United States; four years later that figure had risen to 82.4%.[60]

The decline of Germany's importance in Colombian trade during the first world war and the early 1920s paralleled that of the United Kingdom. It was the fear of German resurgence that contributed to official anxiety. The fact that Germany had been the 'enemy' in the war led American officials to view her as a serious threat to the United States in Latin America; recovery of the German position in the Colombian market by 1935, when she replaced the United Kingdom as a source for Colombian imports, made that potential resurgence a reality.[61]

In the 1920s the State Department was inclined to believe that German business representatives were disrupting American relations with Latin American countries. In September 1927 William R. Castle Jr related to Francis White an interesting conversation he had recently had with retired Colonel John Stuart of Black, McKenny and Stuart, an engineering firm. Just returned from Colombia, Stuart was convinced that German nationals operating there were determined to frustrate the conclusion of Colombian government contracts with American companies. He also claimed American commercial difficulties in Latin America were directly linked to the fact that 'German agents in Latin America ... were stirring up anti-American sentiment.' Consequently, when Hoover, as president-elect, determined to tour Latin America, one of his reasons for doing so was to dispel the anti-American sentiment propagated by the German, Italian, and British-subsidized press as part of their campaign to stimulate trade.[62]

American concern over German activities in Latin America did not become acute until 1938,[63] but it is far too simplistic to suggest that that concern was solely a response to Nazi propaganda. It may have been true that Germany made every effort not to antagonize the United States in her dealings with Latin America because American investment tended to improve German commercial possibilities in the area,[64] but the State Department certainly did not picture the German presence in such terms. On the contrary, U.S. government correspondence and the American press throughout the 1930s were replete with references to the effects of German (and Japanese) commercial activities in Colombia alone, where German influence never approached the level it did in countries such as Argentina, Brazil, and Chile.

Japanese commercial relations with Colombia in the 1930s were marginal in comparison with the commerce of the industrial leaders; her constant search for markets in the area and her conflict with American interests in China, however, distorted, at least from the perspective of the United States, Japan's immediate importance in Latin America.[65]

In 1934 Japan and Colombia established formal diplomatic relations, and commercial activities intensified. Yet the growth of Japanese sales to Colombia in the early years of the depression was not accompanied by increased exports to Japan.[66] The result was that after May 1935 the two countries agreed to continue trade on

a restricted basis for a six-month trial period, during which the Colombian legation in Tokyo and representatives of the National Federation of Coffee Growers
hoped to stimulate coffee sales to Japan. At the same time the Exchange Control
Board established a ceiling on Japanese exports to Colombia. Less than a month
later the Colombian government announced that unless Japanese purchases increased, Colombia would discontinue imports from that country until the end of
October.[67]

There was a definite relationship between the Colombian decision and American policy. Although there is considerable evidence that Colombian business
opinion was unfavorable to continued relations with Japan,[68] the Colombian government took strong action against Japan in part because it believed this move
would please the United States. The State Department certainly wished to improve trade with Colombia, yet it shrank from the prospect of being accused of
interfering in the commercial policy of another country. When the American
chargé informed the department of the Colombian government's action, Herbert
Feis and Sumner Welles were concerned that the United States not get involved.
In a memo to Welles on 18 June 1935, Donald Heath suggested: 'I believe it desirable that no such misapprehension should exist in Colombia or elsewhere, and
do not see why, since we are pursuing definitely a liberal foreign commercial policy, we should not seek in a proper way to gain adherents to that policy.'[69]

Amid professions of good intentions, the State Department did press for the
discontinuation of the acceptance of German 'ASKI' or compensation marks used
specifically by Germany to undercut competition in Latin America. Before the
conclusion of the trade agreement with Colombia, the department instructed
William Dawson to investigate the status of Colombian trade with Germany. The
Department of State had been receiving complaints from American exporters
that the use of compensation marks had enabled Germany to increase its competitive position in the Colombian market; Dawson was directed to determine whether Colombian authorities were facilitating German activities.[70]

Investigation indicated that coffee exports to Germany had increased 50% in
volume in the first quarter of 1935, and Colombian imports from Germany were
up 90% in value over the same period in 1934. The American minister in Bogotá
believed that this increase was primarily the result of the fact that compensation
marks derived from the sale of Colombian coffee to Germany were currently offered at a discount at least 20% below the official rate for the Reichsmark. He
was optimistic that this situation would be temporary, however: 'I am informed
that at present the Colombian Exchange Control [Board] is taking steps to make
sure that coffee shipped to German ports is actually for German consumption,'
and not for resale to other parts of Europe and the United States.[71]

In mid-June Dawson again reported that German interests, using compensated marks, appeared to be on the verge of depriving an American firm of a government contract worth two million pesos for the construction of a pipeline. The department suggested that he raise the issue of German tactics with the Colombian government and emphasize that the United States expected its nationals to receive treatment equal to that afforded other countries: 'It is the Department's belief that the system of exchange control and the restrictive exchange agreements which have grown out of them are responsible in a large degree for the continuance of the depression in world trade.' Hull urged Dawson to stress the 'potentially injurious effects of these practices and their bearing on the American policy of liberal trade.'[72]

Alberto Bayón, the head of the Exchange Control Office, assured Dawson that Colombia did not want to stimulate trade 'through an artificially low medium of exchange.' He indicated that before the Exchange Board's ruling of 25 June, centralizing operations under the Bank of the Republic and its correspondent in Germany, the Dresdner Bank, no Colombian agency had been able to exercise any effective control. Bayón thought that the 25 June action had been a very positive one, since the German government had virtually suspended commercial dealings with Colombia as a result of the clamping down on the use of compensated marks.[73]

In spite of Dawson's optimism in September 1935 that Colombian-German relations were deteriorating, both the German and Colombian governments appeared anxious to continue the compensation arrangement. On 5 November the two governments, in an attempt to stabilize relations, signed a temporary agreement, which both pleased and distressed the United States. In terms of exchange control the November agreement was an effort on the part of Colombia to extend the use of ASKI marks, at the same time removing certain discriminatory features. It took control out of the hands of the Bank of the Republic – a development which disturbed American interests – and provided that any Colombian bank could have an ASKI account with the German bank of its choice. Colombian and German merchants were to enjoy complete freedom, moreover, in selecting the banks through which they conducted business. The last two aspects of the agreement were included to prevent the continued domination of transactions by the Banco Antioqueño-Alemán. The only feature which pleased American officials was that all freight on merchandise of third countries shipped in German carriers was to be paid in free exchange.[74]

From 1935 through 1938 Colombia and Germany continued to conduct trade relations on a compensation basis, and the system enabled the two nations to carry on a lucrative trade. German exports to Colombia showed a steady increase from 1933 through 1936. In 1935 her share of Colombian imports was 18.7%; in 1936 that figure increased to 22.3%.[75] In 1937, although German exports to Colombia declined drastically to 13.5%, Germany still ranked second as a market for Colombian exports.[76]

The importance of the trade agreement with Colombia lies, therefore, at least partially in the impact it had on Colombia's total trade picture. In 1935, before the agreement was signed, Harry Tipper, the executive vice-president of the American Manufacturers' Export Association, expressed the opinion that German and Japanese gains over American exporters in Colombia and Brazil (the only two countries in South America where the United States was being undersold) were temporary, because the Trade Agreements Act promised to undermine the compensation basis of exchange.[77]

Trade statistics covering the period immediately following the conclusion of the agreement with Colombia suggest, firstly, that while there were no startling changes, American exports to Colombia increased markedly in proportion to Colombian exports to the United States, and secondly, that the Colombian industrial sector possessed the capability to compete with imported products.[78] The change in American exports to Colombia relative to Colombian exports and European trade is most significant, since an increase in the volume of Colombian-American trade could have been simply the result of improved economic conditions in 1936.

A comparison of trade in September 1936 with the same month in 1935 reveals that American exports to Colombia increased in value from 3,361,000 pesos to 4,977,000 (the U.S. dollar equaled 1.78 and 1.75 pesos in 1935 and 1936, respectively). Colombian imports from all other countries in that month increased at a comparable rate, from 8,104,000 pesos in 1935 to 12,028,000 pesos in 1936. To consider a broader period of time, in the first ten months of 1936 Colombian exports to the United States declined 3% from the same period in 1935, but its total exports increased 27%. At the same time Colombian imports from the United States registered another marked increase.[79]

A 1937 report prepared by the American legation in Bogotá compared only the months of June, July, and August 1935 with the same period in 1936. It indicated that Colombian purchases of products on which concessions had been granted the United States increased 101.7%; purchases of the same commodities from all other countries declined 34%. The Bureau of Foreign and Domestic Commerce specifically attributed to the trade agreement the increases in American exports to Colombia.[80]

In the first three months of 1937 Colombia began to reap a share of the benefits of the agreement, as the value of her exports to the United States rose 31.3%. Again, however, the greater improvement was in favor of the United States, whose exports to Colombia were 67.2% higher than in the first three months of 1935.[81]

One approach to determining the impact of the agreement is to consider the statistics for individual commodities on which Colombia granted concessions. The legation report mentioned above indicated a substantial increase in Colombian purchases of these commodities, and this is particularly significant when viewed in conjunction with American export objectives in 1936 and 1937.

On 19 March 1936, Secretary of Agriculture Henry Wallace pointed out that production control programs had not removed the chronic problem of agricultural surpluses. 'Export markets for wheat, pork, and tobacco, lost following the enactment of the Smoot-Hawley Tariff of 1930, have only in small part been regained,' he suggested. 'The huge carry-over of cotton ... has not yet been reduced to normal.'[82]

Secretary of Commerce Daniel Roper referred to a similar problem in the cotton industry: 'The ultimate effects upon the South of the gradual alienation of our foreign markets should be well understood ... The serious aspect is occasioned by factors that are causing a decline in cotton exports, concurrently with increasing foreign production.' The secretary was convinced that the trend was not temporary, and that the shift to foreign-grown cotton and self-sufficiency would make it increasingly difficult for American exporters unless something was done to make the price of American cotton competitive.[83]

In the Colombian market for textiles the United States was contesting second place behind the United Kingdom, which dominated the market with 55% of total imports in 1937.[84] In 1935 the United States ranked third behind Japan's 12.7%. The next year a combination of Japanese difficulties in Colombian trade and the implementation of the trade agreement enabled the United States to move into second place in Colombian textile imports with 18.6% of the market. By the end of 1937, the first full year in which the agreement was in operation, American interests had secured 20.2% of total textile imports.

Statistics also indicate that the trade agreement enabled the United States to compete more effectively with Germany for the Colombian market in manufactured goods. In the lucrative machinery and apparatus trade, the American share of Colombian imports rose from 71.9% in 1935 to 75.6% in 1937 at the expense of German exports, which declined from 13.1% to 11.8%. In terms of total Colombian imports of metallic goods, the United States share rose to 54.2% in 1937 from 42.2% two years earlier.[85]

Colombian exports in the 1935-7 period did not increase as much as those of the United States. The fact that in each of these years coffee accounted for more than 50% of the value of Colombian exports and that the balance was completed by crude petroleum and gold, with slight assistance from bananas, hides, and platinum, underlined Colombia's continued dependence on a few major exports. Significantly, Colombian exports to the United States increased only in the case of coffee and bananas, where the value of the increase was much less than the volume indicated.[86]

The Colombian failure to make any major advance in its exports to the United States confirms the impression that the trade agreement was little more than a guarantee of the status quo for Colombia in return for concessions on her part. The short-term effect was to reduce the unfavorable American balance of trade with Colombia by stimulating exports to the south. In 1934 American imports from Colombia had exceeded exports by $42,823,787; three years later the figure was $4,055,427, a major adjustment within a short period of time.[87] Moreover, a comparison of the 1936-7 average with that for 1934-5 reveals that while American exports to Colombia increased 53.6% in the later years, Colombian exports to the United States actually registered a decline of 2.2%.[88]

Repeated efforts by American officials to impress upon the Colombian government the need to 'liberalize' trade methods had a definite impact during these years on the competitive position of the United States in the Colombian marketplace. In October 1937, William Dawson wrote to the Department of State: 'It appears that the Colombian Government's commercial policy is definitely tending to approach the basic purposes and objectives of the trade agreements program of the United States.'[89]

3

Finance diplomacy

A phenomenon closely related to the general commercial relationship just discussed was the expansion of indirect investment by American bankers and citizens during the pragmatic but sometimes 'Polyannic' years which followed recovery from the post-first world war recession. Just as Americans optimistically approached the possibility of new markets in Colombia for United States commodities, so the idea of selling Colombian bonds in the American market caught the official and public imagination. American financial expansion was general in Latin America in the decade after the war.[1] Latin American countries were eager to participate in the sometimes uncontrolled investment surge which earned the epithet 'the dance of the millions,' a phrase exemplifying the often reckless plunge of investors after wealth.[2] Colombians and Americans also, however, shared a belief in the productive power of loans obtained through the sale of government bonds in the United States. These funds were earmarked for precisely the type of development that Herbert Hoover as secretary of commerce and officials of the Bureau of Foreign and Domestic Commerce thought desirable – transportation and other internal improvements desperately needed in Colombia. It was believed that such development, fostered by international cooperation, would bring Colombia and other Latin American societies into the twentieth century and mitigate the effects of international economic disparity. Those who emphasize only the exploitative dimension of the bankers' scramble for business in the 1920s miss the much more important liberal internationalism which motivated policy-makers in this period.[3]

An examination of the Colombian experience underlines the tensions which existed, not only between government officials and bankers, but within these groups and institutions as well. It also reveals the interaction between foreign policy and international financial trends. Regardless of State Department objectives, their realization was largely dependent on appropriate action by central banking institutions and treasuries in Europe and the United States. So closely tied were the economies of countries on the gold exchange standard that uncertainty or crisis in Britain, France, or the United States meant inevitable problems in dependent countries such as Colombia.[4]

Initially hesitant to float bond issues of the Colombian national, departmental, and municipal governments, New York bankers by 1926 became the major source for the financing of Colombian public works. From 1927 to the end of 1928 the total external debt increased 200% to $197,691,000, whereas between 1920 and 1926 Colombia had borrowed a total of only 51,000,000 pesos in the American market.[5] In 1927 alone borrowing reached 67,464,000 pesos, and by mid-1930 there were more than 200,000,000 pesos in loans outstanding.[6] In terms of total borrowing in South America, by 1928 only Argentina, Chile, and Brazil exceeded Colombia in the value of government and corporate securities held in the United States.[7] As a contemporary observer pointed out, 'Of all the Caribbean countries, Colombia seemed to be profiting most by the "new era" and fell most heavily under its spell.' What did not augur well for the future was the fact that 'its borrowings – at least those directly by the central government – tended to be made without the specific guarantees that were still demanded of weaker units.'[8]

A variety of factors accounted for the new confidence of Wall Street in Colombian securities, not the least of which was Edwin W. Kemmerer's 1923 financial mission to Bogotá. The influential Princeton economist had performed similar services for a number of countries. From 1903 to 1906 he served as financial adviser to the Philippines, and from 1917 to 1919 to Mexico and Guatemala. Shortly before his appointment to the Colombian commission he had returned from a tour of Argentina, Uruguay, Chile, and Brazil under the auspices of the Department of Commerce.[9] His rapid but thorough examination of the Colombian fiscal structure resulted in the establishment of a central bank, a concept to which he was strongly committed, and a reorganization of the country's treasury system. As a product of the Progressive era, Kemmerer viewed central banks of issue and rediscount, separate from government and staffed by experts, as essential for the exercise of financial power without political interference.[10] Such stability was also essential for the development of Colombian trade. Prior to the first world war there was no system of discounts and trade acceptances in the country, with the result that foreign trade was financed on long-term credit, with a Foreign Export Commission functioning as banker. The tendency after the war was for closer ties with the United States and the establishment of a system of exchange with shorter credits, a system in which foreign – especially American – banks played a vital role.[11]

As the American role increased in the 1920s, that of the British declined. The sustained effort of the British Foreign Office to make its products competitive in

Colombia was more a symptom of declining power than evidence of a reinvigorated imperialism. Making allowances for the effects of Anglo-American rivalry on his attitude, the 1928 comments of Edmund Monson, the British minister in Bogotá, are indicative of the extent to which Colombia was drawn into the American orbit. 'Perhaps, and with some good reason, Colombia regards as inevitable her eventual engulfment, and has decided to gain what immediate benefit the situation offers ... Whatever the reason,' he noted in closing, 'it becomes daily more obvious that President Abadía's Government have involved themselves in a financial entanglement with the United States from which there is now no escape, and which must eventually deliver the republic bound to the world's rough creditor.'[12]

The Kemmerer mission, funds obtained in the American bond market, the $25,000,000 derived from the Thomson-Urrutia Treaty, and the promising petroleum resources all contributed to a major boom in Colombia in the 1920s. Trade increased, the assets of commercial banks tripled between 1924 and 1928, the construction industry grew rapidly, and prices and incomes rose.[13] The weakness in this boom was not the fact that Colombia was jeopardizing her sovereignty through the American connection, but the fact that the growth was poorly coordinated.

To curtail the chaotic borrowing by departmental and municipal governments, in 1928 President Miguel Abadía Méndez pressed for legislation requiring governors to obtain the approval of the national government before undertaking public works for which external financing was needed. The result, law 6 of that year, was less than effective, however. Theoretically all loans to local governments had to be cleared with Bogotá, and the government was empowered to refuse authorization when the amount required to service the debt constituted more than 20% of the borrower's ordinary revenue. In practice, however, permission to borrow was not denied even under the most obvious violations of restraint. 'The apportioning of railway and road routes,' observed the British minister, 'has become the sport of local politics; a national plan of transport arteries has given way to a mere jumble of disconnected and improductive [sic] works of highly doubtful value and heavy costs.'[14]

Confronted by a proliferation of foreign bonds in the United States, the American government failed to take effective measures to counteract the indiscriminate and unrestrained lending, until the situation reached crisis proportions after 1929. When it did move to publicize the insecurity of some Colombian investments in September 1928, other factors clouded its motivation.

The banker-government relationship is important to an understanding of the development of American foreign policy in the 1920s. The government position on private loans to Latin American countries appears to have been remarkably consistent. Government agencies provided to the American business community financial and political information that made it possible to determine the relative importance and security of investments. The State Department, with the agreement of the bankers, also exercised an informal screening power over private loans; but this does not seem to have been a restraining force in the floating of Latin American government bonds. The 1921 meeting of Harding administration officials with the leading financial houses, and the State Department press release of 3 March 1922 which resulted from the meetings, merely formalized this screening process, since it had long been the procedure of the larger houses such as J.P. Morgan & Co. to discuss major loans with the State Department prior to final approval.[15] The system that evolved, in other words, was a prime example of Hoover's progressivism, in which government functioned as an aid to private enterprise in the productive use of American capital abroad; Hoover viewed such capital flows as vital to domestic economic growth,[16] a sentiment he shared with key figures in the 1920s and 1930s as they attempted to consolidate an 'international legal order of the industrial-creditor nations.'[17]

Both the government and some of the larger, more responsible investment bankers took the initiative in attempting to restrain overborrowing in the United States by Latin American countries. Hoover, as secretary of commerce, continued to emphasize the need for productive loans. And in 1927 Thomas Lamont, speaking to the International Chamber of Commerce, called for a halt to indiscriminate lending abroad and to excessive scrambling for business among the investment bankers. In the Colombian instance, J.P. Morgan & Co. declined to float government bonds because it viewed the credit situation as unstable. The highly influential finance and investment division of the Department of Commerce, under Grosvenor Jones, also tried to impose restraints on Colombia by threatening to discourage investors unless the Colombian government curtailed borrowing by the departments and municipalities.[18] When self-regulation was not forthcoming by 1928, the Department of Commerce determined to take concrete action to warn investors against potential loss.[19]

In the period before the Department of Commerce implemented its intentions, the State Department reluctantly accepted the necessity of distributing to the financial community a special report on the Colombian economy, even if such action meant straining diplomatic relations at a sensitive juncture in the petroleum debate. As S.W. Morgan of the State Department observed, such action would be 'for the protection of the American investing public.' Officials such as Morgan and Julius Klein, head of the Bureau of Foreign and Domestic Commerce, believed that a temporary diplomatic rift was preferable to a financial collapse in Colombia that would threaten the full spectrum of American investments.[20]

State Department officials were especially concerned with the implications of government involvement in foreign bond sales in the United States. Consequently, Secretary Kellogg had on 28 December 1927 issued special instructions to American representatives abroad. 'Special care should be taken,' the circular instructed,

that the record with respect to financial negotiations be clear and self-explanatory and that diplomatic officers in no way inadvertently lend color to claims ... that there exist ... relationships involving the responsibility of the Department in connection with such loans.

The instructions concluded with the assertion that

the Department, in its announcement of March 3, 1922, and its letters to bankers pursuant to the announcement, has uniformly stated that it will not pass upon the merits of foreign loans as business propositions, nor assume any responsibility whatever in connection with loan transactions. [21]

It was thus following a lengthy period of official discussion of loan policy and the condition of foreign finances that the Department of Commerce on 29 September 1928 issued a special circular on the Colombian economy.[22] Prepared by staff member James C. Corliss, it concentrated its criticism on the financial instability of the Colombian government and its ineffectual efforts to maintain control over the financial policies of the departments and municipalities. Corliss argued that the provisions of law 6 of 1928, authorizing the government to reject applications for loans when the servicing of the debt exceeded 20% of the debtor's ordinary revenues, were inadequate because they did not cover the refunding of foreign obligations; the term 'ordinary revenues,' moreover, was open to flexible interpretation in the search of the local governments for funds to finance public works. Corliss indicated that liquor legislation introduced that year in the Colombian Congress, raising prices and controlling the retail of alcohol, also threatened to reduce departmental revenues intended to meet the service on new obligations. In a lengthy statistical analysis Corliss painted a gloomy scene of the security of American investment in Colombia.[23]

Reaction to the Corliss circular was mixed. The Colombian minister in Washington, Enrique Olaya Herrera, protested to Julius Klein what he viewed as a 'hostile statement' of the American government. The director of the Colombian Bureau of Information in New York, Abraham Martínez, in a note to Grosvenor Jones, conceded the accuracy of the circular's statistics but questioned the tone and purpose of the document.[24]

The opposition Liberal party press took advantage of the American action to undermine the Conservatives; but on the whole there does not appear to have been any significant outburst of anti-American sentiment which can be traced expressly to the circular. This can be attributed largely to the growing consensus in Colombian political circles that loans should be curtailed. The secretary of the American legation commented: 'Its reception here ... was marked with a gratifying and most unusual absence of violent denunciation of the United States.'[25]

William J. Samels, manager of the National City Bank in Colombia, depicted public reaction to the special circular as being more hostile; yet he conceded it would oblige the Colombian government to come to terms with the critics of its financial policies. 'There is considerable agitation here,' Samels informed Victor Schoepperle, vice-president of National City, 'and a great deal of criticism of the manner in which the Colombian Government has handled its finances.' Samels added that the public debate occasioned by the bond crisis had given rise to talk in some circles of obtaining a fiscal agent in the United States to handle Colombian issues, but 'in view of the inflammatory speeches of some of the members of Congress against everything American ... any steps ... toward the establishment of a fiscal agency would be met with considerable opposition.'[26]

The British legation in Bogotá viewed the American action from an entirely different perspective. The British minister suggested the intent of the circular was to impress upon the Colombians the power of the United States to affect Colombia's international credit; he further intimated that the State Department planned to use this fiscal instrument as a lever to obtain a favorable settlement of the Barco petroleum concession, in which the South American Gulf Oil Company had been involved for several years.[27]

Monson's allegations contained a kernel of truth. The State Department was at that time involved in a disagreement between the Colombian government and Gulf Oil's operations in the country, and it was anxious for the government to introduce petroleum legislation more attractive to American investment. Yet Monson too readily ignored the fact that the British had also expressed concern at the overextended loan policy of the Colombian government, that it had been equally skeptical of the June 1928 financial legislation, and that British petroleum interests had also been seeking to obtain concessions from the Abadía administration.

This is not to suggest that the American government acted out of disinterested concern for Colombia, but rather that its economic objectives were much broader than Monson intimated. To allow Colombia to continue to regress toward potential default on its external debt threatened not only the investment in bonds but the security of American trade relations with Colombia and the growing American industrial investment in the country. The American government's concern to bring economic stability to the Colombian situation was apparent in a comment by Bert L. Hunt, a former commercial attaché in Bogotá, to Grosvenor Jones. 'It was my feeling all the way through our negotiations,' Hunt recalled on 2 February 1932, that the stopping of loans to Colombia would be a great service to both Governments, and I sincerely believe that the issuance of the Circular ... prevented the further loss to American citizens of several tens of millions of dollars and a saving to the Colombian Government of a much heavier burden in foreign indebtedness than it is at present carrying. It was also the influence which made possible the election of Dr. Olaya with all its attendant benefits [to the United States].[28]

The Colombian government attempted to strengthen its credit standing by reforming those aspects of its fiscal policy which had come under attack. Although the bullish New York market maintained the competitive level of Colombian bonds, the Abadía administration reorganized the public works administration and sought to lessen the impact of the alcohol legislation on departmental revenues.[29] Especially well received was the creation in November of a National Council of Transportation and Communication. R.O. Hall, acting head of the finance and investment division of the Bureau of Foreign and Domestic Commerce, referred to the reorganization of the public works program as 'the key to the present situation in Colombia.'[30]

When the Colombian government replied to the American broadside, it gave indications that it would be interested in expanding Colombian financial ties with England and stimulating its European trade relations. Britain was equally anxious to see administrative reforms effected in Colombia, but British officials in London and Bogotá also hoped to capitalize on this temporary Colombian disenchantment with the United States to obtain for Lazard Bros. of London and Paris the Colombian fiscal agency. The plan which evolved provided that the fiscal agency would be shared by Lazard and the Guaranty Trust Co. of New York. The only major obstacle to the immediate conclusion of an agreement with the Colombian government was the request for broader foreign control of public works. The British government sent a special representative to Bogotá in 1928 to impress on the Colombians the necessity of submitting their projects to a board of experts, whose composition would be determined by the bankers and which would include at least one American and one British member. 'The bankers expect,' the British minister observed in January 1929, 'to exercise sufficient control through this body to safeguard the credit of the republic, and incidentally the security of loans made, for the issue of which they would ... enjoy a virtual monopoly.'[31]

When the British legation discussed the subject with the Colombian government, however, it met with a cool reception; subsequently, the pro-American minister of finance, Esteban Jaramillo, presented the British overture to the Council of Ministers in such an unfavorable fashion that it was summarily rejected. Adding further insult to the British, the Colombian government announced that it intended to appoint Americans to each of the three positions open for foreign advisers on the Board of Public Works. The British minister's indignation was ill-disguised. 'The Council of Ministers,' he wrote, 'consists of a majority of mediocre and half-educated persons, few of whom have had any experience in the outside world.'[32]

Important as the American connection was, however, the Colombian government could not afford to alienate its best European market. Consequently, following further discussions with the British minister, the Abadía administration announced a compromise whereby it would appoint a British adviser for ports and inland waterways, a Belgian for railroads, and an American for roads.[33] This decision marked the nadir of Jaramillo's influence in the Abadía cabinet. When both he and the minister of public works resigned in protest against the compromise, the British Foreign Office was delighted. R.L. Craigie, a clerk in the American department, gloated: 'The Americans were on the point of swallowing Colombia whole, and this sudden change in the situation is really quite dramatic.'[34]

This alternating gravitation between competing imperialisms did little to satisfy Colombia's immediate need for financing. Although Colombia was compelled to pursue a more conservative borrowing policy in 1929 (less than $2,000,000 in Colombian bonds were publicly offered in the United States in the first half of the year), the government required loans to complete essential public works projects and to cover routine expenditures. Yet even those financial institutions which had not been intimidated by the Corliss circular were reluctant to make definite commitments.[35]

This hesitancy was the result of factors far more complicated than the stability of the Colombian government or the failure of the Abadía administration to pass favorable petroleum legislation. From June 1928 to October 1929, the Federal Reserve Banks in the United States raised interest rates to curb speculation in common stock and to close off capital exports, a move that tended to accentuate financial problems. Although the Federal Reserve system was not unanimous on the efficacy of the policy, with individuals in the New York Bank leading the dissent, economists agree that this tightening of credit led to economic stagnation in other countries; it was, in other words, a 'beggar thy neighbor' policy, wittingly or otherwise.[36]

This policy and the general instability of Colombian finances led Lazard and the Guaranty Trust Co. to withdraw from their effort to become the Colombian fiscal agents. Under pressure from the British Foreign Office, Lazard might have held on had their financial role in Colombia been larger. But as the smaller partner, and with the necessity of obtaining the New York market, Lazard followed the lead of the American bankers. This decision was only indirectly related to the continuing debate over Colombian petroleum policy.[37]

In the last months of 1929 and those of early 1930 these issues remained unsettled. The pending Colombian presidential election of February 1930 and the unpredictable political situation caused by the financial crisis and the debate over the United Fruit Company strike of December 1928 precluded any commitments to a policy. The impotence of the Abadía administration led a group of moderate Liberals and disaffected Conservatives to approach Enrique Olaya Herrera, the Colombian minister in Washington, as a compromise presidential candidate. Although Olaya initially rejected these overtures in December of 1929, within a few weeks he yielded. With the Conservative party hopelessly divided between the supporters of Guillermo Valencia and Alfredo Vásquez Cobo, Olaya's candidacy was propitious.[38]

Olaya himself did nothing to minimize his dedication to the American connection. In his major speeches to business audiences he referred repeatedly to the necessity for cooperation with American capital. At Medellín on 25 January he spoke of his approach to investment in terms of an open door for capital so that foreign enterprise could locate in Colombia confident that the Colombian government would grant it security. Should the country make no attempt to dispel the atmosphere of uncertainty and hostility to the United States, Olaya predicted a dismal economic future. In a major address at the Jockey Club in Bogotá on 29 January, Olaya referred to the Corliss circular as evidence of a belief in the American financial community that Colombia was unwilling to grant American capital equal opportunity. 'I cannot understand,' he concluded, 'how it could be advisable to refuse the ... co-operation offered us by a frank and sincere friendship inspired in the interest of maintaining close commercial and economic relations.'[39]

Olaya's references to the United States in his campaign addresses reveal one aspect of his approach to inter-American relations that came to dominate his presidential years. As candidate and as president, he placed unwarranted emphasis on the ability of the United States to counteract Colombia's economic ills. This was partly because he, and most Colombians for that matter, viewed the depression in an insular rather than international context, so that the most significant foreign presence in the country was either damned or cheered for its every action on the grounds that it held the key to economic recovery.[40] Olaya's faith in Yankee omnipotence contributed to his pursuit of a consciously pro-American program, but he operated on the false assumption that his efforts to appease Washington were on a quid pro quo basis.

With electoral victory achieved, Olaya, in the months before his inauguration in August, turned his attention to the republic's financial dilemmas. While he recuperated at Ocaso from his whirlwind campaign, he discussed the nations's finances with members of Abadía's government and with the president of the Bank of the Republic. He then returned to the United States to discuss future loans with New York bankers. During the Ocaso talks and the subsequent trip to New

York from late April until July, Olaya made clear his unequivocal intention to hitch the Colombian future to the coattails of the United States.[41]

The courting of the Colombian president-elect in New York was thorough. Representatives of President Hoover, the departments of War, Navy, and State, and John L. Merrill, the president of All-America Cables (controlled by ITT), formed the official welcoming committee when Olaya landed in a United Fruit Company Steamer on 21 April.[42]

Olaya's presence in New York was occasion for renewed confidence in Colombian investments. Late in April Seligman & Co. agreed to extend for six months the maturity date on the short-term bank liens from the Guaranty Trust Co., the original lender with Lazard Bros. of London. Julius Klein, now assistant secretary of commerce, assisted Kuhn, Loeb & Company in negotiating with Olaya in New York, although the large houses, like J.P. Morgan & Co., were not interested in becoming involved with Colombian finance.[43] When Olaya (in his capacity as Colombian minister to the United States) concluded a contract for a $20,000,000 bank loan it was with the First National City Company and the First National Bank of Boston with the assistance of the Manhattan Trust Company, the Continental Trust Co. of Chicago, and Lazard of London.

The contract with the National City group was further evidence of the determination of the American and British banking communities to grant no credit to the Colombian government without some political control. It required that the government maintain a balanced budget; that it float an internal loan of 6,000,000 pesos ($5,820,000); that it establish government operations on a 'more business-like basis,' and that it reorganize its system of commercial customs collection.[44] To meet the terms of the contract Olaya and officials of the Bank of the Republic sought Edwin W. Kemmerer to conduct a second study of the Colombian economy.[45]

Kemmerer's 1930 work was less significant than that of 1923, when his mission established the Bank of the Republic on the model of the Federal Reserve system in the United States. In 1930 his main task was to devise means of improving government revenues to stabilize the economy.[46] Whether they were dealing with foreign enterprise or attempting to put teeth into Colombia's income tax laws, Kemmerer and his associates were highly representative of the progressive American 'experts' of the 1920s and 1930s. He provided a very accurate expression of his philosophy in commenting on his proposed export tax on bananas.

It is unfortunate for any business to be subject to frequent changes in the rates which are imposed upon it. If changes are frequent it becomes difficult for an industry to make adjustments and to carry out plans and negotiations because of the uncertainty.[47]

Stability, predictability, nonpolitical expertise – these were the key words in Kemmerer's professional vocabulary. He proposed taxes on the capital value of real property, centralization of the income tax collection, increased salaries for officials in a central bureaucracy, creation of a general customs board representative of the leading economic and professional interest groups, and a new organic budget law. Each of the measures received attention from the Colombian government, but they were implemented largely in a piecemeal fashion and with considerable modification.[48]

In spite of the confidence which accompanied the announcement of the second Kemmerer mission and the short-term bank loans, Olaya's four years in office did not promise to be unclouded by financial worries. Indeed, he had been in power only a few months when the negative impact of the depression on the New York bankers became increasingly evident. Following one of Olaya's bitter complaints about his difficulties with his New York creditors, under secretary of state Francis White commented on the general situation: 'The bankers of course are not in business for pleasure, but I think they are sincere in desiring to do what they can to help Olaya at the present time. The truth of the matter is they are up against the toughest financial situation the New York market has faced for a very long time ... The situation in South America,' White added, 'could not possibly be worse with the revolutions in Brazil, Argentina, Peru and Bolivia, and the imminence of default in every one of those countries except Argentina.'[49]

Olaya pressed to fulfill his contractual obligation. He honored both foreign and domestic advocates of progressive reform by appointing a prominent Colombian engineer as minister of public works. With effective rapport now established between the Olaya administration and the Transportation Commission appointed by Abadía, by January 1931 the government was prepared to propose a legislative program; the most important of these bills, a draft law providing for the reorganization of the railroad network, became a sine qua non for the New York bankers.[50] The National City Bank and the First National Bank of Boston insisted on passage of the railroad bill before extending the terms of the short-term credits, and when they later negotiated a new agreement with the government, they reaffirmed the provision in the original contract of June 1930 for a balanced budget and added the stipulations that the railroad system be taken out of the hands of the government and placed under the direction of professional management and that Congress pass a law placing a limit on debts.[51] The bankers' objectives clearly paralleled Kemmerer's ideal of placing financial and economic control in the hands of nonpolitical experts.

Caffery was encouraged by Stimson's news that the banks had yielded on the issue, but he feared that Olaya's prestige had already suffered sufficiently to endanger the continuation of his pro-American policies. 'I am not convinced,' Caffery wrote on 17 March, 'that he will continue to support the Barco contract with the same vigor, and he may not veto all the many objectionable articles in the general tariff bill which is now in his hands for signature.'[52] The following day he added an indictment of American enterprise in Colombia. 'The best efforts of the Department of State and our diplomatic missions ... may be almost nullified by prejudicial activities of American business concerns,' he suggested. 'I do not believe that hostility will ease until some way is found to have American business concerns understand that it is imperative for them to act towards the Governments and peoples south of the Rio Grande in the same manner as ... towards people and concerns in the United States.'[53] Caffery's target represented one of the vital objectives of the State Department in the Hoover-Roosevelt years: an environment in Latin America favorable to American investment and an investment community sensitive to local conditions.

The Department of State pressed the bankers to meet the financial requirements of the Olaya administration, but it was difficult to dispel the hesitancy which had characterized the attitude of Wall Street with respect to the payment of the third $4,000,000. To impress upon the bankers the political and diplomatic ramifications of their actions, on his return from Bogotá George Rublee, Olaya's principal economic adviser in the United States, spoke with representatives of the New York and Boston loan group. 'I thought they realized,' he confided to Francis White on 21 April, 'that they could not afford to let Olaya down. There is no doubt, however, that they have cold feet.' While in Boston, Rublee also urged officials of the United Fruit Company to consider extending a $2,000,000 short-term loan to the Colombian government; not only would it serve to bolster the Olaya government but it could repair the public image of the Magdalena Fruit Company.[54]

While the bankers pursued a cautious policy, Olaya guided through Congress a budget law based on Kemmerer's recommendations of the previous fall. Yet the bankers again refused to release the final $4,000,000 credit because Colombian revenues for the first quarter of 1931 did not match the original estimates on which the contract was based. Olaya warned that further economies, particularly wage cuts, threatened to arouse dangerous social unrest; should the national government be placed in a position where it was unable to continue financial support of the departments, it would result in immediate default on the latter's foreign bonds.

Jefferson Caffery cautioned the State Department to intercede. 'If the bankers drive Olaya from office,' he argued, 'the chances of their ever recovering their fifteen millions already invested will be remote. It is quite clear that after all ... Olaya has done for American interests ... if he turns to Congress with empty hands he cannot retain the presidency.'[55]

The State Department continued to urge the bankers to moderate their demands on Olaya, yet there was some uneasiness in the department that such action was contrary to the traditional policy on loans. Although he was overruled, Feis suggested to the secretary of state that support for Olaya would allow National City Bank to implicate the department in the event of default on the Colombian debt. Both Henry L. Stimson and H. Freeman Matthews, assistant chief of the Latin American division, nevertheless presented the department's views to W.W. Lancaster, counsel for National City, and successfully persuaded bank officials to reduce their demands and extend the final $4,000,000 credit to the Colombian government.[56]

This provided little more than a brief respite for the beleaguered Colombian government. The settlement of the outstanding Barco contract with South American Gulf Oil did not act as the instant tonic to the economy which the Colombian public had been led to anticipate. The choking off of lines of credit to New York and London for the continuation and completion of the public works projects, stagnation in trade, and the inexperience of Bank of the Republic officials contributed to a flight of capital from the country. By September of 1931 the drain on the national gold reserves made the economic situation acute.[57] Economic questions dominated the Bogotá press and the debates in Congress and culminated in the delegation of emergency powers to the president to control exchange, curtail imports, and institute tax increases.[58] The Bank of the Republic also appointed a commission, under Julio E. Lleras, to study the Federal Reserve system in the United States in the hope of further reforming the Colombian banking structure. Nevertheless, these efforts to encourage reform and economic stability enabled the Colombian government to attract only small, short-term loans to cover current expenditures. Faced with ever-increasing economic worries, and with public opinion aroused in opposition to further concessions to American interests, in mid-September Olaya felt obliged to cancel a proposed trip to the United States.[59]

The State Department was clearly in a dilemma, torn between its desire to maintain the strongly pro-American Olaya and a reluctance to deviate from its loan policy. This was particularly evident in Stimson's conversations with George Rublee and in his communications with the American legation in Bogotá. Rublee had been attempting to arrange a Colombian credit from the Federal Reserve Bank of New York, but the bank was not enthusiastic given the uncertain state of Colombian finance and the crisis occasioned by Britain's departure from the gold standard in September. Stimson presented the problem:

It is not a question of letting him [Olaya] down, but of world conditions over which the Department has no control ... The Department ... at no time ... either directly or indirectly extend[ed] any sort of promise on a *quid pro quo* ... Olaya apparently does not understand that not only can the Government not exert pressure of private banks but also that its relationship to the Federal Reserve System precludes it from exerting any influence upon the independent institution.[60]

In 1931 and early 1932 the Colombian government slid toward default on its foreign debt, and its international creditors tightened their purse strings. Initially the government prohibited Colombian departments, municipalities, and corporations from servicing their foreign debts to prevent further depletion of gold reserves. Then, early in January 1932, the government suspended sinking fund payments on the national bonded debt and on the government-guaranteed bonds of the Banco Agrícola Hipotecario.[61]

To obtain operating revenues, the government also leased the national salt mines to the Bank of the Republic for a period of thirteen years in return for a two-year advance on revenues. Olaya took this step against the wishes of the international bankers.

The problems of the Olaya administration were hardly unique to Colombia. In fact, given Olaya's determination to avoid a complete moratorium on the country's external debt service, American bankers and the State Department could find little fault with Colombian intentions. Yet Latin American bond defaults encouraged a public reexamination of United States loan policies in the previous decade;[62] and although the ensuing debate was primarily a political football, it led to developments directly affecting American relations with Colombia.

In December of 1931, Hiram Johnson, the Progressive Republican senator from California, called for a Senate investigation of the sale of foreign bonds in the United States.[63] For the next two months witnesses from the financial establishment as well as from government departments analyzed the events of the previous decade. Although the Finance Committee hearings treated a wide range of bond issues, especially German, attention to Latin America was conspicuous. American investment in Latin America now exceeded that in Europe, and since President Hoover had not extended the moratorium on foreign debts to Latin America,[64] there was considerable concern over the security of investments in government bonds. By the time the hearings opened on 18 December, Bolivia, Brazil, Chile, and Peru had defaulted on their national bonds, and Colombia was faltering.

Johnson's contention was that the State Department had sought advantages for private American companies but had been inactive in protecting American citizens who had purchased Latin American government bonds. He argued that in the Colombian instance the department and the bankers collaborated in the spring of 1931 to bring economic pressure on the Colombian government to settle the Barco petroleum concession in a manner satisfactory to the South American Gulf Oil Company.[65] But Johnson's witnesses lent little credence to his basic hypothesis.[66] Henry L. Stimson, Francis White, and H. Freeman Matthews denied the existence of any connection between the petroleum question and the loan; White argued that the department had approached the bankers because 'it was to the interests not only of the bank but of all American interests down there that American institutions should have a reputation of living up to their contracts.' White concluded in his testimony that 'the bankers were pledged already. The settling of the Barco matter improved Colombia's credit standing for the future. It did not apply to Colombia's credit position vis-à-vis the loan in which there was disagreement ... because that had been agreed to months before.' Matthews later wrote that 'Senator Johnson's thesis had no foundation in fact whatsoever. It rested chiefly upon a chronological coincidence.' Stimson noted in his diary on 13 January that he 'hardly knew that there was such a thing as the Barco concession, and it had been granted and signed long before this affair with the City Bank came up.'[67]

In terms of their impact on Colombian-American relations, the Senate hearings drew considerable coverage in the Colombian press, but the few editorials that examined the testimony tended to 'consider the investigation largely a local political move in the United States.'[68] Nevertheless, the hearings were accompanied by a resurgence of rhetorical anti-Americanism in Bogotá because they revived memories of the petroleum debate and made Colombians acutely conscious of their dependent status. Olaya's pro-American course in general was running into heavy seas;[69] he confided to George Rublee:

Men who followed me with much enthusiasm and resolution in the development of this policy, today appear discouraged and consider that in this aspect of international financial policy ... I am facing failure.

Public pressure for a moratorium on both private and government debts continued to build. Early in April 1932 about one-third of Bogotá's principal general merchants closed their shops in protest against the government's delay. Less than a week later, representatives of the departmental assemblies meeting in Medellín recommended the complete suspension of service on the national external debt.[70]

To appease his domestic opponents, Olaya took steps to reduce both the national government's debt and the pressures of private debts. The most significant movement in this direction was decree 711 of 22 April 1932, which provided for the formation of a Central Mortgage Bank and authorized commercial banks to accept Colombian internal and external bonds as partial payment of debts.[71] The decree operated as a strong inducement to the repatriation of external bonds since they could be redeemed at 80% of par value in Colombia but were selling well below that figure in the United States. By 1936 the government repatriated

$6,000,000 of its external bonded debt, but at the cost of alienating American holders of the bonds.[72]

With some justification foreign banks operating in Colombia were hesitant to participate in the provisions of the decree; their open opposition heightened the tension which had existed with the president since Olaya assumed office. Olaya informed the American legation that the bankers had intimated earlier they would not oppose his move. However, when the finance minister, Esteban Jaramillo, presented the proposal to the board of directors of the Bank of the Republic, the Board of Foreign Banks sent an informal delegation composed of Frank Smith of National City Bank and Fred Dever of the Royal Bank of Canada to see Olaya. The president signed the decree that afternoon, cognizant, therefore, of the foreign bankers' objections.[73]

Olaya continued to reject total default on the government's obligations. The foreign banking community also made a number of concessions which mitigated somewhat the refusal to participate in the formation of the Central Mortgage Bank. Fred Dever indicated that the Bank of Canada frequently went beyond the 50% provision of the decree in accepting government bonds as payment for debts. Local representatives of the National City Bank, restricted by the negative response of New York officials, made every effort to impress upon head office that without cooperation it would find prospects for future expansion in Colombia dismal. National City Bank officials were well aware of the dangers of opposing Olaya but were intimidated by the provisions of decree 711 and by economic conditions in the United States.[74]

At this juncture the Peruvian attack on Leticia, Colombia's isolated Amazon port, vastly altered the Colombian situation.[75] The conflict with Peru absorbed the energies and finances of the country for the next two years and the accompanying resurgence of patriotism directed attention away from the American presence. The need to finance a military campaign, when little emphasis had been placed on military strength for a generation, increased the nation's incapacity to meet its foreign obligations. When the government issued 10,000,000 pesos ($9,500,000 U.S.) in 4% national defense bonds, the Colombian public responded by oversubscribing to the issue the first day it was on the market, an indication of the amount of private capital available to meet the right crisis.[76]

The financial demands of war imposed on an already troubled economy led to a steady succession of government measures designed to achieve temporary relief. On 26 November Olaya signed a private debts moratorium law, which gave foreign banks the alternative of recognizing the moratorium or accepting a 70% cash payment or 40% cash and 60% national government bonds as full settlement of debts. In April of 1933 the government announced its intention to suspend interest payments on the national external debt and the guaranteed bonds of the Agri-

'But why are you worth more than I am?'
'Because, my dear fellow, I am your rich benefactor.'

El Tiempo, 28 September 1933

cultural Mortgage Bank. For the remainder of 1933 Colombia met the interest charges on its 6% national bond issues of 1927 and 1928 by paying two-thirds in scrip and one-third in cash.[77] Though a total default appeared inevitable by the end of 1933, Olaya clung stubbornly to his earlier objective of continuing to meet Colombia's financial obligations to the United States. It is ironic that the Leticia conflict with Peru, which enhanced Olaya's prestige and strengthened his political position, was largely responsible for the ultimate default.

An analysis of Colombian-American financial relations from 1920 to the end of the Hoover administration reveals a number of interesting facts about the significance of the American presence. Terms such as *imperialism* are too simplistic to define the relationship between the two societies, but it is obvious that Colombia found itself in a dependency relationship to the United States. Yet one must reiterate that foreign, especially American, banking institutions and American capital played a major part in making possible the economic boom that Colombians (at least those who were part of the market economy) enjoyed. Colombian economic problems were related more to administrative inexperience and political meddling (if one accepts Kemmerer's view) and to the policies of the Federal Reserve Banks than to any specific State Department policy. It was not United States foreign policy itself that threatened Colombian sovereignty, but the realities of the international financial community. In addition, although some objectives may have been similar, there were substantial tensions between the American government and the international banking community over financial relations with Latin America, tensions that derived largely from the different functions of the two institutions. The question of culpability may not be ahistorical, yet there is reason to believe that some of the defaults on Latin American bonds could have been avoided had some American bankers been more scrupulous and avoided floating bonds which were of doubtful value. As Thomas Lamont commented, the American bond market in the 1920s would absorb 'almost anything.'[78] From the American point of view, however, bankers and government officials agreed that the sale of foreign bonds in the United States stimulated the economy in the 1920s by helping to finance the export of American products.[79]

4

The quest for recovery

As the earlier discussion of loan policy suggests, the problem of guaranteeing the security of Latin American loans was a perennial one, and in the 1920s there was some consideration of alternative approaches to the coordination of loans. In 1920 several large investment houses (including J.P. Morgan & Co.; Kuhn, Loeb, & Co.; the National City Company; Guaranty Trust Company of New York; Harris Forbes & Co.; Lee, Hugginson & Co.; and the First National Bank of Boston) organized the South American Group to coordinate financial activities relating to Latin America. The group disbanded following constant frustration in attempts to restrain Latin American countries from reckless financial policies. Consequently, when Secretary of Commerce Robert Lamont approached J.P. Morgan & Co. in 1930, he found the bankers unsympathetic to either reviving the South American Group or establishing another institution. The secretary clearly hoped for significant cooperation among the bankers for the benefit of American commerce. He wrote to Thomas Lamont: 'Would it be feasible to attempt concerted action with a group of banks working together ... on a sound constructive basis that would also carry some measure of control of financial activities on the part of the Governments until ... their financial structures were in better shape?'[1]

Consideration of a more formal semiofficial entity made little headway until several years of depression had elapsed, and then discussions centered around an organization whose primary responsibility would be to recover defaulted loans. Opinion in the banking community concerning this question evolved from a definite preference for ad hoc committees dealing with specific issues to consideration of something along the lines of the British Bondholders' Council. The change of opinion was largely the result of the growing number of defaults on foreign bonds[2] and some dissatisfaction over the fact that American bankers could not count on the same degree of diplomatic support British bankers received.[3] The result was a concerted effort in the Hoover-Roosevelt period culminating in the formation of the American Foreign Bondholders' Protective Council.

Prior to and following the formation of the council in late 1933, the State Department's role in protecting investors was not as innocuous as some of its public statements might suggest. In the Colombian instance, the department attempted first to discourage the Colombian move toward a debt default; when that failed, the department was instrumental in coordinating discussions which led to the creation of the FBPC as a semiofficial body responsive to American foreign policy objectives and yet not publicly identified as a government agency. The fact that the council worked very closely with the government, although there were often tactical disagreements, tends to negate Cordell Hull's claim that the formation of the council removed the question of debts from the State Department's sphere.[4] From the State Department's perspective, the FBPC also mitigated the disruptive effect of the private bondholders' groups which emerged in this period.

In the Colombian case there were several private groups which represented themselves as spokesmen for the bondholders: the Bondholders' Committee for Republic of Colombia External Dollar Bonds, under a former ambassador to Italy and co-founder of the Council of Foreign Relations, Richard Washburn Child; and the Independent Bondholders for the Republic of Colombia, under Robert L. Owen, a former U.S. senator from Oklahoma.[5] From their inception, these two committees (united in 1935) lacked the confidence of the American bondholders they claimed to represent, the Department of State, and the Colombian government. This was in part the result of the activities of Lawrence de S. Hoover, a member and secretary of the Owen committee, who badgered State Department officials with incessant demands for government support. The Colombian government indicated it had no intention of negotiating with either the Child or Owen committees.[6]

The formation of these two groups coincided with the 1932 elections in the United States. The general economic crisis inevitably made financial questions the subject of campaign oratory; the hearings before the Senate Finance Committee the previous winter and the public interest aroused by the Senate Banking Committee investigation guaranteed that foreign bonds would receive considerable attention from the Democratic candidate. On 20 August in a speech at Columbus, Ohio, Roosevelt criticized the Republicans for complicity in the overextension of credit to foreign governments, and contended that it would 'no longer be possible for international bankers or others to sell foreign securities to the investing public of America on the implied understanding that these securities have been passed on or approved by the State Department or any other agency of the Federal Government.'[7]

Roosevelt's attack on his predecessors and the investment bankers was not entirely campaign rhetoric, as the Securities Act of 1933 demonstrated, but his public posture was misleading. Contrary to the impression Roosevelt sought to create, the Hoover administration had not been idle in dealing with the problem of foreign debts. In fact, it was the seed planted by the Department of State under President Hoover which subsequently bore fruit.

The Hoover administration initiated discussions as early as the spring of 1932 on the feasibility of creating a foreign bondholders' association. Secretary of State Stimson requested Assistant Secretary Harvey Bundy and Herbert Feis to devise a plan for the department's consideration; Stimson and other officials were concerned that if the government did not assume the leadership, the independent bondholders' groups would cause friction between the United States and the debtor nations.[8] With this objective in mind, a group broadly representative of government departments and the private sector met in Washington on 15 April. Among those present were Harvey Bundy and Herbert Feis; Under Secretary of State William R. Castle Jr; Ogden Mills, Secretary of the Treasury; Grosvenor M. Jones of the Department of Commerce; Charles P. Howland of Yale; Pierre Jay, Chairman of Fiduciary Trust Co., New York; Princeton economist Edwin W. Kemmerer;. Thomas N. Perkins, prominent Boston lawyer and businessman; and George Rublee of the Washington law firm of Covington, Burling, Acheson, Shorb & Rublee.[9] This and subsequent meetings led to a proposal for the formation of a committee modeled in general on the British Corporation of Foreign Bondholders.[10] With less than a year remaining to the Hoover administration, however, there was little opportunity for the proposals of this group to find expression in legislation. Economic adviser Herbert Feis proved to be one of the most persistent advocates of the creation of a 'disinterested and independent organization.' Feis's position was especially crucial in the light of his transitional role between the Hoover and Roosevelt administrations.[11] He was not pleased with the direction in which the Roosevelt administration appeared to be moving in early 1933, with respect to the question of defaulted securities; he was convinced that influential individuals within the administration, particularly Henry Morgenthau Jr, head of the Farm Credit Administration until January 1935 when he became secretary of the treasury, and Roosevelt aide Louis Howe, were pressing for a government agency authorized to collect defaulted foreign debts. Although Roosevelt attempted to dispel this impression, other State Department officials shared Feis's apprehension that the president had begun to favor Hiram Johnson's amendment to the securities bill currently before Congress.[12]

The securities bill passed in May along with the Johnson amendment, which became title II of the act. The act to a certain extent reflected Roosevelt's earlier rhetorical stance against big business. It placed control of security issuing under the Federal Trade Commission, required publication of complete information on each issue, and provided that company officials could be held criminally responsible for fraud.[13] Title II of the act was the logical outgrowth of Johnson's criticism of the State Department in the Finance Committee hearings the year before; it provided for the formation of a Corporation of Foreign Security Holders under government auspices, to be put into effect by presidential decree.[14] Under pressure from the State Department and some of the New York bankers who opposed the creation of a government body, Roosevelt delayed implementing title II.

Feis continued to press for the adoption of his proposals. He familiarized Cordell Hull, newly appointed as secretary of state, with earlier discussions and prepared a complete memorandum for Roosevelt on the question of defaulted bonds. Feis recommended that any body organized to deal with the problem not be identified with the banks and financial houses because of the lack of confidence they frequently generated abroad. To be effective an agency would have to possess the sanction of the American government, because private committees were unable to obtain the cooperation of foreign authorities. Such a 'disinterested' body, Feis pointed out, 'has been visualized by the State Department as a step away from dollar diplomacy, and not toward it. In the absence of such an organization it is almost inevitable that the government will be dragged into serious situations in an effort to protect the American investors against unfair or discriminatory treatment.'[15] The formation of such a committee would clearly place the government in a more effective position to control the recovery of loans. It reflected the long-standing commitment of Hoover to loan supervision as well as the internationalist orientation of New Deal diplomacy.

The State Department's determination to avoid diplomatic incidents involving the recovery of defaulted bonds was particularly applicable to the activity of the private bondholders' groups in Colombia. The department's attitude toward these groups was explicit in an exchange of notes between Robert Owen and Assistant Secretary of State Harvey Bundy in February 1933. Owen concluded his request for department support: 'In view of the action of the department in giving its implied assent to the sale of these bonds to the public, we trust that the department will feel an interest and take proper steps to protect our rights.' Bundy replied briskly: 'The business of conducting negotiations with foreign governments regarding loan issues it customarily leaves to the private parties directly concerned ... The Department wishes to deny ... that it gave "implied assent" to the sale of these bonds.'[16]

The department's relationship with the secretary of the Owen group, Lawrence de S. Hoover, was even less cordial. H. Freeman Matthews, for example, made no effort to disguise his irritation with Hoover's solicitations. Matthews was convinced that Hoover was untrustworthy and noted that he had a reputation as a notorious gunrunner in Ireland, an activity for which he had served a prison term. 'I wish to emphasize,' Matthews wrote, that if the Department does eventually say anything on matters of interest to the bond-holders to President Olaya, Mr. Hoover and his committee should not be apprised thereof. Hoover is thoroughly unscrupulous and would most certainly misuse any such information either to acquire the deposit of additional funds or as a means of bringing further pressure on getting publicity.[17]

The State Department grew increasingly anxious to implement a positive policy in Colombia because, while the department delayed, the banks were taking action on their own. Hallgarten and Co., for example, sent a representative to Bogotá to arrange with the Colombian government for the payment of the July coupon and agreed to accept a one-third cash and two-third scrip payment. Believing that piecemeal negotiations would impede a more general settlement, Matthews urged his colleagues in the Latin American division to press the Colombian government for a full cash interest payment.[18] There was also a secondary consideration in pressing for a settlement at this juncture. Both Matthews and Rublee wanted to enter into negotiations while Olaya was still in office. With Alfonso López looming on the horizon as the Liberal presidential candidate, the State Department had reservations about the prospects for future cooperation.[19]

President Olaya, however, continued to argue that the country was financially embarrassed because of the Leticia conflict with Peru and the continued instability in trade and exchange. He added that unless the American government established an official committee with which Colombia could negotiate, he would have to make temporary settlements.[20]

Pressure for a semiofficial body came as well from the Federal Trade Commission. Raymond B. Stevens of the commission presented Roosevelt with arguments similar to those used by the State Department in opposing implementation of title II of the Securities Act. Stevens contended that an official committee would give the impression the government was assuming responsibility for defaulted bonds, and the administration would thus become the target for criticism from parties not satisfied with a settlement. In a constitutional sense, Stevens argued that implementation of title II would be an unwarranted duplication of State Department prerogatives and activities.[21]

Roosevelt forwarded Stevens's comments to Hiram Johnson, adding that he was inclined to sympathize with Stevens. 'As you know,' Roosevelt pointed out,

he [Stevens] is a real progressive and talks our language. If I could get somebody thoroughly trustworthy, like George Rublee, to organize a Foreign Security Holders Committee on a basis of very low cost to the bond holders and wholly nonprofit-making, we could throw the official approval of the Federal Trade

Commission behind such a committee by having the committee ask the approval of the Commission for the issuance of certificates of deposit.[22]

Stevens met with Roosevelt at Hyde Park and, with the president's approval, approached George Rublee and Pierre Jay, who had been active in earlier efforts to organize a committee. Stevens obtained tentative commitments to serve on a council from John C. Traphagen, president of the Bank of New York and Trust Company; Charles Francis Adams, at that time president of Union Trust Co. of Boston; Thomas N. Perkins, a Boston executive; Roland S. Morris, a Philadelphia lawyer; and Newton D. Baker, a former official in the Wilson administration. To offset potential public criticism should title II not be implemented, Stevens recommended that the FTC write the president an open letter outlining its objections to title II and prescribing the formation of an independent bondholders' committee.[23]

Believing he had gained the president's support, Stevens recommended the formation of a small committee to finalize plans, one member from each of the departments of State, Treasury, and Commerce, and one from the FTC. He suggested that a committee comprised of men such as William Phillips, Jefferson Caffery, Dean Acheson, Daniel Roper, and Stevens himself would be sufficient to fill the need. Such a body could 'devise a method by which an adequate private bondholders' committee could be set up under auspices that would not connect it with the Hoover Administration or with Wall Street.'[24]

Senator Johnson remained unconvinced by Roosevelt's assurances; nor was he pleased that the administration would bury his amendment to the Securities Act. He was especially opposed to a suggestion, which he attributed to Feis, that the commission be selected by the National Chamber of Commerce, the Carnegie Foundation, and a few semipublic bodies. 'Bitter experience has taught those whose sole object was to aid Americans who had been swindled,' he wrote the president on 26 August, 'that little dependence could be placed upon an organization chosen by chambers of commerce or other semi-public bodies ... We believed,' he added, 'that within a brief period after such a selection the control of the directors would be the very men who had originally perpetrated the wrong.' Johnson preferred an organization under government control to one 'manipulated and directed by the international bankers and investment houses.'[25]

Johnson misrepresented Feis's position. Feis frequently expressed the conviction that the bondholders' committee should be entirely independent of the banking interests. He argued that any required financing should be handled either by the Reconstruction Finance Corporation or the Federal Reserve Board. That these bodies might share the objectives of the international bankers does not appear to have deterred Feis; the fact remains, however, that he opposed the formation of any government agency which could complicate domestic politics as well as American relations with the Latin American republics.[26] The Feis-Johnson disagreement was clearly one over tactics, not ends.

Feis and Stevens had a definite influence on Roosevelt's approach to the question. The president pointed out in a letter to Senator Frederick Steiver of Oregon that the administration intended to cooperate in the organization of a group 'which shall be entirely independent of any special interests and have no connection with the investment banking houses that originally issued the loans ... Such action,' Roosevelt argued, 'would be entirely in accord with the traditional policy of our government, which has been to regard loan and investment transactions as private transactions to be handled by the parties primarily concerned.'[27] Roosevelt's analysis of the relationship between the government and private financial institutions was of course similar to that advanced by Republican administrations before him; yet the evidence suggests that the government was playing a vital role in the crisis over foreign debts.

In December 1933, the labors of the previous eighteen months culminated in the formation of the Foreign Bondholders' Protective Council, Inc., with Raymond B. Stevens as president. Four men comprised the original executive committee; Pierre Jay, T.D. Thatcher, John C. Traphagen, and Hendon Chubb, none of whom was entirely divorced from the banking interests. Nevertheless, to avoid control by investment houses, financial contributions (on which the council was dependent) from a single donor were limited to $5,000. In personnel the council was increasingly identified with the State Department. When Stevens became ill, J. Reuben Clark Jr replaced him; in January 1935 former Assistant Secretary of State Francis White became executive vice-president and secretary, and later president.[28]

By the time the Foreign Bondholders' Protective Council came into existence, Colombia appeared to be on the verge of a total moratorium on its foreign obligations. In October 1933 representatives Héctor J. Vargas and Moisés Prieto introduced into the lower house a bill providing for the suspension of service on the external funded debt, with the exception of the short-term loan from the New York-Boston-London banking group. The congressional move challenged the determination of Olaya and his finance minister to meet the country's obligations in scrip and was a further indication of public disenchantment with the president's financial policies.[29]

The State Department and the representatives of the banking group expressed concern at this turn of events. The latter threatened to support the bondholders' associations should the Colombian government default on its 1930 loans. Cordell Hull wired William Dawson for an explanation of Olaya's waning control. 'We trust,' Hull commented, 'that the bill does not represent his views. We are aware of no developments of an economic nature in Colombia which would require suspension of the presently extremely reduced debt service payments.' State Department officials maintained that the 15% the Bank of the Republic charged on foreign exchange drafts was sufficient to cover cash payments on the foreign debt. The department also thought Colombian timing was inauspicious because of the impending formation of the bondholders' council.[30]

Embarrassed and discouraged by congressional opposition to servicing the foreign debt, Olaya predicted to George Rublee that complete default was inevitable by 1934 'because of the daily increasing expenses occasioned by [the] ... war adventure in which Peru wishes to involve us.' Confronted with insurmountable political obstacles, Olaya signed a debt law on 30 November, aware of the objections of the State Department to article 2, which provided for payment of obligations in Colombian currency.[31]

Article 2 was the most controversial aspect of the debt law. Although Olaya in a special message to Congress urged that article 2 not be made applicable to national government debts, the bankers were not appeased.[32] The United Fruit Company shared their resentment. It had recently advanced dollar loans to the independent banana planters in the Magdalena region and to the Colombian government; in addition, the law would complicate the long-term contracts between the company and local planters. United Fruit's exchange difficulties were, however, considerably lightened by the fact that the company was not required to return to the country the foreign exchange proceeds of its exports.[33]

The situation in Colombia was highly volatile when the Foreign Bondholders' Protective Council initiated its work. Although the political arena was relatively stable, the country was in considerable financial difficulty; there was a congressional consensus favoring the priority of national problems over the service of the foreign debt; and President Olaya, pro-American as he was, no longer possessed the political authority he had exercised in his first two years of office.

The bondholders' council gave the State Department another vehicle with which to pursue its objectives. Whereas the department had vigorously denied any connection with earlier 'private' bondholders' committees, it now instructed the American legation in Bogotá to inform the Colombian government that the council had the full approval of the United States government.[34]

Early in 1934 Senator Johnson once again entered the fray with a revival of his bill to prohibit financial transactions of Americans with foreign governments which had defaulted on their obligations to the United States. Johnson's bill (S. Res. 682) did not affect Colombia directly because her debts were not intergovernmental. But as the independent bondholders' committees commented during debate on the Johnson bill in the House, the act would induce countries such as Colombia to make greater efforts to service their debts.[35]

The Colombian move toward default on its foreign debts was compounded, in the American view, by the fact that Olaya's term expired in August 1934. Consequently it was the personality and politics of his successor, Alfonso López, which concerned the State Department. López had been vocally opposed to a number of American enterprises in Colombia, particularly the United Fruit Company, and there was consternation in American circles that this antipathy would be accentuated during his presidency. López was, however, primarily concerned with effecting a broad range of domestic reforms; he desired not to achieve a major redistribution of wealth and power in Colombian society but to make the fruits of power available to a larger segment of the Colombian populace. Confronted by a major depression and faced with increasing political and economic radicalism in the labor movement, López moved left in much the same fashion that Roosevelt did. López's domestic program had socialist overtones, but its objectives were no less bourgeois and capitalist than the American model to which he looked for guidance. The influential *Acción Liberal* commented shortly before López's inauguration that although López claimed affinity with 'the spirit of the Mexican revolution,' his program was a pale reflection of the original.[36]

López had, nevertheless, long been a critic of the Colombian government's overextended borrowing for public works, and his own acumen as a banker lent credence to his reservations.[37] Two years before Olaya assumed office, López warned that the Colombian economic structure could not continue to generate the funds to service the debts acquired in the preceding years. As the chairman of the Colombian delegation to the Montevideo Conference in December 1933, López praised Roosevelt's approach to inter-American affairs and spoke in support of Hull's economic resolutions; but the Liberal presidential candidate stressed that he was unwilling to sacrifice the material welfare of Latin American people to the interests of international finance.[38] In June 1934, as president-elect, López made it quite plain to the American legation that he would not allow the financial indiscretions of his predecessors to interfere with his domestic legislative program; in his message to Congress at its inaugural session he lamented the concessioning of the country's natural resources to foreign interests.[39]

Shortly after López assumed office, J. Reuben Clark Jr of the council called the Colombian president requesting information on the government's financial status. Clark indicated that there was considerable public pressure on the council and the United States government to adopt coercive measures, such as a special tariff on Colombian coffee imports. López was not to be intimidated. He replied in detail but refused to commit his government to a course of action. 'It can easily be demonstrated,' he suggested to Clark, 'that Colombia would have been in a position to give better satisfaction to her creditors now if the suspension of the debt service had not been postponed until the last moment when our entire economy had been seriously crippled.'[40]

With the new administration installed, the New York and London bankers raised the question of the short-term banking loans, payment of which had been postponed during Olaya's presidency. National City Bank officials agreed that the moment seemed opportune to press the Colombian government for a settlement; accordingly they sent a representative to Bogotá. The ensuing discussions between Lazard and the American members of the group indicated that the American bankers, relieved of their issuing privileges by the securities legislation of that year, wanted to recover their investment and withdraw, at least temporarily, from Colombia. In the absence of American interest, Lazard became the Colombian government's fiscal agent.[41]

A number of factors clouded the Colombian economic and political picture early in 1935, not least among them the persistent inability of Congress and the administration to reach an accord on the Rio Protocol settling the Leticia dispute, and the insecurity of the coffee industry. Moving to adjust the high import levels that plagued Colombia's balance of payments, the government abolished the time limit for the disposal of foreign exchange warrants; this caused the exchange rate to rise and the peso to seek a more realistic level. This development, the British commercial secretary argued, was 'a healthy departure from the policy of expedients followed by the preceding Administration, under which Colombian importers were encouraged to take more goods from abroad than the country could afford.'[42]

During 1935 the Securities and Exchange Commission investigated the protective committees, in part because of allegations that the bondholders' council was dependent on funds from New York and Chicago issuing houses. That fall, James M. Landis, chairman of the Securities and Exchange Commission, notified the State Department that the commission intended to hold public hearings on defaulted Colombian bonds. One of the commission's objectives was to justify the existence of the council by demonstrating that the independent committees had not operated in the interests of the bondholders. State Department officials were sympathetic but concerned that publicity on the activities of such groups would retard passage of the recently concluded United States-Colombian Reciprocal Trade Agreement. J. Reuben Clark suggested that as long as the SEC kept the enquiry discreet the investigation might encourage the Colombian government to negotiate with the council. But the State Department was not convinced. The trade agreements program had greater priority in American policy at this juncture, and the department was unwilling to sacrifice its trade objectives to the interests of the bondholders. Edwin Wilson accordingly requested the SEC to delay the hearings until later in the year.[43]

During its investigation of Colombian bondholders' committees (which continued sporadically from late December 1935 to the spring of 1937), the SEC examined a possible conflict of interest between the Owen committee and Standard Oil of New Jersey.[44] Three of the six original members of the committee were involved in Standard Oil operations: Frederick Bradford, a salaried director of Standard Oil; James Hayes, an attorney for the corporation at the time he joined the committee; and Harrison K. McCann of McCann-Erickson, an advertising agency which did much of Standard's work. The Owen committee for eleven months occupied rent-free office space in the Standard Oil Building at 26 Broadway in New York. Evidence presented to the SEC suggests that some officials of Standard Oil had thought that cooperation with the Owen committee might be advantageous. The SEC learned that Frederick Bradford in 1932 informed the Standard president, Walter Teagle, that the corporation's personnel had become involved in the committee largely at the insistence of Hayes. Bradford pointed out to Teagle that he had been 'assured that such a committee would not be detrimental to any of the interests of our people in Colombia or to the Republic of Colombia – on the contrary that it could very readily turn out to be of real help.'[45]

Although the testimony before the Securities and Exchange Commission did little to improve the image of the bondholders' committees, the hearings also had little effect on the willingness or ability of the Colombian government to resume payment on defaulted bonds. J. Reuben Clark Jr continued to argue that this reluctance was economically unwarranted and that the position of the Colombian government was the result of the fact that López, bitter about the obstructionism of the Santos wing of the Liberal party, was satisfied to leave the debt as a legacy to his successor. Clark may have been more 'stubborn and acquisitive' than some of his former associates, but his analysis of López's attitude toward the centrist Liberals was essentially correct.

The State Department maintained a more flexible stance. The chief of the Latin American division, Laurence Duggan, suggested that the public statements of the Colombian minister of finance indicated a willingness to negotiate; he received support from the American minister in Bogotá, who contended that President López was prepared to settle the issue provided it could be isolated from the domestic political context. Reluctant to exert overt pressure on the Colombian government, however, the department continued to anticipate the Colombian initiative. There the situation rested until 1937 brought a united effort from the Foreign Bondholders' Protective Council and the Department of State.[46]

In 1937, the State Department arranged a leave of absence from Yale for Dana Munro, a former chief of the division of Latin American affairs, to undertake a mission to Colombia on behalf of the bondholders' council. Munro had performed a similar function in Cuba, and, as Hull explained, 'the Department would welcome a mutually satisfactory adjustment of this debt situation, both because of the benefit to American investors and because its continued unsettlement is an unsatisfactory element in its relationship with Colombia.'[47]

Munro twice traveled to Bogotá that spring and summer in an effort to bring negotiations to a conclusion. Exploratory conversations in May with President López and the minister of foreign relations convinced Munro that Colombian intentions were sincere, and he accepted López's invitation to return in July or August to make final arrangements for an agreement with the bondholders.[48]

In spite of his warm reception on both occasions, Munro made little progress on the debt question. President López repeated his professions of good intentions but pointed to the complications of domestic politics. When Munro first met with Carlos Lleras Restrepo, the comptroller general, on 31 August, Lleras confirmed the president's hesitations to attempt a settlement at that juncture. Eduardo Santos, Lleras informed Munro, was certain to succeed López, and the *Santistas* in Congress would combine with the Conservatives to defeat a López-proposed agreement rather than be forced to function under a burdensome financial settlement. Even had López been prepared to conclude an agreement with the FBPC there was no assurance that he could have imposed its terms on Congress. By 1937 López's reform program, La Revolución en Marcha, had alienated the conservative elements in both parties; in the congressional elections of that year the swing of the political pendulum returned a majority of pro-Santos Liberals. Under the circumstances Munro, for a second time, was obliged to leave Bogotá without an agreement.[49]

The López administration was not wholly responsible for the failure of the 1937 Munro mission. The council was, for one thing, perhaps trying to drive too hard a bargain, since Munro rejected as impractical a proposal that Carlos Lleras Restrepo thought very favorable. In addition, following the inconclusive efforts by Munro, it was Francis White, now president of the council who discontinued discussions with Colombia on the ground that Brazil's withdrawal of price supports for coffee would unsettle the Colombian economy. There were also internal Colombian problems related to the efforts of entrenched bureaucrats to prevent further economies which could threaten their positions.[50]

By the spring of 1938 an increasingly impatient Francis White was once more urging the Colombian government to make a definite offer. 'The important thing,' he wrote to the Colombian minister in Washington on 21 April 1938, 'is to have negotiations. The promise of such negotiations has been held out to us as a possibility for the last 4 years ... We are at your disposal.'[51]

When a settlement was achieved, it was due essentially to the determination of the departments of State, Treasury, and Commerce to bring the Colombian government and the American FBPC to terms in the interest of hemispheric security.

From the Colombian perspective the gratification of earlier creditors meant subsequent opportunity to borrow in the United States. The opportunity to obtain loans from the United States was particularly important to President Santos, who was being criticized by both Conservatives and the left of his own party for granting concessions to the American government without reciprocal benefits.[52]

Secretary of the Treasury Henry Morgenthau Jr indicated the connection between financial solidarity and hemispheric security. Although Morgenthau's objectives were in harmony with those of the Good Neighbor, his initial tactics were not. On 7 June 1938, for example, he recommended to Roosevelt a bill authorizing the Treasury Department to make foreign loans when the president believed that

by reason of a threatened violation of the Monroe Doctrine, or by reason of a threatened disturbance of the peace of nations of the Western Hemisphere, an emergency exists and that financial assistance to any government in the Western Hemisphere will, in the interests of the United States, aid in the preservation of the Monroe Doctrine and the peace of the Western Hemisphere.

Morgenthau argued, in defense of his suggestion, that the financial difficulties experienced by the South and Central American countries exposed them to foreign interference. It was not the validity of Morgenthau's argument, but the potential consequences of articulating such a policy which the administration felt constrained to oppose. Under Secretary of State Sumner Welles moved immediately to block Morgenthau's initiative, and Roosevelt informed the secretary of the treasury that the State Department feared that his proposal would be viewed by Latin America as a 'resumption of dollar diplomacy.'[53]

Morgenthau's proposal failed to materialize in the form he envisaged; yet his concern with general hemispheric conditions found expression in negotiations over the outstanding Colombian foreign debt. As well as desiring to foster the expansion of American markets in Latin America, Morgenthau took an increased interest in the activity of the FBPC in Colombia where, as table 2 indicates,[54] Americans had a major interest in the resumption of payments on the external funded debt.

Morgenthau appears to have been one of the more aggressive members of the Roosevelt administration in attempting to expedite a settlement with the Colombian government to restore Colombian credit and take advantage of the trade increments he was certain would follow. At a meeting in the Treasury Department early in January 1939, Morgenthau suggested that a loan from the Export-Import Bank would enable the Colombian government to meet its external obligations and stimulate demand for American products. Herbert Feis countered that in-

TABLE 2
American interest in Colombian bonds in 1939 (estimates, in U.S. dollars)

Bonds	Total outstanding	Held by American interests
National government	51,223,500	26,555,000
National government scrip	2,616,030	1,600,000
Agricultural Mortgage Bank	10,288,500	4,115,000
Departmental bonds	59,988,000	56,988,000
Municipalities	22,149,900	21,041,000
Bank bonds (not guaranteed by the national government)	12,416,000	4,955,000
TOTAL	158,681,930	115,254,000

creasing exports at that moment was not vital to American interests, and that it would be preferable for the Colombian government to take the initiative on the debt question without further foreign financing. There was considerable disagreement over Feis's position, however. Morgenthau was convinced, and he received support from Ambassador to Colombia Spruille Braden, that it was illogical to restrain the Export-Import Bank in anticipation of a settlement of debts to private American interests.[55] In general, this perspective was consistent with the State Department's approach to the debt question; its primary consideration in the debt settlement was the pursuit of broader American political and economic objectives, among them the protection of trade and investments and the prevention of European interference.

The catalyst to settlement was the Colombian government's need for new loans and its inability to obtain financing in London.[56] By the fall of 1939 the Colombian economy was in desperate need of support. The outbreak of war in Europe once again severed Colombian access to its coffee markets in England and on the continent, with the result that by May 1940 Colombian coffee prices were one third lower than the previous September.[57] This contributed to a general recession throughout the economy and placed the government increasingly at the mercy of its foreign creditors.

A second development which facilitated settlement was the formation of an interdepartmental committee in the United States to establish guidelines for handling requests for loans from other American republics. Again the initiative came from Morgenthau. The committee which evolved from Morgenthau's suggestion was composed primarily of Morgenthau, Jesse Jones from the Department of Commerce, and Sumner Welles from State; but there was disagreement over the inclusion of other groups. Roosevelt initially urged that the Securities and Exchange Commission be represented in 'any matters involving new securities or investments in Latin America'; Welles, however, was less enthusiastic about the Securities and Exchange Commission and was strongly opposed to including the Foreign Bondholders' Protective Council, largely on the grounds that one of its members, John C. Traphagen, was believed to be politically opposed to the New Deal. Since this friction was essentially political, the Treasury Department was able to facilitate effective communication among the groups.[58]

On 5 December, Welles, Jones, Warren L. Pierson (president of the Export-Import Bank), Joseph P. Cotton Jr of the State Department, and Esteban Jaramillo, former Colombian finance minister and representative on the Inter-American Financial and Economic Advisory Committee, gathered in Morgenthau's offices to consider future Colombian financing and past debts. This meeting established the precedent for a series of discussions over the next eight months. Throughout these crucial months of negotiation, Morgenthau was the most persistent advocate of settlement of Colombia's outstanding obligations, anticipating that the termination of past grievances would enable the American government to resume normal commercial relations with Colombia and extend additional credits.[59]

By February 1940 the interdepartmental committee had persuaded a reluctant Foreign Bondholders' Protective Council to accept a Colombian proposal for a temporary settlement of the 1927 and 1928 dollar loans, based on the payment of interest at 3% on the 1940 coupons and the allotment of $400,000 from the budget for the amortization of the bonds. The Export-Import Bank now honored the Colombian request for a $10,000,000 loan to the Bank of the Republic. Although the bondholders' council declined to accept a permanent settlement on the same terms, with the unofficial approval of the departments of State, Treasury, and Commerce, the Colombian government proceeded to incorporate the provisions of the most recent discussions into a final settlement of the national government's dollar bonds. The State Department agreed, in addition, to accept a reservation on the part of the Colombian government that should national customs revenues fall below 25,000,000 pesos per annum ($14,286,000 U.S.) no payment on the external debt would be required.[60]

The bondholders' council viewed this provision of the Colombian proposal as an insufficient guarantee to the bondholders,[61] but the State Department proceeded to announce the proposal. The draft of the department's press release was revealing in its reference to the government's role in the negotiations:

The Treasury Department, the Federal Loan Agency, and the Department of State have not been, and are not now, parties to the proffered settlement. They have acted only as friendly intermediaries ... (However, in view of their detailed knowledge of every aspect of the Colombian debt situation, and of their concern at continued failure to reach a permanent settlement, these agencies recommend the present offer to the consideration of the bondholders).[62]

The diplomacy surrounding the issue of Colombian finance, and especially the question of default on government bonds floated in the United States, absorbed the entire depression period, in large part because the financial dimension was so closely related to a broad range of issues affecting the two societies. The recession after the general expansion of the 1920s placed the Colombian government in an increasingly insecure commercial and financial situation. The commercial crisis contributed initially to protectionism in tariff policy followed by negotiations leading toward a bilateral trade treaty and ultimately the conclusion of a Reciprocal Trade Agreement, as chapters 1 and 2 outline. But the overexpansion of indebtedness in the 1920s led to Colombian default on its foreign bond issues early in the 1930s. Olaya's administration, with its firm belief that default would further weaken Colombian credit abroad, attempted to steer against the current of public and Congressional opinion in delaying default until late in his term. Olaya capitulated only when confronted with what appeared to be insurmountable Congressional momentum toward default.

In the aftermath of the default, a number of private bondholders' groups formed in the United States. The initial organizations received little government assistance and no official sanction and were greeted with alarm and suspicion in Colombia. Unlike the Foreign Bondholders' Protective Council established early in the Roosevelt administration, these groups were concerned only with the recovery of financial losses. Without recognition and support from either government, however, these initial committees floundered helplessly in a diplomatic vacuum.

The government of Alfonso López inherited both the legacy of default and the newly formed Foreign Bondholders' Protective Council in the United States. The council, as the material above suggests, was a nongovernmental organization, officially sanctioned by the Roosevelt administration and staffed largely with former government officials. Given what was a clearly semiofficial status, the council exercised more influence on Colombia and possessed as well a greater sensitivity to the broader exigencies of American foreign policy objectives in Latin America, sympathetic as it certainly was to the plight of individual bondholders. The United States had consistently attempted to maintain a friendly and solvent power adjacent to the Panama Canal, and with the deterioration of diplomatic relations in Europe and the outbreak of war in 1939, the realization of that objective became more acute. As Secretary Morgenthau's somewhat aggressive rhetoric suggested, some American officials also believed, as did the Colombian government, that it was essential to resolve Colombia's outstanding foreign debt in order to extend new credits and to encourage the expansion of American exports. Under the direct guidance of the departments of State, Commerce and Treasury, representatives of the bondholders and the Colombian government reopened effective negotiations in 1939. In the process the United States made explicit its desire not to allow the debt issue to hamper the realization of commercial expansion and strategic security, both of which remained fundamental objectives of the Good Neighbor policy in Latin America.

5

American enterprise and
Colombian petroleum

The close relationship in United States foreign policy between economic expansion and strategic security was particularly striking in the case of American involvement in the Colombian petroleum industry between the wars. At the conclusion of the first world war Colombian fields were in the early stages of exploration and development and were yet to be exploited at commercial levels of production. The belief among American entrepreneurs that Colombian petroleum reserves were promising, and the fact that the Colombian shipping points were twelve to twenty-four hours closer than Tampico, Mexico, to eastern United States refineries combined to make the development of Colombian petroleum of considerable strategic and economic significance to the United States. Because of the desire of petroleum enterprises from the United States and Western Europe to obtain Colombian concessions and the United States preference that such concessions be held by American interests or those of nations friendly to the United States, petroleum became one of the most vital areas of international economic rivalry in the post-1919 years.[1]

The political debate in Colombia over the granting of petroleum concessions to foreign enterprise followed a pattern similar to that characteristic of the commercial and financial events discussed in earlier chapters. The experience of the first world war made American officials more sensitive to the importance of controlling foreign petroleum reserves, and they consequently urged national enterprise to expand abroad. With the conclusion of the Thomson-Urrutia Treaty in 1922, Colombian official opinion was sympathetic to that expansion and remained so until 1927, when the minister of industries under Miguel Abadía Méndez, José Antonio Montalvo, along with critics of the Conservative government, urged a cessation in the granting of liberal contracts to foreign firms and a general reappraisal of Colombian petroleum laws. There followed more than ten years of political and diplomatic conflict over Colombian petroleum policy, a conflict aggravated by the post-1929 depression, which drove down the international price of crude oil and discouraged American interests from exploiting their holdings. The dispute was mitigated, on the other hand, by a broad consensus among Colombian elites and American officials, who perceived foreign capital and entrepreneurship as the most pragmatic route to modernization. There was no sustained, radical alternative to the pro-American position to which Colombian moderates adhered. Those measures which were adopted were only partially sensitive to the desires of some groups for greater autonomy in economic development. To a certain extent, of course, the failure of the nationalists was due as well to the very successful diplomacy of the United States in supporting those political elements most sympathetic to the American presence. United States officials sought to ensure that American firms did not antagonize the host country and defended private investment against what was perceived as the 'Bolshevist' example of Mexico, which nationalized most of its petroleum operations in 1938.[2]

THE SEARCH FOR A PETROLEUM POLICY

By 1940, there were eleven major petroleum concessions in various stages of development in Colombia, but for twenty years two of them, the Barco concession (see map 1) and the De Mares concession (see map 2) dominated the political, diplomatic, and economic picture.

The former was operated under a thirty-year government contract of August 1919 by the Tropical Oil Company, originally formed in 1916 by the prominent Pennsylvania oilman Mike Benedum, who subsequently sold control of the company to Standard Oil of New Jersey. Jersey Standard then reorganized the International Petroleum Company, Ltd. (Canada) to include the operations of Tropical as an affiliate. In the period before the second world war, Jersey Standard's Canadian affiliate, Imperial Oil, which held a controlling interest in IPC, was relatively independent of Jersey in its operations. In Colombia, however, Tropical Oil officials were dependent upon decisions made by the parent firm. Because Imperial had little experience in exploration and production, Standard personnel largely staffed the operations on the De Mares concession. Jersey always maintained an executive representative in Bogotá to function as a liaison officer in government relations. The Andian National Corporation, a Canadian subsidiary of IPC,[3] operated the pipeline from the concession to Cartagena, some 350 miles to the north along the Magdelena River. The presence of both Andian and Tropical Oil resulted in a certain diffusion of authority within Colombia. Each of these entities, the executive office in Bogotá, the Andian National Corporation in Cartagena, and the Barrancabermeja refinery, reported directly to Toronto in those years. The importance of the Toronto offices need not be overemphasized, however. In the

MAP 1

Uribia

Santa Marta

Barranquilla

GUAJIRA

Cartagena

MAGDALENA

PANAMA

BOLIVAR

(BARCO CONCESSION)

Turbo

VENEZUELA

Cúcutá

See inset map for detail

Bucaramanga

ANTIOQUIA

SANTANDER

Arauca

ARAUCA

Medellín

Puerto Carreño

CHOCO

Quibdó

CALDAS

CUNDINAMARIA

BOYACA

VICHADA

Manizales

Ibagué

Bogota

Villavicencio

VALLE DE CAUCA

Buenaventura

TOLIMA

Cali

META

CAUCA

Neiva

Popayán

HUILA

Calamar

VAUPES

NARINO

Florencia

Pasto

Mocoa

CAQUETA

PUTUMAYO

ECUADOR

La Pedrera

AMAZONAS

BRAZIL

PERU

POLITICAL SUBDIVISION OF COLOMBIA
(INCLUDING MAJOR PETROLEUM CONCESSIONS, 1939)

Petroleum concession

––––– Oil pipeline

0   100   200   300   400

MILES

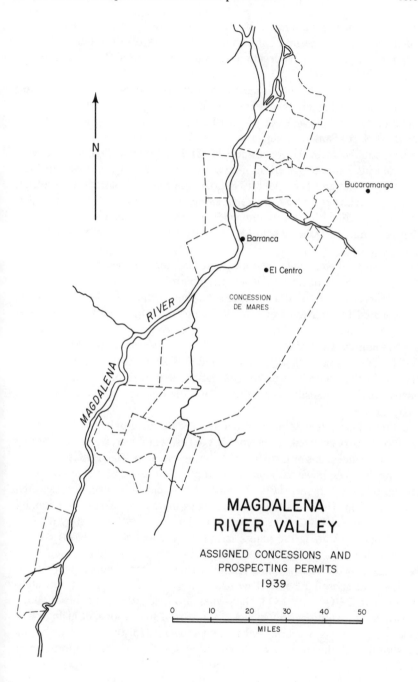

Bucaramanga

●Barranca

●El Centro

CONCESSION
DE MARES

RIVER

MAGDALENA

**MAGDALENA
RIVER VALLEY**

ASSIGNED CONCESSIONS AND
PROSPECTING PERMITS
1939

0　　10　　20　　30　　40　　50

MILES

N

absence of a Canadian diplomatic presence in Colombia, and since Tropical Oil was identified as an American company, the executive office in Bogotá worked entirely through the American legation when dealing with the Colombian government.[4]

The Colombian Petroleum Company, a subsidiary of South American Gulf Oil, held title to the second major concession, the Barco concession, which comprised some two million acres of potentially rich oil land in what is now the Department of North Santander adjacent to the Venezuelan border. The concession had been acquired from the government in 1905 by General Virgilio Barco, who in turn sold his rights to American interests during the first world war. In 1918 the Carib Syndicat and H.L. Doherty & Co. organized the Colombian Petroleum Company of Delaware and a Colombian subsidiary to develop the local properties. Early in 1926, with a conflict impending between the company and the Colombian government, Doherty sold his 75% interest to the South American Gulf Oil Company.[5]

This conflict between the government and the company became the keystone in the debate over the operations of American petroleum companies in Colombia. For five years after the transfer of ownership, the question of title to the concession dominated the political arena. As H. Freeman Matthews wrote at the end of the Hoover administration: 'From 1926 on the Barco concession played a role in Colombian politics which it would be impossible to exaggerate; it became a "Muscle Shoal" of Colombia.'[6] That the conflict culminated in the conclusion of a new contract with the Colombian government favorable to the Colombian Petroleum Company was to no small extent due to the diplomatic activity of the State Department.

The Colombian intent to articulate a definite resource policy to control the petroleum industry emerged at the time of the first world war, when the granting of major land concessions made national direction essential. The legislation passed in subsequent years, however, contained no provision to restrict exploitation or ownership of subsoil rights to Colombian nationals, and laws generally respected private ownership. The one attempt to move in a more nationalistic direction, by President Marco Fidel Suárez in 1919, was declared unconstitutional by the Colombian Supreme Court in the same year; his presidential decree had reserved all subsoil wealth for the nation. Law 120 of 30 December 1919 consequently generally adhered to the court's ruling that the surface owner of property possessed the rights to its subsoil minerals. Law 120 established that on property privately owned prior to 28 October 1873, the owner also held title to the subsoil; however, with respect to property which was still part of the national domain or had become private property subsequent to 28 October 1873, the law vested rights to the subsoil with the state. Law 120 nevertheless recognized the importance of national mineral deposits to the country's development and provided that the industry of exploiting hydrocarbons and laying petroleum pipelines was of public utility.[7]

With the optimism that accompanied the Colombian boom of the 1920s, it was not until mid-decade after Tropical Oil began commercial production that the Colombian government moved toward a more antionalistic petroleum policy. Several factors contributed to this reevaluation of policy: a fear of loss of sovereignty; the belief that the society would not reap the rewards of direct foreign investment; and an ambiguous popular anti-Americanism, which seems to have been readily available to feed the ambitions of Colombian politicians.[8]

Although the minister of industries under Miguel Abadía Méndez, José Antonio Montalvo, took the initiative in adopting a hard line against foreign exploitation, it would be misleading to view this nationalist phase in Colombian economic history as a private crusade. Montalvo may have been, as the American minister suggested, an 'ambitious' and 'small man,' but his policies received significant support from a wide cross-section of the Colombian political spectrum, and Colombian-American relations in the interwar years likely reached their nadir at the time of the petroleum debate.[9]

The first action in the general movement to tighten control over the exploitation of petroleum by American companies in fact preceded Montalvo's appointment. In February 1926 the Conservative government of Pedro Nel Ospina revoked the Colombian Petroleum Company's title to the Barco concession for alleged failure to comply with the terms of the concession. Several months later Montalvo supplemented the nullification of the Barco concession with the introduction of a more comprehensive petroleum law. When Congress in 1927 failed to pass Montalvo's legislation containing retroactive provisions for the confiscation of rights to subsoil mineral deposits, the government implemented emergency legislation (law 84 of 17 November 1927), which went into effect under the provisions of decree 150 on 28 January 1928.[10]

The foreign companies strongly objected. Decree 150 required companies holding title to lands to submit documentary evidence of ownership to the Ministry of Industries within thirty days. Because of the complicated transactions which had followed the original granting of a land concession to a Colombian national, the companies argued that compliance with the law within the required time limit was virtually impossible. The companies were also displeased with the imposition of an additional royalty of 10 to 20% on concessions in which the landowner's title predated 1873. The aspect of the decree which most disturbed the companies, however, was the delegation to the Ministry of Industries of authority to pass on the validity of land titles, a function which the companies argued was the prerogative of the courts.[11]

Representatives of the American petroleum companies in Colombia conceded that Colombian laws had long needed updating to establish a more uniform regulatory system, but they objected to the apparently intentional harshness of the 1928 provisions. They were also concerned that the anti-Americanism of the minister of industries would operate to the advantage of British petroleum companies, which had in 1926 demonstrated a timely interest in obtaining a concession.

Significantly, the State Department and the British Foreign Office demonstrated more interest in the jockeying for position in Colombia than did the companies themselves, a fact which emphasizes the strategic significance of petroleum in international relations. This was particularly true of Tropical Oil, which was not entirely pleased with its monopoly on Colombian marketing in the interwar years, since monopoly conditions neither were conducive to good public relations nor facilitated price increases on gasoline and fuel oil.[12]

When the Anglo-Persian Company's representative, Colonel Henry Yates, concluded a contract with the Colombian government for the development of a concession in the Gulf of Urabá area near the Panamanian border,[13] the State Department protested. Secretary of State Frank Kellogg cabled the United States minister in Bogotá, Samuel Piles, outlining the American position. 'This Government,' he advised, 'would view with concern any action which would tend to create a substantial monopoly or even to alienate such a considerable proportion of available oil lands as to exclude American interests from reasonable opportunity to participate in the future development of petroleum resources of Colombia.'[14]

Secretary Kellogg's cable was an example of his overreaction to events in Latin America. Although Montalvo and the Colombian government were anxious to achieve a diversification of foreign investment in the country, they did not intend to exclude American interests. There was a distinct relationship, however, between the negotiations with the British company and the passage of new petroleum legislation in 1927. As the local representative of Tropical Oil suggested: 'The ... so-called "nationalistic" policy in oil matters, in my opinion was originally started as a shield to secure the delivery to an English company of large oil reserves to counteract the "American" progress in the field of endeavor.'[15]

The British cast the American in the role of villain. Tropical Oil may have welcomed competition, but it was reluctant to lose its advantage in the market. The Foreign Office noted that Sir Arnold Wilson of Anglo-Persian had been verbally threatened by an official of an American oil company active in Colombia, and on 15 May 1928, referring to the Tropical Oil Company, T.M. Snow of the American department of the British Foreign Office commented: 'It is disconcerting that American opposition to the Anglo-Persian contract should disguise itself behind a Canadian facade.'[16]

It is doubtful if the American opposition to the Yates contract was the crucial factor determining its ultimate rejection by the Colombian Congress. Anglo-Persian itself was disappointed in the results of initial geological surveys of the concession area, and the company failed to take advantage of the favorable position it enjoyed with the Colombian minister of industries. The Colombian Congress based its final rejection of the contract on the fact that Colombian law prohibited the granting of a concession to a foreign government and the British government held a majority interest in Anglo-Persian's common stock.[17]

After meeting what it viewed as a British challenge to the American presence in Colombia, the State Department concentrated on the petroleum legislation and the Barco concession. The American minister, hesitant to make the issue one of major importance in United States relations with Colombia, advised the department that it would be preferable to await the outcome of the petroleum company's legal proceedings in the Colombian courts.[18] Samuel Piles was an elderly and mild-tempered man; he was not a career diplomat, but had developed a very cordial relationship with Colombian officials during his appointment, removing some of the Colombian bitterness over the earlier loss of Panama. He was now reluctant to offend his friends of several years' standing, and his procrastination brought him into increasing disfavor with Washington officials. Just four days after Piles advised the department to delay taking coercive action, Kellogg, at the insistence of Allen Dulles, attorney for the Carib Syndicate, instructed the American minister to press the department's point of view on the Colombian president. 'It is believed,' he emphasized, 'that much good might be accomplished if the President would decide *voluntarily* to set aside the regulations or to modify them so as to remove the features which the companies think impracticable.'[19]

As the news leaked to the press that the State Department had actively opposed the Colombian petroleum legislation and the cancellation of the Barco concession, there was an indignant flurry of nationalist rhetoric. With few exceptions the press rallied behind the Colombian government. The two Liberal organs of Bogotá, *El Tiempo* and *El Espectador*, found Montalvo's desire to diversify foreign investment in the petroleum industry to be in conformity with their own cautious view of the American presence. *El Tiempo* defended decree 150 as a necessary intervention of the state into the nation's economic life on the grounds that it was designed to ensure a wider distribution of the benefits of the development of natural resources.[20] In an editorial on 22 February 1928 entitled 'A Question of Sovereignty,' *El Espectador* pointed out that the American government had no jurisdiction whatever in Colombian petroleum affairs. Further to the left, *Claridad*, the organ of Colombian syndicalism, argued: 'What interests us in Colombia is not the question of whether the Americans or the English are to dominate the situation, or whether the sphere of influence is to be divided ... the important and vital concern is to conserve and develop the natural wealth for the benefit of all Colombians.'[21]

More ambiguous in its posture was the Conservative paper *El Debate*, closely identified with the Church, which often adopted an anti-American position in these years. Its initial response to the American pressure was similar to that of the Liberal press of Bogotá, but by the summer of 1928 it had moderated its position. The paper warned that Montalvo had placed too much confidence in British intentions and had deliberately attempted to incite an Anglo-American conflict over the granting of petroleum concessions in the hope that the Colombian government would benefit by the increased competition for its patronage. 'It is necessary to restore our relations with the United States,' the paper editorialized on 22 December, 'if we wish to defend our economic and political interests ... Panama was lost through our nationalistic intransigence.' A possible explanation for this ideological wandering is that one of the paper's major shareholders was Jesús M. Marulanda of Antioquia, the minister of finance in the previous administration and a persistent congressional critic of Montalvo's economic policies.[22]

Through the spring of 1928 the State Department was opposed to the Colombian course of action but restricted its activity in the case of the Barco concession to that of mild diplomatic pressure, preferring to offer the South American Gulf Oil Company advice than to involve the American government in diplomatic intervention. It was consequently encouraged when the Colombian foreign minister's son mentioned privately to Piles that if the State Department could arrange for an old friend of the minister's, Jordan Herbert Stabler, to represent the Gulf interests in Bogotá then the matter might be quietly patched up. The department responded quickly to this overture from the Colombians. It instructed Piles to arrange for direct negotiations between Clarence Folsom, Gulf's local representative, and the Colombian government and made arrangements for Stabler's trip to Bogotá; but it explicitly requested the American minister not to become involved in the discussions.[23]

In the interval Piles grew concerned that the enforcement of the provisions of decree 150 prohibiting drilling without permit on property to which title was in question would result in a serious setback to American petroleum interests.[24]

The State Department immediately reiterated its position on the crisis and instructed Piles to present the department's memorandum to the Colombian government. It read in part:

The American oil companies earnestly desire to co-operate with the Colombian Government in good faith to contribute to the constructive development of the natural resources of Colombia. In view of the very large investments these companies have already made in Colombia, the Government of the United States feels that it is only just that further consideration be given to these measures before the effort is made to put them in effect.[25]

Once again Piles acted in a manner which Kellogg thought too conciliatory. When the American minister talked with President Abadía, the Colombian president agreed to respect the wishes of the United States government but convinced Piles that it would be more feasible politically for him to suspend the decree on the petition of the petroleum companies than under pressure from the State Department. Much to the dismay of both the department and the companies, Piles chose to respect the request of the Colombian president and withdrew the memorandum.[26] Within the week Piles received a sharp note from the department. 'If, when you receive this telegram,' the secretary of state cabled,

the President has not carried out the assurance which he gave you that the decree would be suspended, you are instructed immediately to return the memorandum to him, and you will not withdraw it again unless the Department authorizes you to do so.[27]

Jordan H. Stabler, who had reached Bogotá on 5 May, was equally displeased with the conciliatory approach Piles appeared to be pursuing. That Stabler should have found Piles wanting in backbone was not surprising. A former State Department official, Stabler was considered by some of his associates 'one of the last of the old imperialists.'[28] On 24 May he communicated to Assistant Secretary Francis White his vexation with Piles. On the one hand he thought that the Colombian minister of industries was 'insane,' and on the other he advocated the immediate recall of the American minister for accepting the return of the department's original memorandum. 'His elimination,' Stabler claimed, 'is most necessary if [the] United States wishes to maintain respect for its representatives and its own prestige.' Stabler conceded that through his personal charm Piles had done much to mitigate the anti-American residue of the Panama seizure, but he maintained that the situation demanded a stronger man. Two days later, in a letter to Francis White, Stabler urged the department to press its advantage with the Colombians:

The Government of Colombia is apparently very afraid of the 'bugaboo' of Diplomatic Intervention in this matter and we have tried to avoid even a mere reference to such a course of action, but an informal, private enquiry cannot be considered by them as the dread 'intervention' and will do a great deal to bring them to their senses.[29]

Constant American pressure soon took its toll. On 1 June the Colombian government suspended decree 150 pending a Supreme Court and Council of State ruling on the constitutionality of law 84 and the decree itself. The suspension of the decree marked a temporary decline in fortunes for the Colombian minister of industries, but it did not alter the government's intent to regulate the petroleum industry or its stand on title to the Barco concession.[30] Official suspension of the decree in fact appeared to be essentially a diplomatic maneuver intended to appease the State Department, since local government officials continued to enforce the provisions of law 84 and thus to impede the operations of American companies. In response to a complaint from the Sinclair Exploration Co., the Bureau of Foreign and Domestic Commerce commented: 'It might be worthwhile to enquire whether the Colombian Government is throwing obstacles of this sort in the way of American interests who are in good faith endeavoring to meet the requirements of the Colombian law.'[31]

In his attempt to effect a settlement of the Barco concession, Stabler enjoyed even less success. His presence in Bogotá was from the beginning an embarrassment to the Colombian government; his outspoken criticism of Colombian policies aroused such intense public hostility that to rescind the forfeiture decree on the Barco concession in the spring of 1928 would have been political suicide for the Abadía administration. When Congress discovered the objectives of Stabler's visit to Bogotá, it cited the minister of industries to appear before the lower chamber to explain the government's relationship to the Stabler mission. Both Montalvo and subsequently the foreign minister, Carlos Uribe, whose son originally suggested that Piles arrange for Stabler's trip, denied any accountability for the American's presence. Stabler was now a political liability and for several days before his departure in July he was unable even to obtain an interview with the president through the American minister.[32]

Following Stabler's capitulation, the dispatches from Washington and the Bogotá legation assumed a more menacing tone. H. Freeman Matthews advised the division of Latin American affairs late in July: 'I feel certain that the President will not rescind the expropriation decree unless he is forced to do so by a strong definite demand to that end, especially in view of the present political attacks on his administration.'[33] After further consultation with Piles the department adhered to Matthews's advice, recommending that the legation inform the Colombian government that after prolonged consideration of Gulf Oil's position on the nullification of its concession rights, the United States government was 'convinced the decree of nullification was unjustified and should be rescinded forthwith.'[34]

The Colombian government replied through an official resolution rejecting the company's appeal.[35] The government justified its position on the ground that the company had failed to begin exploitation within the time stipulated by the contract, that it had violated its contract by failing to conduct exploitation at certain periods since 1918, and had not paid its 5% royalty requirement. These assertions were, in Piles's opinion, spurious, since the 1918 contract had not stipulated exploitation every year, and because there had been no production on which a royalty could be levied.

Nevertheless, the resolution reflected the prevailing sentiment within the administration. The antipathy toward American interests which had arisen as a result of the Stabler mission and what Colombians viewed as diplomatic intervention made it essential for Abadía to adopt a position which would rally his supporters. 'In Government circles,' Piles commented, 'it is considered as an open defiance of the United States.' Nevertheless, as the British minister suggested, the Colombian fight against the State Department and Gulf Oil had 'rather the appearance of the struggles of a fly in a spider's web.' Montalvo's victory, like his earlier setback, was temporary.[36]

The American oil companies were determined to continue their development of Colombian petroleum, and as popular enthusiasm waned for the more intransigent approach of the minister of industries, they set out to educate the Colombian public on the mechanics of petroleum exploitation.[37] Late in August Samuel Haskell, the local representative of the Texas Petroleum Company, arranged an open lecture in Bogotá's municipal theatre; he outlined the basis on which American companies believed they could equitably operate in Colombia and followed his lecture with a film provided by the U.S. Bureau of Mines on the technical aspects of the industry. Montalvo and a number of congressmen who attended the session were clearly impressed by the American's presentation, and the normally hostile Bogotá press was notably subdued the following morning. *El Tiempo*, for example, went so far as to challenge Haskell's contention that the Colombian government had demonstrated opposition to the operation of American enterprise in the country.[38] Colombian officials were impressed with Haskell's arguments, but they were not yet prepared to allow American interests to proceed at their own pace and at the possible expense of Colombian resources.

At this juncture the Chamber of Representatives chose the Tropical Oil Company as its next target. Because of its special contract with the government, Tropical had not been directly concerned with the conflict over the Barco concession or with the general petroleum legislation of 1927, except insofar as it affected expansion of Standard Oil operations.[39] Since 1926 the Colombian government had not collected its 10% royalty on the production of the De Mares fields because of the uncertain price of crude petroleum on the world market. In late August 1928 the Chamber appointed a committee to investigate the payment of royalties and to determine whether the 1919 transfer of the concession to the company had been valid.[40]

A month later the committee completed its study of Tropical Oil. Significantly, both the majority and minority reports adopted a critical posture. The majority report, written largely by Pedro Juan Navarro, an outspoken Liberal critic of the American company, claimed that the original concession contract had lapsed prior to transfer to Tropical Oil in 1919, and that because the 1919 contract with the Colombian government modified the earlier contract it should have been approved by Congress. The report accordingly recommended to the Chamber a bill of two articles, one invalidating the contract of transfer, the second authorizing the government to conclude a new contract with the company. The minority report, signed by the chairman of the committee, the Conservative Próspero Márquez, repeated the recommendations of the Navarro group, but added allegations that Tropical had not adhered to the spirit or letter of its contract.

The tone of the reports owed much to the climate of public criticism of American enterprise in Colombia in the 1920s, but it was perhaps more significant that both the Navarro and Márquez reports recommended that the government conclude a new contract with Tropical Oil. Tropical had a better relationship to the press, to the government, and to the public than did Gulf Oil during the debate on the Barco concession. The fact that Tropical rapidly and efficiently placed the De Mares concession into production and established a refinery to supply the domestic market made the company commercially important to the Colombian economy. As a result, the critical dimension of the two reports met with little approval outside Congress, and even in the Chamber they did not reach first debate. The president himself had been a member of the cabinet which approved the 1919 contract and he was not disposed to reverse his earlier decision. The result was the Colombian government's acceptance of Tropical's interpretation of the royalty clause.[41]

Abadía's scuttling of the Chamber committee reports did not mean the abandonment of efforts to regulate the petroleum industry. Following the suspension of decree 150, the government devised new legislation and in September presented it to Congress. The legislation was an imaginative attempt to nationalize future petroleum exploitation on a basis of profit sharing between the government and private enterprise; the latter would participate in petroleum development on the national domain through 'semiofficial companies.' The major aspects of the proposals were these: a single company's grant was not to exceed 75,000 hectares; the state would control 20% of the shares and no other single entity could hold more than 10%; all pipelines outside actual concessions would be controlled by the state but would be financed and operated by private capital; undeveloped property held by a concessionaire would be heavily taxed to encourage production; the state should construct at least one national refinery to ensure a domestic supply of petroleum products. Finally, as the bill applied to private lands, royalty

requirements were substantially reduced and no permits were required for exploratory drilling – a further indication of the government's determination to combine national controls with an encouragement to private industry.[42]

The reaction to the proposals, particularly from the petroleum interests, was
not enthusiastic. Sir Arnold Wilson of the Anglo-Persian Petroleum Company,
Ltd informed the Foreign Office that the bill contained 'many objectionable features,' even though in an interview with the Colombian minister of industries on
15 September he had praised Montalvo for devising a bill which 'was new, original
comprehensive and consistent – qualities exceedingly rare in oil legislation.'[43] An
official in the Foreign Office commented: 'I should imagine that if companies are
tempted to take up concessions on these terms they will find that in most cases
they fail to make a profit, while developing Colombian resources.' Wilson was, of
course, speaking in terms of profit motivation rather than controlled resource
development (with considerations of political and economic sovereignty) when
he objected to the Colombian legislation, but from a Colombian perspective the
bill had much to commend it.[44]

Shortly after the government introduced the legislation, however, another diplomatic 'incident' occurred to draw congressional and public attention away from
the merits of the bill. Two days prior to his departure for the United States on
17 September, the retiring American minister in Bogotá presented a sharp note
to the Colombian foreign minister reasserting the intention of the United States
government to protect American interests involved in the Barco concession and
criticizing the Colombian government for its failure to respond to a 'simple enquiry from the American Legation ... with regard to the rights of American oil
producers.'[45]

The revelation of the contents of the American note of 15 September aroused
widespread indignation in Bogotá. *El Tiempo* carried the story on 21 September
and supplemented general coverage with a lead editorial urging the government
to resist American capitalism. In the public clamor which ensued, Congress sum-
moned the ministers of industries and foreign affairs to explain the circumstances
in which the government had received the American protest. Uribe's assurances
that the reply to Piles's note would conform with the requirements of national
dignity drew warm applause from Congress, which passed a resolution affirming
'its irrevocable support for an international policy capable of rejecting at
all times, as has the present Government, the intervention of any foreign
power.'[46] Matthews observed on 22 September that 'the Government and
Congress have been aroused to a dangerous state of defiance and self-confidence
which if unchecked may result in serious injury to American interests.' From
Montevideo, the American minister informed the State Department that the
Uruguayan press was giving the dispute with the petroleum companies

prominent coverage, and the headlines had been notably unfriendly to the Americans.[47]

The American protest also received considerable attention in nongovernment circles in Colombia. On 23 September a number of priests, at the instruction of the Archbishop of Bogotá, denigrated the morals of American society in general, criticized the American presence in Colombia, and equated Americanism with Freemasonry. In some sermons priests referred specifically to American intervention in the Barco conflict. The following day a large student demonstration converged on the Plaza de Bolívar, and the crowd moved from there to the Presidential Palace to express its approval of the government's stand against American 'imperialism.' Taking advantage of his opportunity to establish closer ties with the student sector, Abadía spoke briefly, urging the students to maintain calm and insisting that there had in fact been no diplomatic intervention; he added that the State Department had merely requested information and the foreign minister had received a conciliatory telegram from the department explaining its intentions.[48]

Matthews urged the department not to knuckle under to the public protest. 'I wish to emphasize,' he wrote on 27 September,

that the Colombian Government deliberately stirred up the present incidents for its own political ends, that it will stop at nothing it can get away with in its attack on foreign interests to increase its popularity at home and that the Department's explanations are interpreted here only as signs of weakness and do not help the situation. It is my calm and unbiased opinion that the Department will shortly be compelled to decide whether to protect legitimately established American interests in Colombia by means of strong pressure, financial, economic or otherwise, thus losing a large part of the Colombian market for our manufacturers and at the expense of American bondholders or else to forego such protection with ... serious loss of prestige.[49]

It is in the light of this statement that one should view the issuing of the Department of Commerce special circular on Colombian finances, with the blessings of the State Department,[50] on 28 September. It indicates that while the circular may not have been intended to support American petroleum interests, the relationship between Colombian finance and politics and the petroleum crisis was so close that the publication of the special circular and the difficulties of the petroleum companies were not merely chronological coincidences. The State Department failed to take further action until Jefferson Caffery reached Bogotá in late November to replace Piles. The Bogotá representative of Tropical Oil commented in a note of 16 December 1928 to the Toronto office:

The situation as I view it is that the new American Minister ... will carry much prestige with the Government. The report of the Department of Commerce, with the overwhelming success of Mr. Hoover in the recent election, plus the Catatumbo matter, has had a remarkable effect on local policies. Doctor Urueta [attorney for Tropical Oil and close confidant of the Colombian Minister in Washington] is convinced that if Mr. Caffery will make some insinuations or evidence interest in the protection of our interests there will be perhaps a good chance of obtaining in the next Congress ... a legislative enactment definitely terminating any defects or rather alleged defects in our title.[51]

Caffery stood in almost direct contrast with Samuel Piles. A professional diplomat with seventeen years' service (much of it in Latin America, first in Caracas and later in El Salvador) prior to his Bogotá posting, Caffery was more polished and more skilled in the diplomatic process than his amiable predecessor. In both Bogotá and Havana, where he replaced Sumner Welles in 1933, Caffery demonstrated an acute ability to operate at all times close to the seat of power, and he was unrelenting in his defense of American interests. Partly because of this latter trait, he never attained (or probably sought) the popularity of men such as Josephus Daniels, who attempted to implement a less business-oriented Good Neighbor policy in Mexico than was generally characteristic of the Hoover-Roosevelt years. While ambassador to Mexico, Daniels wrote of Sumner Welles and Caffery:

They ... are of the old school of diplomats, who never saw anything wrong in the sort of diplomacy which cost us the confidence of the people of Pan America in the past years. What we need in all Pan American Embassies and Legations are men of our type, who will change the whole atmosphere and have welcome in their hearts for a New Deal in those countries such as we wish for our own.[52]

The American companies were concerned that, in the absence of an American minister, British interests would enhance their position with the Colombian government. The American companies were not satisfied that the termination of negotiations (on the Yates contract) between Anglo-Persian and the Colombian government the previous summer was conclusive evidence that British involvement in Colombian petroleum was a dead issue. W.B. Heroy of the Sinclair Petroleum Co. suggested on 9 November:

If the representatives of Anglo-Persian and the Colombian Government were ... working harmoniously with reference to Decree 150 at a time when it was being assailed by American petroleum interests, it seems quite reasonable that the proposed ... petroleum law might also have received advance approval from the British, especially as the conditions under which joint companies will be formed would ... be more favorable to a British company than the Yates contract was.[53]

Although he was mistaken in his view of the British response to the earlier Colombian legislation, Heroy was accurate in his contention that the British government was reluctant to abandon its hope of obtaining a petroleum concession for the Anglo-Persian Company. British despatches from Bogotá and Foreign Office minutes for late 1928 and early 1929 contain frequent reference to this objective and to attempts by the British minister and Arnold Wilson of Anglo-Persian to shape the new legislative proposals to modify law 120 of 1919 to enable companies which had the financial participation of a foreign government to obtain Colombian concessions. In fact it would appear that Wilson had largely won his point with the Colombian government, when domestic legislation (the administration's so-called anti-Bolshevik bill to curb rising labor radicalism) intervened to disrupt Congress. With the refusal of the minority party to participate in Congressional debate, Congress was adjourned.[54]

In addition to their efforts to undermine British petroleum interests, the American companies expressed concern over the Mexican influence on Colombia. As if to lend substance to American fears, late in October the Colombian Ministry of Industries published a study entitled *The Controversy Over Mexican Petroleum Legislation*, written by Julio Corredor Latorre. In his preface, Corredor dedicated the volume to Montalvo for his attempt to regulate Colombian petroleum development. In the spring of 1929, following publication of the Mexican study, the assistant chief of the Mexican Department of Petroleum, Santiago González Cordero, visited Colombian officials and offered assistance. During his brief stay in Colombia, Cordero was outspoken in his criticism of the contracts with Tropical Oil and the Andian National Corporation, and he was appointed to the committee set up that spring to study the industry. Moreover, the influence of the Montalvo faction within the government was sufficient for Corredor to be appointed consul general in Mexico in September 1929.[55]

CONSOLIDATION OF POWER

In 1929 the Abadía administration turned to foreign advisers for assistance in drafting new petroleum laws. The government obtained the services of H. Foster Bain, a former director of the U.S. Department of Mines and Petroleum; J.W. Steel, an official of the U.S. Geological Survey; H. Ibarra, an American expert on United States and Mexican petroleum; Sir Thomas Holland of Great Britain; Santiago González Cordero of the Mexican Department of Mines and Petroleum; and Auriel I. Ancoulesco, a Rumanian lawyer and specialist in petroleum legislation.[56]

Bain came to dominate the group. Scrupulously honest, he adhered stoically to the Colombian government's request that members of the committee not discuss their progress with foreign companies, with the result that even the anti-American Liberal press found his work commendable.[57] Largely for the same reason, private petroleum interests were critical, arguing that Bain's experience was too theoretical and that he was isolated from sources of practical information in Colombia, especially at the local level. A vice-president of the Texas Petroleum Company commented that Bain's technical inexperience resulted in an overly theoretical analysis. The Texas Company believed that Bain's background as a government employee had left him 'saturated with the U.S. Government viewpoint' embodied in the American mineral leasing act of 1920, which gave considerable control to the federal government over all public lands, restricted the size of leased lands, and established minimum periods for exploration and drilling. American petroleum interests contended that this type of approach was impractical in Colombia given the nature of the topography and the unproven state of much of the potential petroleum lands.[58]

Whether or not United States experience was applicable in the Colombian context, the British minister was convinced that the Americans dominated the committee of international advisers preparing the legislation. Monson indicated that the committee continued to meet following Sir Thomas Holland's departure for England; in these subsequent meetings the American bias of the other members was left unchecked.[59]

The Ministry of Industries' petroleum bill contained a number of the recommendations of the Bain group. The more important changes were as follows: the bill eliminated the concept of semiofficial companies but specified that 20% of stock issued by a company had to be offered to Colombians for a minimum period of ninety days on the Bogotá Exchange; it required a minimum of 10% Colombian employees in the first three years of a company's operations, with an increase subsequently to 25%; companies were required to locate their head offices in Bogotá; should the company be owned by foreign interests, it would have to obtain corporate status under Colombian law; instead of an absolute royalty payment there was now a sliding scale of royalties which took operational variables into account; on both public and private concessions owners were required to submit a detailed technical plan to the government prior to undertaking exploitation.[60]

Once again the legislation met both business and congressional opposition, with the result that by early September it was apparent that Congress would not likely pass the bill in that session. Not only were the Liberals, led in Congress by Antonio José Restrepo, outspoken critics of Montalvo's proposals, but factionalism also erupted in Conservative ranks because of the impending conventions for presidential nominations.[61]

The opposition of the oil companies contributed to further delay. The companies opposed the Montalvo bill in anticipation of better terms following the 1930 presidential election and as the depression made Colombia more desperate for economic stimulus. In addition, world overproduction of crude petroleum made the exploitation of the Colombian fields at that juncture not only unnecessary but detrimental. Clarence Folsom, the local representative of Gulf Oil, for example, indicated that his principals, W.L. Mellon in particular, were determined to obtain the validation of their title to the Barco concession but would keep it in reserve until world prices were more attractive.[62]

The embattled petroleum bill of 1929 had little chance of success. In the absence of a specific legislative enactment, the companies continued to function under emergency law 84 of 1927, which was found constitutional by the Supreme Court in November 1929.[63]

As with other areas of friction in United States-Colombian relations in the late twenties, the petroleum situation entered a new phase with the election of Enrique Olaya Herrera in February 1930. Although he did not assume office until August, his activities in the first part of the year moved the republic toward a settlement of the Barco dispute and passage of the long-awaited petroleum legislation. The fact that one of Olaya's closest confidants, Carlos A. Urueta, was a former minister to Washington who had represented both Standard Oil and Gulf on various occasions and had been for several years on intimate terms with the American legation strengthened the American hand. Urueta was, as Jefferson Caffery informed the Department, 'our one outstanding friend in Colombia.'[64] Olaya's election, moreover, mitigated the influence of Abadía's anti-American minister of industries until a cabinet reshuffle in April brought to office a former member of the Congressional Petroleum Committee, Francisco José Chaux.[65]

Olaya's determination to deal equitably with the United States was apparent in his months as president-elect; his return to New York in May 1930 to arrange financial support and to discuss the petroleum situation with American interests indicated his priorities. Although the Ministry of Industries concluded a contract with the Unión Colombiana de Petróleos (Standard Oil with essentially Antioqueño capital) in March for the development of the Carare area, the majority of American oil companies continued to denounce the current legislation as unworkable, and the president-elect was convinced that the alleged inability of the law to encourage foreign investment in the industry was largely responsible for the country's weak credit position.[66]

Olaya's conferences with Gulf Oil officials in the United States with respect to the Barco concession and the petroleum laws were not entirely amicable. The company was highly encouraged by Olaya's attitude toward the contract, but it was not in full sympathy with his insistence that should the contract be approved the company would immediately have to bring a well into production. The com-

Olaya Herrera and Secretary of the Treasury Andrew Mellon (settling the Catatumbo Concession)

Colombia Nacionalista, 22 June 1935

pany claimed this would necessitate the curtailment of production in other fields, given the current world situation. Gulf did not, however, foresee that this stipulation would be a major obstacle. The company was sufficiently determined to obtain a satisfactory settlement that it suggested to Matthews that if the Colombians did not act quickly 'diplomatic intervention' should follow. Matthews of course did not concur in this, yet he did nothing to sway the company from its position.[67] 'The Gulf,' he noted, 'are proceeding on the basis that if they can't get what they want they can fall back on the Department.'[68]

The lack of cooperation from American oil interests was not unanimous in the spring of 1930. Tropical Oil made considerable effort to accommodate the incoming administration's need for economic support. In May the company agreed to assist the government over its financial difficulties by advancing $500,000 on its next royalty payment and on its 1929 income tax. Its affiliate, the Andian National Corporation, consented to advance $150,000 in lieu of the government's transportation rights on the Andian pipeline, and $500,000 on its 1929 income tax. Tropical was also, of course, concerned about the state of finances in the Department of Santander. The governor of the department indicated to Tropical's executive representative in Bogotá, H.A. Metzger, that the department needed national financing for public works projects to prevent the three thousand unemployed in the area from creating social unrest which would also influence Tropical's labor relations.[69]

Olaya received additional encouragement from the Department of State. While the president-elect was still in the United States, Joseph P. Cotton Jr, the under secretary of state, arranged for him to meet with George Rublee of the law firm of Covington, Burling, Acheson, Schorb & Rublee. Rublee had recently completed duries as adviser to Dwight Morrow while the latter was ambassador to Mexico, and the department was anxious for him to use his Mexican experience in Colombia.[70] Olaya shared the desire to obtain the advice of someone like Rublee who had an established reputation, was in the confidence of the Department of State, and yet was competent to be objective in his appraisal. He anticipated, as did the department, that Rublee would function 'somewhat ... as a buffer between the oil companies and the Colombian Government.'

Rublee subsequently accepted the responsibility. 'Formally,' Rublee later commented, 'I was to be an advisor to the Colombian government but informally I was to advise Mr. Cotton and the State Department. That was understood by Olaya.' Rublee, Francis White informed the American minister in Bogotá, was a 'man who will give Olaya and Colombia excellent service ... will solve a major difficulty for us, and keep the oil question there from becoming acrimonious and a subject of newspaper discussion throughout this hemisphere.'[71]

Once established in office Olaya initiated the study of a new petroleum bill. On the advice of Carlos Urueta, he also reorganized the Ministry of Industries to eliminate the anti-American Montalvo appointments. Olaya soon discovered, however, that the pessimists among his advisers were correct. His long absence from Bogotá made it difficult for him to readjust to the contours of Colombian domestic politics. In fact, within a month of his inauguration he had become so disillusioned by the obstacles confronting him that he expressed thoughts of resignation to his closest friends.[72]

In spite of his domestic political problems and Gulf Oil's attitude, Olaya continued to cooperate fully with Caffery. When the government completed its study of a petroleum law that fall, Olaya submitted a copy to the American legation for comment before he took further action. Generally satisfied with the Colombian proposals, the legation, after consultation with H.A. Metzger and Urueta, suggested some minor alterations.

Olaya's strategy was to present the bill to Congress prior to Rublee's arrival in Bogotá in order to avoid public criticism that the legislation was the creation of an American lawyer. 'The representatives of the American oil companies will all be very much disappointed,' Caffery noted, 'when they find out they are not to have an opportunity of expressing themselves on the bill.' Caffery's comment was not only premature but inaccurate, since Metzger of Standard Oil had been frequently involved in earlier discussions and since Olaya made a distinct effort to approach the companies in the early weeks of October to test the climate of opinion.[73]

Unlike Olaya, Caffery was optimistic at the turn of events. When the right-wing Conservative Silvio Villegas attacked the administration for its close cooperation with the United States and referred to the Rublee mission, Eduardo Santos, the foreign minister, and Chaux, the minister of industries, successfully defended the government's activities in the field of petroleum development. 'We have probably a unique opportunity during this Congress,' Caffery cabled on 13 October, 'for securing a variety of much desired legislation of far-reaching effects on American interests.'[74]

With Rublee's arrival on 27 October, meetings between the American legation and the Colombian government increased in frequency. Rublee was apprehensive about his knowledge of the petroleum industry, but this deficiency did not concern the State Department; Rublee was an excellent intermediary.[75] After discussing the legislative proposals of the Colombian government with Metzger and Urueta, Rublee and Caffery called on the president. The first week Rublee met Olaya daily to rework the legislation and invited representatives of the American companies to present their views. By this juncture Rublee anticipated only two major objections to the legislation – a parallel system of reserves and the question of compulsory production levels. Rublee and Metzger were prepared to accept the Colombian position that the legislation should include a device to ensure minimum production to guarantee the government a relatively constant income from royalty and tax payments. Nevertheless, they could envisage no way in which the companies could be compelled to produce beyond the capacity of the world market.[76] Whether developed by foreign or domestic enterprise, in other words, the Colombian petroleum industry would remain sensitive to international prices and demand.

The new petroleum bill modified the 1929 legislation in several respects. With regard to the national reserves it opened the eastern Llanos to exploitation but restricted the Department of North Santander, which contained the yet-contested Barco concession. It reduced royalty payments and placed them on a scale ranging from 2% to 11% depending on the distance of the wells from a seaport and on whether the lands were public or private; it reiterated the concept that the petroleum industry was a public utility; and it limited concessions to 50,000 hectares except in the Llanos, Putumayo, and Amazon regions, where the limit was 200,000, and prohibited the transfer of a concession to a foreign government. Article 6 provided that Colombians receive priority in hiring and equality of pay with foreigners. The legislation suspended export duties in petroleum for the first thirty years of a concession's operation and required companies to operate wells at a minimum of one-quarter capacity.[77]

Reaction to the petroleum bill was mixed. Rublee was generally satisfied that he had accomplished as much as possible within the limits of Colombian politics. Anglo-Persian's local representative was also encouraged by the prospects of development under the legislation and suggested that the provisions were 'much more favorable to foreign companies' than earlier measures had been. The American companies were less confident. H.A. Metzger argued that the terms were not sufficiently lenient given the unfavorable world situation, although the removal of exchange restrictions on petroleum exports was a distinct assistance to exportation.

Some members of Colombian society would have preferred to see a more stringent clause covering the employment of national labor. Press agitation during the congressional debate stressed this, but a floor amendment establishing quotas on foreigners at laborer and employee levels failed to pass.[78]

Caffery perhaps best described the role of the American legation in the controversy:

Dr. Olaya might have left both matters [the legislation and the Barco Concession] drop for the present as, although he continues to have tremendous good will for the United States and our interests, he seems more and more inclined to let matters drift when there is no impelling reason for him to do otherwise ... It has been clear for a long time that, even with the amazing change throughout Colombia in sentiment in our regard, those two projects could never be put through Congress unless an effective driving force of the Executive Power were put behind them.[79]

Rublee's presence reinforced the efforts of the State Department and the Colombian government to seek a middle course between the extremes of nationalism and the preferences of the petroleum interests. At the same time Rublee, like Bain before him, encouraged a more favorable Colombian attitude toward American assistance. As the British commercial secretary suggested: 'Colombians are now beginning to appreciate the difference between the views of representatives of American interests and those of impartial or academic American experts, and ... to better understand the President's pro-American leanings.'[80]

While Congress debated the petroleum bill, Rublee and Olaya turned their attention to the problem of achieving a reconciliation with Gulf Oil interests in the Barco concession. The State Department was afraid that Olaya was in sufficient domestic difficulty that a complication in the discussions with Gulf would lead him to allow the Colombian courts to resolve the dispute. As a result Rublee sought to prevent any clashes among the participants in his conversations with Clarence Folsom, Olaya, and Roscoe B. Gaither, representative of American Maracaibo, which had an interest in the concession. This was not an easy task because of the additional tensions which existed between Rublee and the Gulf Oil representatives resulting from Rublee's earlier association with Dwight Morrow's actions in Mexico.[81]

The principal point of contention between South American Gulf Oil and the Colombian government was the amount of royalty the company's subsidiary would have to pay on its operations. Gulf offered 5½% of the value of crude petroleum at seaport; the Ministry of Industries contended that less than 6% was neither economically nòr politically feasible. With the area of disagreement relatively marginal, Folsom successfully appealed to head office for a compromise, and Francis White reinforced the request by calling the vice-president of South American Gulf, William Wallace.[82]

In mid-February President Olaya expressed a desire to add two clauses to the proposal, one establishing minimum production levels, the second limiting the exploration period. Olaya indicated that the inclusion of these two clauses was essential to overcome the belief in some congressional circles that the foreign companies wanted the concessions to hold in reserve rather than for rapid development.[83] Convinced that unless Gulf readily agreed to Olaya's recommendations the president would discontinue the discussions, Rublee and Caffery recommended acceptance. They thought that had Olaya not believed he was acting in conformity with the State Department's wishes he would have been more inclined to negotiate with one of the non-American companies interested in the concession.[84]

Certainly Gulf remained attracted by the Barco concession. The company feared that political stability in Venezuela was too dependent on the longevity of Juan Vicente Gómez, dictator since 1908; should its Venezuelan properties be threatened, Gulf wanted to have a concession on the Colombian side of the border.[85] Nevertheless, Gulf officials remained opposed to the Colombian proposal to limit the exploration period to ten years; and after further debate Olaya conceded. Gulf agreed to begin commercial exploitation when an output of 3,000 metric tons of crude oil per day was reached and to put a pipeline into service within three years of that development. The road to the successful conclusion of Rublee's mission now seemed open. At the end of February Henry L. Stimson cabled to Caffery: 'The Department, of course, does not undertake to pass upon the contract as a whole; nevertheless, it hopes that these offers of the company will make it possible for the two parties to reach a satisfactory agreement at an early date.' The secretary of state's optimism was not ill conceived; on 4 March Clarence Folsom and the minister of industries signed the contract restoring to Gulf what was believed to be a potentially rich area for exploitation; in fact, the new contract contained an additional 35,000 hectares.[86]

American interests considered the results a Gulf victory. Metzger commented that the contract was considerably superior to Tropical Oil's. It was, he claimed, 'the best contract I have seen come out of Colombia; it is wonderful.' American financial interests evidently agreed with Metzger's assessment, since the conclusion of the Barco contract coincided with approval of a $4,000,000 installment on a short-term loan to the Colombian government from a consortium headed by the National City Bank of New York.[87]

The congressional hurdle remained, and in spite of Olaya's efforts to placate opponents of the contract, by mid-April he was beginning to despair of achieving ratification in that session. For three months following the signing of the agreement the administration and its supporters portrayed ratification as vital to Colombia's economic and financial stability, in an effort to win congressional leaders to the government's side. In the debate which ensued, public sentiment reached a pitch which observers compared to activity at the time of the Panama revolt.[88]

The most consistent advocate of the contract was *El Tiempo*, which, under the direction of Eduardo Santos, moved steadily into the president's camp. Although the paper occasionally vacillated during the debate, it never recommended more than minor modifications of the contract. Its editorials persistently criticized what it considered excessive nationalism on the part of other papers and congressional critics.[89] Slightly to the left of *El Tiempo*, *El Espectador* remained critical of the bill for its failure to provide specific guarantees that the company would put the concession into operation within a reasonable period of time. The other leading Liberal paper of Bogotá, *Mundo al Día*, played both sides of the debate; at times it carried critical articles by prominent Colombian writers yet, as the end of the debate in Congress neared, the paper praised Olaya's administration for its persistent efforts at economic recovery and echoed the president's assertions that approval of the contract would reassure foreign capital.[90]

The response of the Conservative press was less uniform, but the support of papers such as Bogotá's *El Nuevo Tiempo* indicated the growing sympathy of moderate Conservatives for the Olaya administration. *El Nuevo Tiempo* took a generally conciliatory stand on the petroleum question in the late 1920s, but the introduction of the Chaux-Folsom contract initially aroused its opposition. One plausible explanation for the paper's ultimately sympathetic position is that Olaya offered Roberto Urdaneta Arbeláez, a prominent Conservative associated with the paper, a political position if he would mute the critics of the contract. On 6 April the newspaper began to publish a series of letters between William Wallace and Urdaneta. In July Urdaneta became foreign minister.[91]

To the extreme right of *El Nuevo Tiempo*, a Conservative Medellín daily, *La Defensa*, espoused a fanatically anti-American position often tinged with overtones of anti-Semitism. The paper was consistently hostile to the terms of the agreement itself and to the president's attempt to stifle congressional opposition.[92]

Outside Congress and the editorial pages of the Colombian press, the public reaction to the debate on the Barco concession was vigorous but of little political significance. By the end of March street demonstrations were commonplace, and hostile handbills were prominent on walls throughout the capital. In a rather ineffectual effort to coalesce the opposition forces, on 27 March Luis Rueda Concha, a young Conservative later associated with Laureano Gómez, presented a public lecture at the Municipal Theatre; following his talk, a small group of one hundred marched up the Carrera Séptima to *El Tiempo*'s offices shouting 'Down with the contract, down with Olaya Herrera.'[93]

It was in Congress that the crucial confrontation took place. In the Chamber of Representatives, where the Liberals held a majority, most of the party rallied to the administration, with the exception of a prominent Manizales representative, Aquilino Villegas, minister of public works from 1922 to 1926. With its narrow Conservative majority the Senate was another matter, however, and once more Olaya was obliged to make liberal use of his patronage to obtain a favorable Senate report on the Barco bill.[94] In mid-June Olaya signed the bill restoring the Barco concession to the Colombian Petroleum Company.[95]

Although the transfer of the concession was thus complete by mid-1931, both the heated debates of the previous five years and the operation of the concession itself remained active issues in Colombian politics and society. The Catatumbo region of Colombia never proved to be the commercially rich petroleum reserve which its publicists envisaged. Moreover, Gulf interests in Colombia were unable to equal the relatively sound relationship which Tropical Oil developed with the Colombian government in the 1930s. As the minister of industries commented to Jefferson Caffery in September 1932: 'The difficulty with the Gulf people is that they attempt to treat us like Venezuelans and that simply won't do here.'[96]

The Department of State was distressed by Olaya's evident belief that the department was a party to the settlement. Stimson protested that 'while the Department discussed the matter with the Gulf, it did not attempt to carry on negotiations with that organization with respect to the terms of the contract, which it considered to be a matter between that organization and the Government of Colombia.' The secretary's objections are misleading. The department was more than a neutral third party during Rublee's talks with Colombian officials and representatives of the American companies; and Caffery had substantially facilitated negotiations between Olaya and the company. Nor was the State Department entirely free of responsibility for the pervasive rumor that the development of the Catatumbo region would improve the nation's financial position. Olaya was the major propagandist for this interpretation, but Caffery and Gulf often expressed similar sentiments. During the debate on the Chaux-Folsom contract, for example, Folsom informed the legation that the Mellon interests would be prepared to support Olaya's efforts to obtain American loans once the contract was approved; it is improbable Olaya was unaware of Gulf's position.[97]

TRADE COMPLICATIONS

Throughout the depression years there was a distinct relationship between the development of Colombian petroleum and the domestic policies of the American companies which held title to the reserves. The Colombian experience underlines the difficulty experienced by capital- and technology-poor nations anxious to develop natural resources without sacrificing sovereignty.[98] Certainly the Colombian government would have been equally affected by international price fluctuations of crude petroleum had it introduced more rigid controls over production, exportation, and marketing. But in the absence of such controls the government was virtually at the mercy of corporate and government decisions beyond its borders, and its balance of payments tended to be unpredictable.

The international petroleum industry was faced with mounting difficulties in the late 1920s as overproduction and depression conditions pushed crude oil prices downward. In the United States one response to the crisis was a changing attitude toward the value of foreign oil imports. The United States government and affiliated agencies, such as the Federal Oil Conservation Board, and the Fuel Administration in the first world war, had long supported substantial petroleum imports as one method of protecting American reserves. Mark Requa, for instance, head of the petroleum division of the Fuel Administration and active in petroleum matters in the Hoover years, had urged American companies to seek concessions abroad to avoid the exhaustion of American resources. The impact of the depression and the discovery of the rich East Texas oil field, however, temporarily altered his perspective. This was reflected in the sharp reversal of position of the Federal Oil Conservation Board between 1929 and 1932. In its annual report for

1929 the board advocated increased importation. The report read in part:

The effort should be made to propose measures that will minimize and delay the undesirable future outcome of this excessive drain upon a limited though admittedly large reserve ... The depletion rate of our own resources which represented 18% of the world total can be brought more into accord with that of foreign resources only in one way – by importing a greater quantity of crude petroleum ... Co-operation in the development of foreign oil fields, through technical assistance and the further investment of American capital, would seem to be a logical conservation measure.

In 1932, on the other hand, the board urged the state governments to restrict local production and the federal government to place a quota or tariff on foreign petroleum imports.[99]

Demands from the independent producers that the federal government take steps to curtail foreign imports were constant in the depression period. Reluctant to involve the federal government in the direct regulation of the industry, President Hoover encouraged conservation and efficiency in production; after March 1929 the government prohibited the issuing of new leases for exploitation on public lands, but this did little to meet the larger problem of overproduction.[100]

With both President Hoover and Secretary of the Interior Ray Lyman Wilbur opposed to a tariff on petroleum imports, mid-continent producers lobbied in Congress for the passage of legislation regulating the industry. In March 1930 the Senate rejected a proposed oil tariff; another measure, introduced by Senators Capper and Shortridge the following January, also failed to pass in that session. Urged to take the initiative, President Hoover succeeded in having the industry's leaders agree to voluntary production controls, which were in effect from April through June of 1931.[101]

Nevertheless, when a tariff on crude petroleum ultimately passed Congress in 1932, Hoover felt obliged to sign the bill. The president and Wilbur remained concerned that a petroleum duty would damage trade relations with Latin American oil-producing nations since Standard Oil of New Jersey and Gulf were the two largest exporters from the southern continent. In reporting on the tariff bill to the Senate Committee on Commerce, Secretary Wilbur emphasized:

A tariff on crude oil with proper compensatory duties on oil products would assist the oil producers and I favor it; but it would injure the oil industry if the law does not safeguard against destruction of our exports.[102]

Other members of the Federal Oil Conservation Board shared Wilbur's hesitation.

In a memorandum to the secretary of the interior, the secretary of the FOCB, E.S. Rochester, commented earlier:

Concerning the foreign trade phase, I may say that we have at stake a two billion dollar a year trade balance with Latin America. The effect of a tariff 'discrimination' at this time against Mexico, Venezuela, Colombia, Peru, and Ecuador would have serious consequences ... It might be well to remember ... that ... this is no time to give Latin American countries substantial evidence of what many in those countries term our 'trade selfishness.'[103]

Mark Requa also supported Hoover and Wilbur. Requa argued consistently that a tariff would not rectify domestic overproduction, and that it was 'childish' to place the blame for the industry's crisis on South American developments, although he admitted that foreign production was a factor in the crisis.[104] He suggested that as part of a larger program the importation of South American oil might be restricted, but he added in an open letter to the American Petroleum Institute:

It is not for lack of a tariff on oil that the petroleum industry finds itself in its present plight. It is due primarily and solely to domestic cut-throat competition in production, refining and distribution, carried on without regard to economic consequences. If and when the industry formulates a program that comprehends more satisfactory service to the public over a longer period of time ... it may well demand action that will check unlimited flow of foreign oil into the United States.[105]

After he left office, Hoover continued to voice opposition to regulation of the petroleum industry, especially to the controls instituted by Franklin Roosevelt under section 9 of the National Industrial Recovery Act in 1933.[106] Under the direction of Secretary of the Interior Harold Ickes, who served also as oil administrator, imports were limited 'to an amount not exceeding the daily average imports of petroleum and petroleum products during the last six months of 1932.' The codes also authorized federal control over domestic production, wages, and prices within the industry, and interstate commerce in 'hot oil,' that is oil produced in excess of state laws. In addition a half-cent per gallon duty on crude petroleum and fuel oil, instituted under the Revenue Acts of 21 June 1932, remained in effect until 1939. When the NIRA was declared unconstitutional in 1935, the controls were incorporated into the Connally Act the following year. Roosevelt, like Hoover before him, was nevertheless reluctant to become involved in a debate on an oil tariff;[107] as in the Hoover years, the primary emphasis was on conservation rather than government control of the oil industry.

Since Tropical Oil was part of Standard Oil's international operations, U.S.

restrictions on crude petroleum imports had repercussions in Colombia. With over-production a crucial factor in the United States, Standard Oil had agreed to ad-here to Hoover's request early in 1931 to impose voluntary restraints on its ac-tivities abroad. Although Imperial Oil and the International Petroleum Company in Toronto directly controlled Tropical's activities and were relatively indepen-dent of Standard's policy decisions before the second world war, the Canadian companies could hardly be immune to the developments south of the border. In March the Toronto office of International Petroleum cabled H.A. Metzger that it intended to cut back production in Colombia and reduce wages to Colombian la-bor.[108] By the end of the month Tropical reduced production from 54,500 bar-rels a day to 48,000, without informing the Colombian government of its inten-tions. The government, involved in its efforts to pass new petroleum legislation and to restore the Barco concession to Gulf Oil, was distressed by what it viewed as a lack of cooperation from the only productive company in the country. It was also, of course, concerned that Tropical's reduced production would affect royalty payments to the government. Since Olaya was using the development of the national petroleum resources as a bargaining weapon in negotiating loans in New York, this further loss in government revenue threatened to weaken his posi-tion, as did the possibility that Tropical Oil would simply discontinue production altogether should the level of world prices further deteriorate.[109] Only after ex-tended consultation with George Rublee and James W. Flanagan, president of the Andian National Corporation and a director of IPC, was Stimson able to obtain the company's agreement to continue production at reduced levels.[110]

The Colombian petroleum industry remained sensitive to external develop-ments. When the U.S. Congress in 1932 did restrict foreign petroleum imports, Tropical Oil brought pressure on Olaya to protest the American action.[111] Pro-duction statistics for 1929–35, as tables 3 and 4 illustrate, reflect the impact of world conditions on Tropical Oil's activities in Colombia. In 1929 Colombia pro-duced over 20,000,000 barrels of crude oil and exported more than 18,600,000 with a value of $27,172,869.40. In 1933 total production fell to 13,157,642, barrels of which the company still exported 11,805,000 barrels with a value of $8,971,921.60. In the same year Colombia's total petroleum production fell be-low 1% of world production for the first time since 1926. The recovery of oil prices after 1934, however, brought an increase in production. By 1 May of that year the Andian National Corporation's pipeline was running at 52,000 barrels a day, and the value of exports in 1934 was nearly double that of the previous year. By the end of 1935 Colombian production represented 1.1% of the world total, which placed it third in Latin America behind Venezuela and Mexico.[112]

As the only producer of petroleum products for Colombian consumption, Tropical was in a sensitive position, and throughout 1933 the company continued to come under public criticism.[113] On 15 November, H.A. Metzger replied to

TABLE 3
Colombian oil production

Year	Crude oil produced*	Place of Colombia among oil producing countries	Average monthly production*	Number of producing wells	Exported crude*	Value of exported crude (U.S. $)	Refined crude*
1921	67		6	3			6
1922	45		27	4			200
1923	323		35	6			341
1924	425		37	16			335
1925	1,007		84	67			587
1926	6,444		537	139	4,642	9,461	337
1927	15,002	8th	1,250	225	13,679	22,507	1,206
1928	19,896	8th	1,658	338	17,911	25,780	1,475
1929	20,385	8th	1,699	461	18,601	27,173	1,668
1930	20,346	8th	1,695	578	19,113	26,351	1,230
1931	18,237	8th	1,520	622	16,989	15,761	1,260
1932	16,417	8th	1,368	654	15,322	16,482	1,017
1933	13,158	10th	1,096	668	11,806	8,972	913
1934	17,341	8th	1,445	697	16,477	16,972	1,532
1935	17,598	9th	1,466	738	15,949	15,757	1,593
1936	18,756	9th	1,563	781	16,437	16,136	2,395
1937	20,298	9th	1,691	847	17,732	20,092	2,783
1938	21,582	9th	1,798	954	18,453	20,747	2,762

* thousands of barrels of 42 U.S. gallons

SOURCE: Félix Mendoza and Benjamín Alvarado *La Industria del Petróleo en Colombia* (Bogotá 1939), adapted from table 19

Tropical's critics in a lengthy open letter in *El Tiempo*. He pointed to the difficulties of producing for the Colombian market from the relatively isolated refinery at Barrancabermeja, but stressed the company's cooperation with the Colombian government in its conflict with Peru; he argued that although gasoline prices in Bogotá were 1½ cents per gallon higher than in New York, the difference in price was largely the result of high Colombian sales taxes.

Metzger's reasoned analysis of the Colombian market did little to end the criticism of Tropical Oil. Yet Tropical was not the only target worthy of attack. As Olaya's detractors pointed out, his administration, in its eagerness to pull Colombia out of depression and attract American capital, had accomplished very little toward the effective regulation of the petroleum industry. In part because of the nature of the international corporation in extractive-export industries, decisions relating to economic development in Colombia were relegated to foreign centers, where first priorities were not necessarily the needs of Colombian society.

TABLE 4
Colombian crude oil exports by countries (thousands of barrels of 42 U.S. gallons)

Year	Argentine	Aruba	Belgium	Canada	Cuba	Czechoslovakia
1926	87			89		
1927	167			4,104	53	
1928	98		199	4,348	40	
1929	313		220	3,987		
1930	91		250	3,110		
1931	211		187	5,097		
1932	281	1,273	140	2,158		
1933	148			2,841		
1934		4,858		4,243	59	
1935		5,850		3,295		
1936	168	8,923		4,067	52	
1937	273	9,651		3,652	58	95
1938	83	8,470		6,035	42	81

Year	England	France	Germany	Holland	Italy	Norway	United States
1926	224						4,242
1927	797			14	169		8,375
1928	903				134		12,189
1929	1,300				202		12,578
1930	182				342		15,138
1931					250		11,244
1932					512		10,957
1933		700	52		426		7,640
1934		2,650	125		521		4,020
1935		2,578	68		345	36	3,779
1936		2,671	58		403	96	
1937		2,794	67		651	61	431
1938		2,876			733	132	

SOURCE: Félix Mendoza and Benjamín Alvarado *La Industria del Petróleo en Colombia*
(Bogotá 1939), adapted from table 22

THE LOPEZ TRANSITION

As the Olaya years drew to a close, there was some anxiety in American circles
that Alfonso López would give free rein to the critics of American enterprise.[114]
Like American representatives in Bogotá before him, Sheldon Whitehouse dis-
trusted López, but also like his predecessors he tended to misinterpret López's
liberalism. What antipathy López felt toward American enterprise was directed

primarily toward the United Fruit Company. Prior to his election he was on excellent terms with H.A. Metzger of Tropical Oil; and his objections to the presence of American petroleum companies were restricted to specific areas of conflict. The comments of the British minister in Bogotá in 1936, M. Paske-Smith, were most accurate:

> Dr. López shows no hostility to foreign capital ... although he is determined that it shall never obtain monopolistic concessions such as the ones granted by the Conservatives ... to the Tropical Oil Company and to one or two English railway companies. So long as he is in power, he once said to me, no new concession will be approved under which Colombia cannot obtain her fair share of her own riches.[115]

Nevertheless, López was displeased with existing petroleum legislation, and as president-elect he appointed a committee to study the question; it was composed of Felipe Latorre, a legal adviser to Olaya, Miguel Arteaga, the governor of Cundinamarca, Jorge Soto del Corral, the manager of the Bank of Colombia, and Luis Eduardo Gacharna, a Bogotá lawyer and politician.[116] From this group stemmed many of the ideas for his later approach to the petroleum industry, especially his interest in the development of a Colombian-owned and -operated refinery.

Conservative predominance in both major parties and divided loyalties in the Liberal ranks between López and Olaya undermined López's legislative program. Nor did he aid his popularity when he attempted to discredit the former president shortly after the inauguration by reviving the issue of Olaya's relationship to the oil interests in 1930-1. The fact that López used his old friend Conservative senator Laureano Gómez as the spokesman for the attack on Olaya did little credit to either man. Olaya, of course, vehemently defended himself, and the ensuing debate dragged Congress through forty unfruitful days. The State Department furnished the foreign minister with cables supporting Olaya's position, and the Liberal press rallied to his side.[117] It is in this political context, prior to Olaya's untimely death in 1937, that one must view Lopez's efforts to revise the petroleum laws.

With domestic factionalism still disrupting Congress, the administration introduced a bill in the Senate authorizing the government to establish and operate a refinery as a public utility. This bill reflected the persistent belief of the moderate nationalists that greater autonomy in the industry through the elimination of Tropical's monopoly on marketing would result in lower gasoline prices to Colombian consumers. It was, the American chargé wrote 'known to embody ideas entertained by many persons desirous of reforming the petroleum legislation.'[118] In an effort to stop the bill, H.A. Metzger discussed it with members of the Senate Petroleum Committee. Whether his representations were decisive or not is difficult to determine, but the committee submitted a congressional report largely favorable to Tropical's objections. The report suggested that in the event the bill passed, the government would be confronted with a loss of royalties from the Tropical refinery and Andian's pipeline; that Tropical would abandon plans to expand its own refining operations and increase the importation of gasoline from its affiliates. The unfavorable report was sufficient to sway Congress from its support of the bill, and it was shelved until revived in 1936 by a more radical Congress.[119]

While the government was trying to establish a national refinery, Jorge Soto del Corral, now President López's minister of finance, challenged the tax returns for 1933 of both United Fruit and the Andian National Corporation. In Andian's case the law establishing a tax on pipelines postdated its contract with the government, and the company had operated on the assumption that its tariff payments to the government were in lieu of the law's requirements.[120]

Andian submitted the question to the courts; in the interval Olaya was able to moderate the approach of the government to the companies concerned. Entering the cabinet as foreign minister early in 1935 to facilitate congressional acceptance of the Rio Protocol ending the Leticia dispute, Olaya insisted on a more conciliatory approach to foreign enterprise as the price for his cooperation. 'The more or less public campaign against these companies appears to have been checked,' the American chargé noted in April.[121]

Through Olaya's efforts and those of Raymond Dodson of the Andian Corporation, who spoke to the Bogotá Rotary Club on the problems confronting petroleum companies in Colombian development, there was a temporary easing of tensions. Because Colombians in general seemed to view Tropical Oil as representative of American enterprise, the American legation viewed this development as a sign of improvement in Colombian-American relations. A few days later the Supreme Court added further credence to this assessment when it decided the tax suit between Andian and the Colombian government in favor of the company.[122]

Olaya's influence over the López administration shortly began to wane, however, and the administration immediately appealed the decision of the Supreme Court. By April 1935 Olaya and his supporters seemed to be losing ground, and the way was cleared for a second attempt to revise the petroleum laws.[123]

There was nevertheless little effective progress toward a legislative proposal until late 1935, when labor unrest and social conflicts in Barrancabermeja served as a catalyst in stimulating renewed criticism of Tropical Oil in Congress. Critics came from both parties, but a small core was led by Pedro A. Jaimes of Bucaramanga, Gustavo Uribe Aldana of Bogotá, and Gabriel Sanín Villa of Medellín, whose position was moderately nationalistic, concentrating on the desirability of a Colombian refinery. By mid-November the orators were spent, and the Chamber sent an investigating committee to report on the extent and causes of labor radicalism in the oil fields.[124]

The committee spent more than three weeks touring the operations of Tropical and the Andian National Corporation before submitting a highly critical report that concentrated on the social and hygienic inadequacies of Barrancabermeja, where Tropical's Colombian laborers lived (it was not company property). But the report also recommended three pieces of legislation which had wider application to the problem of foreign enterprise: the creation of a national refinery; the stricter national regulation of labor relations; and the control of medical and health services in industry and agriculture. In addition the committee suggested the repeal of the companies' exemption from departmental and municipal taxation.[125]

Building on the recommendation of the congressional committee and encouraged by the sympathetic climate of opinion it had created, the López administration believed the time opportune to propose revisions to the 1931 petroleum legislation. The government was not convinced that the 1931 law had been tested sufficiently to require wholesale alterations, but it proposed a modification of the provisions dealing with refineries, taxes on petroleum reserves on private property, and time allotted for exploration.[126]

The legislation which took shape in the course of 1936 evolved largely without consultation with the American companies or the United States legation, unlike that of 1931. It would be misleading, however, to interpret López's independence as a sign of hostility to American investment in the petroleum industry. Although both the president and his minister of industries in 1936, Benito Hernández Bustos, were anxious to achieve greater control over resource development, they were no less convinced of the necessity for American participation.[127]

Law 160 of 14 November 1936 did not radically alter existing petroleum legislation; yet it was technically more sophisticated than the 1931 law and, in the opinion of the companies, generally more attractive to foreign investment. The British minister to Bogotá heralded its passage as 'very striking evidence of the Government's determination to lay real foundations for the development of the petroleum industry by the adoption of far-sighted and stable legislation.'[128]

Briefly, the more significant aspects of the law were as follows. Article 3 qualified the size of concessions by restricting length to no more than two and one-half times the least width. Article 4 extended the exploration period but specified that drilling activities had to commence six months prior to the expiration of the first three-year exploration period. Companies were required to submit detailed plans for future exploration, and these plans had to include provision for drilling a minimum of two new wells – a provision which Tropical Oil considered 'onerous.' Articles 6 and 7 redefined the procedure required to obtain permits to develop private lands, a liberalization which pleased the Texas Petroleum Company in particular because it had invested heavily in private lands. Article 7 also provided that should the Supreme Court determine that land under consideration belonged to the nation, the government could negotiate a contract with the applicant allowing the latter to continue operations. Other sections of law 160 provided for 'substantial' reduction of taxes on privately owned petroleum properties and a liberalization of royalty payments. It exempted from import duties machinery and equipment imported for the construction and operation of refineries; exempted from taxation crude oil produced in Colombia for domestic consumption; and reduced royalties on crude oil produced for export.[129] Noticeably missing from the law was any provision for the construction of a state-owned and -operated refinery.

A companion piece of legislation, law 149 of 1936, attempted to strengthen the position of Colombian labor. Law 37 had stipulated only that 'preference' should be given to Colombians for appointment to higher positions 'provided that their qualifications are not inferior to those of the foreigners.' Law 149 required that 'no industrial, agricultural, commercial or any other enterprise' with a monthly payroll in excess of 1,000 pesos could hire more than 20% foreign employees or 10% foreign labor. It further provided that 70% of the total payroll of such companies had to be paid to Colombian employees and 80% of the payroll to Colombian labor. There were nevertheless several qualifications to the general law. Article 2 allowed companies to appeal to the Ministry of Industries and Labor for permission to employ foreigners in excess of the quota in cases where skilled technicians not available in Colombia were required. Moreover, article 5 defined as a Colombian national anyone with ten years' residence or who was married to a Colombian.[130]

As with the 1931 legislation, the oil companies objected to the limitations on acreage. But they were sufficiently pleased with their progress not to challenge formally the government's position. One of Tropical Oil's Colombian lawyers wrote on 2 April 1937: 'I believe ... that nothing would be more dangerous for the interests of the Company than to create situations capable of justifying a popular and governmental reaction against it.'[131] Austin T. Foster, counsel for the Socony-Vacuum Petroleum Company, informed department official Laurence Duggan that the company was satisfied with the attitude of the Colombian government toward foreign investment, and shortly thereafter South American Gulf Oil announced its intention to construct a pipeline from its producing fields to the coast.[132] In the year that followed passage of law 160 foreign investment in the petroleum industry showed a marked increase;[133] some years later an official of Tropical Oil referred to the years after 1936 as 'the second epoch of exploration in the country.'[134]

The 1936 legislation was thus convincing evidence that the López administration was committed to a policy of industrial development with the technical and financial assistance of foreign enterprise; but it also indicated that, unlike his predecessor, Alfonso López was unwilling to assume the role of sacrificial lamb to American interests. Although the end results may have been similar, in terms of the economic impact of American capital on the Colombian petroleum industry, López at least attempted to maintain a policy free from the direct interference of the Department of State. In pursuing his objectives in this way the president managed to avoid much of the bitterness which had characterized the debate on the Barco concession and the petroleum legislation of 1931. At the same time, the events of the López years removed much of the instability and unpredictability of petroleum exploitation in Colombia as the country appeared to follow a conscious path leading away from the Mexican experience. On 14 June 1938, three months after Mexico nationalized most oil properties, the director of the petroleum department of the Ministry of Industries, César A. Pedraza, issued an official statement to *El Tiempo* affirming that all petroleum contracts in Colombia were secure.[135]

By 1938 the United States had achieved its ultimate objectives – American predominance in the Colombian petroleum industry and relatively favorable conditions for private investment. Ambassador Spruille Braden continued to press for modification of existing laws during Eduardo Santos' administration, but the modifications tended to be details, such as hectarage limitations, rather than questions of principle.[136] On the brink of the second world war, American officials could feel relatively confident that American strategic interests in Colombian petroleum were secure. The primacy which American interests had acquired owed as much to State Department initiative as to the superiority of American technology and the general acceptance by Colombian elites of foreign investment.

Although this study is not directly concerned with the economic significance of the petroleum industry in Colombia, the subject warrants brief consideration.[137] Tropical Oil was the only commercially productive oil company in Colombia until shortly before the second world war. With a very marginal domestic demand for petroleum products in Colombia, it was natural that the industry should function primarily in an extractive-export capacity. Regardless of the political significance of foreign ownership, in an economic sense absentee ownership meant less interest in the development of related industries in Colombia and a corresponding lag in technological advancement. The exemption from municipal and departmental taxation made the companies less responsive to the needs of their immediate environment than might have been the case; but for this Colombian authorities alone were responsible.

The evidence suggests that the industry contributed to the economic well-being of Colombia in the 1920s and 1930s.[138] Royalty payments and income taxes, which the American companies paid more faithfully than did most members of the Colombian upper class, were important elements in national government revenues, and to the departments in which development took place, since they received a share of national revenue.[139] Income from the industry eased the Colombian economy over several difficult years in the depression, when coffee prices were unstable, and likely delayed the default on the national foreign debt. In addition, the exportation of petroleum seems to have enabled Colombian exchange to maintain a relatively strong position in the 1930s.[140]

In the area of labor, the record of the oil industry is a mixed one. The López administration attempted, in law 149 of 1936, to restrict the number of foreign laborers and to promote the advancement of Colombians to management positions. The dearth of Colombians skilled in petroleum technology and the escape clauses in the law permitted violation of the spirit if not the letter of the legislation. Like most foreign enterprise, Tropical Oil paid relatively high wages; after the initial stages of development, however, the industry is not very labor-intensive. In all of its Latin American operations, Standard Oil of New Jersey had only 7,900 employees in 1931 and 33,000 in 1940. In Colombia, Tropical Oil in 1939 employed 3,400 Colombians and 200 North Americans on the De Mares concession, and related activities involved another 1,000, compared, for example, with over 5,000 nationals employed in the manufacture of cigars and cigarettes in 1938.[141] Although more thorough investigation is needed to develop this analysis, the higher wages available on the public works projects in the 1920s and in the oil industry appear to have diverted workers from the coffee plantations.[142] Whether this transfer of labor was permanent and how it affected the general structure of the economy remains to be seen.

Important as the domestic economic dimension is, the main concern in this chapter has been the nature of American policy as it related to the petroleum industry. American officials worked to smooth the way for U.S. investment, to prevent the granting of concessions to European and Asian enterprises, and to bring American corporations into line with the broader objectives of United States Latin American policy. The State Department achieved its objectives largely by reinforcing the Colombian political center in its own effort to advance the cause of modernization along lines compatible with American objectives.

6

Bananas and politics

Of the major international corporations operating in Colombia in the 1920s and 1930s none aroused greater animosity than the United Fruit Company. As a visible manifestation of the American presence the company's Colombian subsidiary, the Magdalena Fruit Company, was an obvious target for anti-American sentiment.[1] Yet, as the Colombian instance demonstrates, opposition to the activities of the Magdalena Fruit Company was as much a reflection of emergent economic and political nationalism as of anti-Americanism. United enjoyed a marketing monopoly on Colombian bananas, the country's third largest export, and was less than conciliatory in its reaction to competitors, whether the source of competition was Colombian or foreign. The company exercised considerable control over the economic, social, and political affairs of the Colombian department in which it operated, and yet it jealously guarded its independence from Colombian authorities. In the depression years the relationship between United Fruit and Colombian society was particularly strained; the stirrings of nationalism and the muscle flexing of an embryonic labor movement brought a reassessment of the company's contribution.

Frequent labor conflict characterized the United Fruit Company's operations in Colombia. Disputes with local planters over prices for produce and the system of marketing were common; disagreement over the control of transportation in the banana zone and over irrigation strained the company's relations with the Colombian government. The State Department at no time became as intimately involved in these disputes as it did in the petroleum debate, largely, it would seem, because of the absence of a strategic dimension to United's operations. The American legation nevertheless sought to mitigate Colombian hostility to the company and to bring the company's activities into conformity with a policy designed to repair the American image in Latin America. In its dealings with the Magdalena Fruit Company the State Department, in agreement with Colombian authorities, supported a moderate labor policy, one which would dampen the appeal of communist and anarcho-syndicalist elements active in the banana zone yet promote the development of a responsible organization.[2]

United Fruit first entered Colombia in the late 1890s (when Panama was still part of Colombian territory) following the acquisition of the British-owned Colombia Land Company by Minor C. Keith, an American railroad financier active in Central America. Primarily interested in the development of railroads, Keith gained control of the Santa Marta Railroad, another British enterprise, which had been used for sugar transit in the Santa Marta area since the 1880s. When he amalgamated his interests with the United Fruit Company in 1899, the latter thereby acquired a monopoly on railroad transportation in the Department of Magdalena. By 1925 the Santa Marta Railroad had 176 kilometers of line in operation, used almost exclusively for shipping bananas to Santa Marta for export.[3]

In Colombia the United Fruit Company initially concentrated on controlling banana exports rather than developing its own plantations as its enterprises had done in other Latin American countries. Nevertheless, by 1929 and throughout the subsequent decade the company owned or directly controlled 20 to 30% of producing banana lands in the department; the remainder was divided among some four hundred private Colombian planters.[4] From the company's perspective this system permitted operation with a relatively small capital investment; and since at this juncture Magdalena Fruit held a marketing monopoly it was assured of a constant supply of produce. From the Colombian perspective, United's operations provided local planters with a large and efficient international marketing structure, but at the same time the planters found themselves virtually at the mercy of United Fruit's policies, price structure, and transportation facilities.

The explosive nature of United's situation in Colombia was especially apparent during a long and bitter strike which hit the Magdalena Fruit Company and the large domestic planters late in 1928. The Department of Magdalena had experienced political instability for some time prior to the strike; rampant political factionalism and feuding over control of the governorship of the department debased the democratic process and severely reduced the administrative effectiveness of local government in the area. These local political problems combined with grievances against Magdalena Fruit to create a highly volatile atmosphere.[5]

Magdalena Fruit was Colombia's largest single agricultural employer in 1928;[6] yet because of its contract labor system it refused to comply with social insurance legislation. Colombian planters were equally guilty of exploiting the largely migratory work force, but this in itself did not divert animosity from United.

In spite of the transient nature of the work force in the area, the strike of 1928 was more than a spontaneous, chaotic outburst of frustration. This is significant in the light of the fact that the Colombian labor movement was in 1928 still in an embryonic state, partly because of official pressures against organization. The right of workers to form unions was not recognized until 1931, and even then there were severe restrictions.[7] Nevertheless, the intellectual ferment of the 1920s and the attraction of Socialism for many young left-wing Liberals led to the establishment in 1926 of a moderate Socialist labor party, the Partido Socialista Revolucionario (PSR) and the parallel development of a left-wing labor movement. The inability of the radical anarcho-syndicalists to dominate the labor movement resulted in further splintering late in 1925, leading to the formation of the Unión Sindical de Trabajadores, which concentrated in the coastal regions of the country and assumed a prominent role in the 1928 strike.[8]

Italian and Spanish anarchists were active in the banana zone in the 1920s and organized some of the workers in the small community of Guacamayal. The 1928 strike, however, was an indigenous movement, led by Colombian nationals. The leftist Marxist faction which remained in the PSR viewed the agricultural labor force as a significant source of support once the workers were organized. Accordingly several PSR members, including Torres Giraldo and Maria Cano, were by 1928 on the north coast attempting to coordinate the diverse labor groups involved in the banana industry.[9]

In the fall of 1928 dissatisfaction with working conditions on the banana plantations led to a series of conflicts culminating in a large-scale strike on 11 November. United from the outset pursued a rigidly anti-labor position. Company officials refused to listen to a petition of grievance when first approached in early October, and when they finally granted an interview to workers' representatives, they indicated that since the workers were not direct employees of the company there was no legal responsibility to negotiate.[10] United officials charged, with support from the American vice-consul, that workers' representatives were professional agitators who had incited an essentially content populace. Intensely anti-labor in his outlook, the vice-consul, Lawrence Cotie, viewed the petition of grievances as 'a clumsy piece of Soviet literature.'[11]

There was some justification for the company's allegations that the leaders were radical and drawn from outside the banana zone, but this obscures the validity of the discontent and the degree of solidarity in the strike movement once it gathered momentum. In fact, the PSR-affiliated Unión Sindical de Trabajadores de Magdalena urged prudence until the rank and file demanded action. The strike was already underway by the time one of the prominent PSR leaders of the strike, Alberto Castrillón, arrived in the zone.[12]

The company received full support from the governor of Magdalena, José Maria Núñez Roca. Núñez and the local manager of United Fruit, Thomas Bradshaw, informed labor delegates they would not negotiate until the strikers returned to work. The one Colombian official in Santa Marta prepared to recognize the legality of the petition, the head of the Ministry of Labor Office, was arrested shortly after the strike began, for interfering.[13]

A delegation from the Ministry of Industries was no less disdainful of the Colombian workers than were the management of United Fruit and the American vice-consul. Yet the head of the department of labor in the ministry, José Rafael Hoyos Becerra, and the counsel for the department, Miguel Velandia, were also struck by Bradshaw's arrogance. Hoyos and Velandia attributed the strike to three factors: the lack of diplomacy on the part of company officials; the desire of local merchants to capitalize on an opportunity to compete with the company's commissaries (which the labor department claimed provided reasonable facilities); and the presence of Communist agitators. They conceded the strike had wide popular support – hardly surprising given the deplorable working conditions of Colombian labor in the zone. Still, the delegates were not prepared to support the workers' request for a salary increase. 'The lack of organization and morality among workers in this region,' the delegates concluded, 'makes any wage increase useless, since any surplus over a subsistence wage will be spent on unhealthy vices.'[14]

The Liberal press perceived the potential political value of the crisis as an opportunity to discredit the Abadía administration. But the fact that large Colombian planters as well as United Fruit were the targets of the strike tended to moderate the harshness of their editorials. *El Espectador* on 19 November endorsed the workers' demands but urged caution in handling a potentially subversive group.[15]

To *El Diario Nacional* (24 November), the Conservative government and its press (*El Debate*) was distorting the nature of the dispute in Magdalena. It was hostile and somewhat racist in its portrayal of the foreign presence:

The ... patience of the proletariat which labors under the direction of United Fruit has at last expired, jolting the Saxon indifference of its fair-haired overlords.

Their just complaint, the human demand for an improvement in working conditions, was sufficient to provoke the angry rejection of the petition by the Saxamerican owners, for whom nothing exists but the cult of their niggardly capitalistic interests.

The paper remained the leading critic of government policy. On 4 December it warned against the violent suppression of the strike and lamented the fact that some supported the foreign company rather than Colombian labor. Since there were only a few hundred troops in the area compared with thirty to forty thousand workers, of whom ten thousand were already on strike, the governor urged

Bradshaw to make concessions until reinforcements could arrive. Early in December the company agreed to consider the improvement of living quarters on its own plantations, the establishment of a six-day week, the construction of more hospitals, the abolition of company commissaries which controlled the distribution of foodstuffs, the full payment of wages in cash rather than scrip or credit vouchers valid only in the commissaries, and a 50% wage increase for the lowest-paid workers. United refused, however, to consider the demand for collective insurance and declined to submit the question to mediation.[16] For the moment, however, no concrete steps were taken to implement these provisions, largely because the Colombian government, afraid that a successful strike in Santa Marta would bring similar movements throughout the country, quietly requested the company not to increase its wages – already high by Colombian standards.[17]

The American vice-consul was particularly alarmed. Following discussions with Bradshaw and the governor, Cotie urged prompt suppression, as the company recommended. Cotie worked closely with Thomas Bradshaw, who, like many of United's employees, was a British national. Bradshaw's unyielding attitude and alarmist statements did much to incite anti-foreign sentiment. When he cabled the company's representative in Bogotá recommending that the government be urged to take immediate action or the company would request outside assistance, the company promptly reprimanded him, but could not erase the damage already done.[18]

United temporarily resumed operations in December, using strikebreakers under the protection of Colombian soldiers. The situation remained extremely tense, however. Cotie noted pessimistically: 'Feeling against the Government by the proletariat which is shared by some of the soldiers is high and it is doubtful if we can depend on the Colombian Government for protection.' He recommended that the American government place a naval vessel with a 'small armed force within several hours calling distance'; when this proposal was subsequently rejected, he curtly responded: 'I was justified in calling for help and I shall welcome the opportunity to defend the position that I took on the morning of the sixth and until the afternoon of the eighth.'[19] Cotie's insistence on intervention struck a sensitive nerve in departmental policy. It was unlikely, given the desire to achieve a lower profile, that the United States would contemplate intervention of any nature.

The Colombian decision to provide adequate protection for American interests was premised on a fear of United States intervention.[20] On 5 December the government declared martial law and placed General Carlos Cortés Vargas in control. Censorship was imposed and control tightened over individual movement in the district.

The first major armed clash between strikers and troops took place the follow-

'The Atonement' in the aftermath of the 1928 United Fruit Company strike

El Tiempo, 29 March 1929

ing morning in Ciénaga, along the coast south-west of Santa Marta. In a tragic moment, which might have inspired the moving scenes in Gabriel García Márquez's novel *Cien Años de Soledad*, Colombian police and troops fired on a tightly packed and noisy crowd they had ordered to disperse. From this moment the strikers fought a retreating battle, fleeing southward along the tracks of the Santa Marta Railroad toward Sevilla, where they were again routed. Within a few weeks the Colombian military had broken the resistance, although sporadic disturbances in the spring of 1929 were a foreboding of conflicts to come.[21]

Politically the strike remained a live issue through the presidential election of February 1930. The Liberal press and politicians continued to draw public attention to the way in which the government had handled the crisis. *El Tiempo*, which maintained a cautious silence during the strike, suggested in an editorial on 26 December that the government investigate the rumor that the American vice-consul had requested American military intervention. *El Tiempo* discounted the likelihood of intervention, yet was apprehensive that avowed 'interventionists' should be given diplomatic postings in the country. The editorial concluded, ironically, with praise for United Fruit officials for their patience and restraint in handling the strikers.[22] Less conciliatory was its editorial cartoon (9 March), which depicted President Abadía being branded with a skull and crossbones and the initials of United Fruit.

The political implications of the strike became more explicit in the summer of 1929, when a young Socialist representative reported on his personal investigation into the government's suppression of the strike. Jorge Eliécer Gaitán provided the essential spark to bring the debate into national prominence. Dynamic and principled, Gaitán called for a parliamentary investigation into the events of the strike; on the basis of the evidence he presented in July, the Chamber requested the Judiciary Committee to conduct hearings on the government's actions.[23]

The American minister, Jefferson Caffery, criticized Gaitán for his opportunism and praised the government's efficient response. He claimed Gaitán had 'interviewed only agitators and individuals on the strikers' side.' With some justification, Caffery accused Gaitán and other Liberal-Socialists and dissident Conservatives of using the incident to arouse hostility to the government and to American interests in general.[24]

Although there was certainly justification for Caffery's accusations of opportunism, Gaitán's recommendations to Congress were characterized by explicit sympathy for the problems of Colombian labor and a perceptive awareness of the precise areas of tension in the banana industry. The chronic socioeconomic difficulties of the banana zone had long drawn the attention of the national government, yet supervision of the industry had been minimal. Gaitán stressed the need for Colombian officials in Magdalena to act more responsibly, and for the improvement of communications between the department and Bogotá, government control of irrigation, an export tax on bananas, a revision of the United Fruit contracts with Colombian planters, the encouragement of Colombian growers, enforcement of labor laws, and more systematic regulation of unions.[25] Each of Gaitán's recommendations was essential to both an understanding and a rectification of the sources of conflict in the industry. The strike in 1928 had been the manifestation of discontent resulting from the domination of Magdalena by an economic and social elite; as Gaitán fully recognized, the monopoly of the United Fruit Company was only one obstacle – although an important one – to the creation of greater economic and social justice in the area.

Gaitán's campaign had little immediate effect on the banana industry; the political storm which he helped to arouse, however, was largely responsible for the resignation of the minister of war in September when Congress began hearings on his possible misuse of funds. In October a combination of Liberals and Vasquistas (the Conservative adherents of Alfredo Vásquez Cobo) passed a resolution in the lower Chamber providing for the appointment of a committee to investigate the president's conduct during the 1928 crisis. Although the committee reported the following month that Abadía had acted entirely within his constitutional limits, the party's political fortunes were damaged as the nation prepared for the February elections. The passage of legislation reducing the strike leaders' sentences was further evidence of the shifting political balance of power. It is significant in terms of Colombian political development, and ironic in the light of subsequent developments, that the pro-American Liberal candidate for the presidency in 1930, Enrique Olaya Herrera, received considerable support from some of the leftist elements which had supported the strikers in 1928.[26]

United Fruit's monopoly on banana marketing in Colombia was a persistent source of irritation to Colombian entrepreneurs who found themselves dependent on United's marketing facilities. On several occasions domestic planters and foreign competitors of United Fruit attempted to shake the company's domination of the Colombian industry – with limited success.

In 1928 Colombian banana planters were a diverse group with little sense of common interest. The one point on which they agreed was the necessity to achieve greater independence of action from the American company, particularly from United's contracts. These protected the company from loss in the event of any transportation failure resulting in spoilage of the crop, and established quotas on purchases from local planters because of United's need to coordinate its international supply. The contracts specified as well that agreements were void should the United States impose an import duty on bananas, and they required domestic planters to absorb any local export taxes.[27]

One of the earliest efforts to break United's monopoly in Colombia came from Samuel Zemurray's Cuyamel Fruit Company, by 1927 United Fruit's major competitor in Central America. In cooperation with the Atlantic Fruit Company, Cuyamel contacted the Cooperativa Bananera Colombiana de Ciénaga. This independent cooperative was under the direction of Roberto Castañeda, who was equally anxious to diversify Colombian exports and break into United's marketing monopoly. Initially the cooperative was optimistic, but continued effective opposition from United obliged Cuyamel to discontinue its efforts. From Zemurray's perspective, his attempts to challenge United were not futile, since they made his operations increasingly attractive to his competitors and culminated in a merging of Cuyamel with United the following year. From a Colombian point of view, however, the failure of the powerful Cuyamel to crack United's Colombian operation underlined the difficulties confronting independent planters.[28]

In 1930 a group of prominent Colombian planters under the leadership of Juan B. Calderón organized the Cooperativa Bananera Colombiana and concluded a four-year contract with the Liverpool firm of Robert Brining Company Ltd, which agreed to purchase the cooperative's bananas for the British market at a price 25% higher than that offered by United Fruit. When United acted to prevent the continued shipment of the fruit, the dispute rapidly evolved into a political issue.[29]

In Santa Marta Bradshaw continued the hard-line policies characteristic of his behavior during the 1928 strike. He accused the head of the cooperative of economic opportunism and of attempting to oblige United to purchase his inferior properties at high prices. Bradshaw saw Calderón as a 'disreputable' personality and castigated the minister of industries, Francisco Chaux, who had given the cooperative assistance, as equally undesirable. In statements to the press, the United manager denied any opposition to local exporting efforts; yet his actions belied those assurances.[30]

United informed the British Leyland Line, which was transporting the Brining fruit, that it was handling produce already under contract. United's agents refused to negotiate directly with Calderón and attempted to have the local land commissioner, José Antonio Sánchez, impose restraints on the cooperative. Sánchez rejected the request, and the minister of industries endorsed his decision. Reluctant to take legal action in the Colombian courts, United launched a suit against Brining in England, where the cooperative's bananas were embargoed and then turned over the United agents.[31] This decision to bypass the Colombian courts was an open violation of Colombian sovereignty in the settlement of a dispute which the Colombian government was attempting to mediate. As Caffery commented: 'While [the] company is clearly within legal rights in asking [an] English embargo, their action is most inopportune for our interests at this time: [the] President had hoped to submit [the] oil bill and Barco matter ... at a very early date.' 'Also,' he added, 'their attitude if persisted in may seriously endanger their future interests here.'[32]

El Tiempo, in an angry editorial on 12 September, presented the embargo as another defeat for Colombian planters' attempts to diversify economic power in the industry. 'On two occasions,' *El Tiempo* concluded, 'United has succeeded in eliminating competition with the support of foreign courts.'[33] *El Espectador* accused United of failing to fulfill its obligation to the government and added: 'Companies such as this one are those which make American capital so despised in our country. There was no necessity for United Fruit to proceed in the improper manner it has, in antagonism toward the initiative of the Colombian Cooperative.'[34]

To appease his congressional critics, the minister of industries informed the company's representative that he intended to issue a press statement and inform Congress that United had negotiated in bad faith. Thoroughly alarmed, Bradshaw appealed to the American legation for assistance. Caffery explained the situation to the Colombian executive, and on the evening of 27 September the foreign minister, Eduardo Santos, and Chaux discussed the situation with Olaya. Subsequently the government determined not to take further action.[35]

With this decision the initiative returned to Congress. On 1 October the Chamber appointed a bipartisan three-member commission to prepare a report on the banana industry, including the relationship between domestic and foreign enterprise in the zone. A former Bogotá representative of United Fruit, H.C. Woodsum, expressed some concern to the American legation that the investigation might provoke further dispute, particularly if the commission revived the sensitive issue of irrigation and water control – a subject which he had previously managed to keep out of politics.[36]

The commission's report was temperate considering the extent of the public agitation which characterized debate on the industry.[37] It touched on all major aspects of the banana industry, including the relationship between foreign and domestic enterprise, irrigation, and labor, but its conclusions on the United-cooperative dispute were hedged with ambiguities. The commission implied that greater domestic participation in the marketing of bananas was desirable, yet it argued that the cooperative under Calderón had clearly infringed on the legal rights of United Fruit by purchasing bananas under prior contract. The report concluded, in fact, with unqualified support for responsible foreign investment:

Colombia requires for its development and progress the immigration of capital to develop its industries and of people who will establish in our midst the technology which made possible the development of higher civilizations. It would be contrary to a rational, constructive policy of national regeneration to erect obstacles which might divert the flow of capital and energy to other areas ... We must provide foreign investment with full guarantees.'

The authors of the report expressed some doubt, however, that United Fruit represented the ideal in foreign investment. 'The United Fruit Company,' it concluded,

taking advantage of the privileged position which it enjoys in the zone ... imposes excessive obligations on the private growers, obligations which could not feasibly be included .in the contracts if there were other sound and reliable entities in the region ... willing to purchase fruit from the growers.

The commission also emphasized the organization of labor in Magdalena as a prerequisite for undermining the contract labor system which enabled United Fruit to avoid compliance with Colombian social laws.[38]

Following the recommendations of the report, Congress introduced several bills, none of which substantially altered the economic balance of power in the banana industry. The president of the Chamber of Representatives ruled out of order Gaitán's motion that a fine be imposed on any foreign company convicted of attempting to appeal a dispute beyond the jurisdiction of national authorities. The one measure which did pass in that session, that imposing a two-cent per stem export tax on bananas, had been recommended by the 1930 Kemmerer mission and was designed to provide stability to the industry, not to penalize United Fruit. The bill made an effort to prevent United from passing this tax along to the Colombian producer by declaring void the clause in United's contracts with local producers requiring the latter to absorb export duties. However, the bill prohibited local governments from collecting additional duties.[39] In general the congressional investigation emphasized the Colombian desire for responsible foreign investment; yet its recommendations led to little tangible reform of the banana industry, nor did the national government act decisively to reduce United's domination of Colombian planters and labor in the zone.

Labor disputes and crop failures plagued the industry in 1931. Financial insecurity impelled national growers to turn for assistance to the government and the American company after a hurricane in the summer of 1931 destroyed crops and reduced prospects for a good harvest. With little undamaged fruit available for export, United suspended shipments until September.

The curtailment of exports brought hardship to national growers and to Colombian labor, victims of both natural disaster and United's ability to control marketing in the area. United's near-monopoly on the marketing of Latin American bananas enabled it to maintain prices in the United States at close to pre-depression levels. From over 65,000,000 bunches in 1929 United States imports of bananas fell to less than 40,000,000 four years later. United was also able to affect Colombia's trade patterns. In 1933 and 1934, for example, Colombia exported 2,348,026 and 2,613,692 bunches respectively to the United Kingdom because the customary source, Jamaica, suffered crop damage. In 1937, however, when the company shifted again to the Jamaican source, the value of Colombian banana exports declined 1,223,218 pesos from the previous year.[40]

Faced with the possibility of a major confrontation with unemployed workers in Santa Marta and the dissatisfaction of the local planters, United honored contracts with the growers and distributed bananas and meat to the families of the unemployed. At the same time, however, it gave notice that it would have to reduce wages and was unable to extend recovery loans to the planters.[41]

The possibility of a threat to American property once again raised the question of American intervention; as in 1928, when the State Department under Frank Kellogg rejected the request of the Santa Marta vice-consul to send a warship, in 1931 the department was loath to become directly involved in the dispute. On receipt of notification from the Department of the Navy that United Fruit desired protection in the event of violence, State Department officials debated alternatives. Initially the Navy Department drafted a cable to the commander of the Special Service Squadron in the Carribbean instructing him not to send a ship to Santa Marta but to 'keep himself discreetly informed of the situation.' After further consultation with H. Freeman Matthews and Francis White, however, it was agreed not to send the cable in consideration of the possible diplomatic repercussions.[42]

In the absence of a diplomatic 'incident,' such as the one that had occurred in 1928, and with more tactful individuals involved, the 1931 dispute ended without a major confrontation. Following a flare-up of tempers when United considered closing the port during a rumored outbreak of yellow fever, the unemployed dockworkers agreed to a 40% wage reduction when operations resumed. In return, the company continued to provide support for their families.[43]

Since the depression brought a 30 to 40% reduction in wages in most Colombian industries by the end of 1932, it would not be just to fault United Fruit for the introduction of economies. Workers in the larger American companies, such as United Fruit, tended to receive higher wages than those employed in domestic enterprise. But the predominance of foreigners in the higher-paid supervisory positions in United emphasized the difference in living standards between foreign and domestic workers. A farm overseer, for example, could earn up to $220.00 monthly, in contrast with the common laborer who received less than $1.50 for a ten-hour day.[44]

Continued friction in the banana zone placed Olaya under constant pressure to reform the industry. As in other areas, however, the president moved cautiously, testing State Department reaction to every initiative. In addition, he was anxious to obtain financial assistance from United for the sagging Colombian economy. He consequently delayed action on a request from the Minister of industries to establish stricter control over irrigation in Magdalena and referred the question to one of his legal advisers.[45]

In other areas Olaya was more decisive. Faced with the reluctance of United to finance domestic planters, the Colombian government assumed greater financial responsibility; in 1932 the Agricultural and Industrial Credit Agency signed an agreement with the independent planters providing for the formation of a cooperative, a development which in fact pleased United officials, because it enabled Colombian planters to assume a larger share of economic responsibility in the industry.[46]

The American company also reached a favorable settlement with the Colombian government on the almost decade-old dispute over control of the Santa Marta Railroad. The Colombian Supreme Court in 1925 ordered United to turn over the railroad to the government, for failing to meet payments to the government for the subsidization of construction and for not completing the line to the Magdalena River. During the Abadía administration the company unsuccessfully attempted, with State Department support, to obtain a reversal of the 1925 decision.

In 1932 the Colombian government offered to lease the railroad to United for thirty years in return for 10% of the gross revenues. These terms were to a considerable extent the result of the financial insecurity of the Colombian government. Following the conclusion of the dispute with the government, United advanced $750,000 for local public works; a short time later the company advanced on equal amount against accruing export taxes and rental of the railroad.[47]

Control over natural waterways and irrigation canals in the banana zone was a particularly sensitive issue. During the Abadía administration José Antonio Montalvo, the minister of industries, prohibited the company from drawing water for irrigation from several rivers in the district. Montalvo subsequently introduced a measure in the Chamber of Representatives granting the government authority to nationalize irrigation canals, financing their acquisition through land taxes on the serviced properties. Although the Abadía administration agreed to oppose any legislation 'detrimental to American interests' in the banana zone, it was not until late in Olaya's presidency that a settlement was arranged.[48] By executive resolution Olaya granted permission for United and other private entities to use national irrigation canals for fifty years, at the end of which time control of the canals would revert to the nation.[49]

The inauguration of Alfonso López in August 1934 marked a shift in the Colombian government's attitude toward United Fruit. López did not eschew confrontation with United, as his predecessor had done,[50] yet in retrospect his policy had no major impact on the economic balance of power in Magdalena. In fact, it was not until reforms had been effected in other areas of the economy in the first two years of his administration that President López turned his attention to congressional recommendations for the banana industry.

López's flirtations with the radical left and his avowed support for organized labor brought his government into friction with United Fruit and the Colombian planters in the zone. When renewed labor disputes erupted in the fall of 1934, López sent the minister of war, Marco A. Auli, to negotiate a settlement between workers and planters in Magdalena. Auli arranged with the manager of the Cooperativa Bananera de Magdalena, José Garcés Navas, for a minimum wage increase from 80 centavos daily to 1.20 pesos. The planters gave added assurances that they would make every effort to improve working conditions; but in the months which followed their failure to do so brought persistent strife to the district.[51]

United officials, apprehensive over López's leftist inclinations, shared the opposition of Colombian landowners to the wage increase. The local manager of the company, George S. Bennett, reasoned that the leaders of the strike had achieved considerable prestige among the workers as a consequence of the favorable wage settlement. Early in January 1935, Bennett warned President López that unless the Colombian government adopted a less conciliatory attitude toward labor and brought stability to the industry, the company would withdraw from the country. López replied that dissent was a sign of a healthy society and that it was virtually impossible to prevent public hostility to such a powerful economic entity as Magdalena Fruit.[52]

A congressional commission sent to the banana zone to report on labor unrest was sympathetic to the complaints of the private planters and United Fruit. Both majority and minority reports were critical of the ineffectualness of the departmental government and its failure to enforce social legislation. The commission deplored the working conditions on Colombian plantations and praised the medical facilities provided by the American company. Both reports were critical of labor radicalism and the threat it posed to foreign investment in the industry. The minority report, prepared by Benjamín Burbano of Nariño, drew attention to the efforts of Colombian planters to establish cooperatives independent of the United Fruit Company and recommended additional government financing for such projects. Burbano noted that the United Fruit Company had contributed significantly to flood control in the banana zone through its construction of a canal on the Aracataca River, and that its irrigation system was 'a work established in good faith.' Yet he added that the company exercised excessive political and economic power in the department. Six years after the bloody suppression of the 1928 strike, the authors of the minority report again recommended that the company deal directly with workers rather than through contractors.[53]

Not until 1936 did political conditions enable the López administration to achieve legislation on the banana industry. Law 149 of October, restricting the percentage of payrolls which could be allocated to foreign workers and employees, brought spontaneous opposition from United's officials. Eugene Le Baron Jr, the company's Bogotá representative, indicated that compliance with the law would require a reorganization of some facets of United's operations in Colombia. When questioned on the possibility of diplomatic assistance, however, both Sumner Welles and Laurence Duggan opposed State Department involvement in a dispute which was clearly domestic in nature.[54]

At the same time the Senate passed a bill placing a two-year limit on contracts for the sale and export of bananas, and authorized the government to establish a national inspection service. To reduce the foreign indebtedness of the domestic planters, the bill also provided that the Magdalena Banana Cooperative could accept twenty-year 8% mortgages from district landowners. Although Congress ultimately revised the bill to allow the executive to approve contracts in excess of two years, Magdalena Fruit remained apprehensive about the possibility of government interference in the company's activities.

The company hastened to conclude a series of five-year contracts with the majority of local planters before the bill became law on 22 January 1937, a move which aggravated López's irritation. To offset criticism, the company altered its long-term contracts to enable Colombian planters to share in international price increases.[55] Shortly after the passage of law 1 of 1937, and partly in response to United's efforts to defeat the spirit of the law, the minister of industries and labor sent a bill to the Senate requesting extensive government control over the banana industry in both production and marketing; it also provided for possible expropriation of property on the grounds of 'public utility and social interest.'[56]

Officials of the Magdalena Fruit Company were noticeably shaken. F.N. Riley, United's Bogotá representative, claimed that the legislation reflected the influence of the manager of the Magdalena Banana Cooperative, José Garcés Navas. A vice-president of United, Joseph Montgomery, discussed the company's difficulties with Sumner Welles. At the same time United's Santa Marta manager testified before the Colombian Senate Committee on Agriculture, Commerce and Industries. The protests had the desired effect; on the recommendation of the Senate committee, the Senate amended the bill, rejecting as unconstitutional the first article, which empowered the government to acquire or lease agricultural lands.[57]

While debate on the bill continued, the American minister requested permission to use the good offices of the legation in United's behalf. The department reemphasized its directive of the previous year, that the dispute was one of a constitutional nature in Colombia and in view of this the department would not interfere; the State Department adhered rigorously to that position throughout 1937.[58]

Confronted with opposition to the measure, the ministers of agriculture and industries, Nicolás Llinás Vega and Alejandro Bernate, drafted a more carefully worded bill for submission to Congress. The revised bill retained the provision granting extensive powers to the government in the direction of the banana industry.[59]

The measure was not premised on anti-Americanism, contrary to the claims of its critics. *El Tiempo*, as the organ of the Santos faction of the Liberal party, inaccurately described the legislation as 'confiscatory' and called attention to the negative response in New York financial circles. Prior to the bill's passage, Gabriel Turbay, the foreign minister, informed the American legation that President López wished to assure the United States of his good intentions, and that the banana legislation was directed toward the rectification of a specific problem. Turbay added that the president felt obliged to assume a more active posture with respect to the banana industry because of the lack of cooperation on the part of United Fruit.[60]

López persevered in the face of opposition, and although the legislation may not have been intended as an anti-American measure, public disaffection with the United Fruit Company was a factor in the administration's favor. At the height of the Senate debate on the bill, the minister of industries announced that his department had evidence implicating Colombian officials in questionable relations with United Fruit. The fact that Rocha's list included several individuals closely connected with the Olaya administration (Esteban Jaramillo, Alfonso Villegas Restrepo, Luis Felipe Latorre, Pedro Maria Carreño) suggests that the publication of the information was designed to discredit the *Santistas* as much as United Fruit. Dubious as the charges may have been, late in October the Senate approved a resolution calling for an investigation into the company's activities.[61]

Concerned that the Colombian trend would lead to repercussions in other Latin American countries, United sent a special envoy to Bogotá to represent the company's position. It was to no avail; on 26 November Congress passed pending legislation as law 125.[62] In the meantime the national police arrested Bennett, initially for 'theft of a public document,' and subsequently for bribery of a public official. Although these charges were dismissed the following spring, they indicated the deteriorated state of relations between the government and the company.[63]

One of United's vice-presidents, Turnbull, warned López in Bogotá that the company would not cooperate with the government until such time as the Bennett case was settled satisfactorily; he added that United would be unable to offer higher prices to the domestic planters in 1938, and pointed out that foreign investment would be hesitant to enter the Colombian market under the threat of possible expropriation. United would not expand its operations or commit the financial resources required to combat the spread of Sigatoka disease (leaf blight) as long as the expropriation clause remained effective. The Colombian president, in response, assumed complete responsibility for the legislation.[64]

Although President López would not yield in the few months before the inauguration of Eduardo Santos, the government caused United no further anxiety. Even the prospect of a pro-American president and frequent verbal guarantees from President Santos that the right of expropriation would not be exercised failed to relieve United's concern, until in 1939 the Supreme Court declared unconstitutional the more important features of law 125.[65]

There was, of course, some justification for United's uneasiness. Never in possession of an unblemished public image, the company suffered further damage when strikes again hit the zone and the Senate pursued impeachment (retroactively) of Pedro María Carreño for receiving legal fees from United at the time that he was in Olaya's cabinet. As a Conservative, Carreño may have been a victim of political infighting; but his censure by the Senate after Santos took office pointed to the enmity the company's presence had aroused. As a committee report to the Chamber of Representatives in March indicated:

Much more serious than the activities of ex-Minister Carreño is the conviction at which we have arrived ... that the foreign company has exercised bribery and coercion as its common weapons in the struggle to preserve a monopoly in the banana industry in Colombia and for the evasion of all instruments of our sovereignty.[66]

On 10 April the Communist weekly *Tierra* added a condemnation of foreign investment.

It is the all-powerful capital of the large financial oligarchies which emigrates to countries which have yet to experience the industrial revolution and takes possession of their markets; it is the invading capital which is designated as loans and in this manner ties itself to the ruling elites of the invading nation; it is the large concessionary companies which invest their capital in the exploitation of our primary resources on the basis of cheap labor; it is the planters of colonial orientation, and in general the capitalist rulers, who undermine our national sovereignty.

State Department policy toward the United Fruit Company in Colombia was consistent throughout this period. Largely because of United's unfavorable public image, the department found it necessary to move with discretion in its efforts to protect American investment in the banana industry. During the volatile situation at the time of the 1928 strike, the department refrained from intervention and assured Colombian authorities of its support. Representatives of the Department of State nevertheless actively sought to mitigate the effects of United's frequently hostile attitude toward Colombian labor and competition. During the Olaya administration, American ministers in Bogotá assisted in obtaining settlement of the outstanding disputes over the Santa Marta Railroad and irrigation. Under Alfonso López, United's position was more precarious. Although the State Department was equally concerned about the implications of the agrarian legislation of the 1934–8 period, it did little except encourage more conservative Colombian political groups.

The department was pleased when Eduardo Santos assumed the presidency and gave full cooperation to Ambassador Spruille Braden, a hard-liner on the question of United States private investments. Unfortunately for the Colombian banana industry, domestic political problems and the disruption of international markets during the second world war delayed a conclusive reconciliation between the government and United and prevented the institution of a full-scale program for the control of Sigatoka disease. By concentrating on its own investments, United strengthened its position relative to Colombian planters during the war, although the company suspended exports in 1942 because of the international shipping crisis.[67] Whether this sequence of events would have been avoided had Colombian authorities pursued a more liberal foreign investment policy is questionable. United was deterred not by the harshness of agricultural legislation but by the uncertain investment environment. Ironically, as in other areas of American investment, Colombia accepted the presence of United States capital in the banana industry and sought only economic and political diversification of power in the banana zone. The United States, on the other hand, although it perceived little immediate strategic significance in United Fruit's political and economic hegemony on the Caribbean coast of Colombia, was sympathetic to the company's efforts to combat both domestic and foreign competition but also attempted to mitigate the political repercussions of the often abrasive tactics followed by the American firm.

7

The SCADTA phantom

A blending of the strategic and commercial dimensions of American relations with Colombia, similar to that which characterized petroleum diplomacy, was evident as well in the reaction of the United States to the expansion of commercial aviation after 1919.

The development of domestic and especially foreign-controlled airlines in Latin America generally (see maps 3 and 4) and specifically in Colombia threatened to provide competition for private American enterprise and to place in jeopardy United States hegemony in the Panama Canal Zone and the Caribbean and on the west coast of South America. The historiography of inter-American aviation rivalry has tended to neglect the degree of continuity which in fact existed in United States policy objectives between the world wars. Historians have demonstrated the prominent role which the United States government assumed in gaining for American airlines a major place in inter-American aviation during the formative years of the 1920s. They have also drawn attention to the State Department's campaign to 'de-Germanize' commercial aviation in the Western Hemisphere in the late 1930s and during the second world war.[1] Yet the two phases have tended to be treated as distinct phenomena. The wartime anti-Axis period in particular has been portrayed as a diplomatic and military response in Latin America peculiar to the exigencies of the war experience rather than a logical culmination of earlier policy objectives.

The evidence in fact suggests an alternative analysis. American officials in the aftermath of the first world war evinced a markedly negative attitude toward European initiatives to establish aviation enterprises in Latin America. Their attitude was especially pronounced in the case of Germany, which United States civil and military officials continued to identify as a strategic and commercial threat to American interests in Latin America. Although this perspective intensified in the course of the 1930s with the rise of Adolf Hitler, it was clearly manifest in the 1920s as well, evolving as it did out of the experience of the first world war and traditional sphere-of-influence and neo-mercantilist ideas.[2] The result was consistent support for the primacy of American aviation interests in the Western Hemisphere and explicit diplomatic support prior to the end of the 1920s for Pan American Airways as the enterprise deemed most able to meet the competitive challenge of Europe. In this light Americanization for strategic reasons after 1939 was little more than an extension in wartime of a traditional policy objective and was very much consistent with what earlier chapters suggested was applicable for petroleum, commerce, finance, and the activities of the United Fruit Company in the banana industry.

One dimension of this policy was the relationship between Pan American Airways and the Colombian line SCADTA (Sociedad Colombo-Alemana de Transportes Aéreos),[3] which operated in Colombia from 1919 until its absorption into the Colombian national airlines, Avianca, in 1940. SCADTA's resistance to the expansion of Pan American was a catalyst in the formation of United States policy. Colombia's proximity to the Panama Canal and its command of both Pacific and Caribbean coasts in northwestern South America necessitated Colombian adherence to a pro-American position. Following Pan Am's maiden flight to Havana on 19 October 1927, the State Department viewed its predominance in Latin America as vital to the economic and strategic interests of the United States.

The timing of Pan American's flight to Havana in late 1927 itself reflected the American preoccupation with the activities of SCADTA in the Caribbean. In the mid-1920s SCADTA's president, Peter Paul von Bauer, an Austrian national, requested permanent landing rights in Panama but met with opposition from the United States until Colombian officials intervened. In possession of temporary permission to land in the Canal Zone in 1925, von Bauer sent two planes through Central America to Havana and then sought extended service to Key West, Florida.[4] Throughout these negotiations Peter von Bauer and his brother, Victor, assured American officials that they would cooperate with American capital and that the company had no 'political or other aims inimical to the United States.'[5]

The SCADTA initiative served as an impetus in the formulation of American aviation diplomacy. On 14 August 1925 the secretary of war, Dwight Davis, expressed his concern that SCADTA represented a potential threat to American interests in the Caribbean. 'It would appear to be highly desirable,' he informed the secretary of state, 'to formulate a national policy in regard to American dominance of aerial commercial and postal activities in Central America, and to determine ways and means by which this policy may be made effective.' The State Department concurred and instructed its representatives in Latin America to report on the operations of the German-Colombian company.[6]

By mid-1927 SCADTA's determination to develop a Central American line led

FOREIGN AIRLINES
IN
LATIN AMERICA
1928

French controlled companies
———— Operating
— — — Under organization

German controlled companies
▭▭▭ Operating
▭◻▭ Under organization

U.S. Foreign air mail system
▬▬▬ Operating

Source : DS 810. 79611. Pan American / 1306

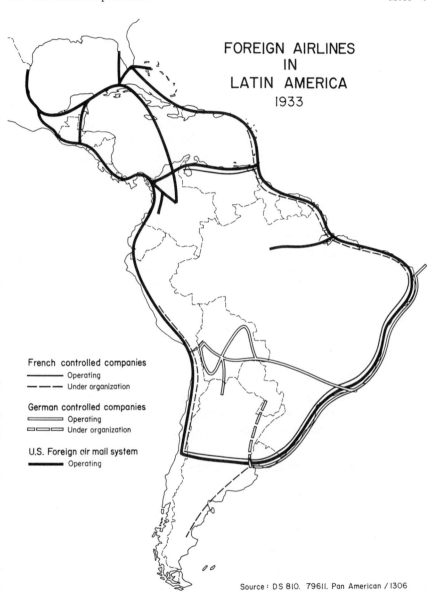

FOREIGN AIRLINES
IN
LATIN AMERICA
1933

French controlled companies
———————— Operating
— — — — Under organization

German controlled companies
⊏════⊐ Operating
⊏═⊐⊏═⊐ Under organization

U.S. Foreign air mail system
━━━━ Operating

Source : DS 810. 79611. Pan American / 1306

to the formation of the Compañía Aeromarítima de Colombia, designed to operate from Barranquilla to the Canal Zone; SCADTA itself controlled 48% of the new company's stock and individual Colombians the balance. Six of the eight directors and the president, Alberto Osorio of Barranquilla, were Colombian. The operations manager, however, was Hermann Kuehl, a German national appointed by SCADTA.[7]

The opposition of the American government to the company's requests for landing rights in Colón precipitated a resurgence of popular anti-Americanism in Colombia. While an interdepartmental committee, composed of the departments of State, Treasury, Navy, War, and Post Office, met in Washington to discuss airmail routes, American hostility to SCADTA's expansion received considerable attention in the Colombian press. SCADTA itself and business interests in Colombia and Panama equally anxious to profit from increased commercial activity were the source of much of the agitation.[8]

The Bogotá press vehemently supported SCADTA's petition for an extension of its service to Panama. On 22 November, *El Tiempo* headlined its front page story 'Yankees will deny ... permission ... because Scadta would compete with North American lines.' The following day all Bogotá papers carried a full page Aeromarítima advertisement appealing to Colombian nationalism. It read in part:

Colombians:
The extension of our commercial air lines from Barranquilla to Cristobal, C.Z. (Colón) ... is on the verge of aborting.

It is, therefore, the patriotic duty of each citizen to ... assert the Sacred Right of the Colombian nation to extend its air line network to neighboring countries, based on the outstanding achievements of Colombian commercial aviation.[9]

The same morning *El Tiempo* commented:

American hegemony over the Canal Zone would not be challenged by allowing Colombian planes to land in the Bay of Colón. As for competition with American lines – that problem too is non-existent since there are as yet no American companies in the area and little prospect of one of the immediate future.

El Diario Nacional, a leading leftist Liberal organ of Bogotá, echoed *El Tiempo*'s sentiments in a 23 November article entitled 'The Yankee Attitude to Our Aviation.'[10] It argued that the dominant financial interest of Colombians in the company negated the American objections to its operation and raised a very delicate question of sovereignty. The following day it suggested:

The Compañía Aeromarítima de Colombia is a purely commercial venture ... If such an action is taken in the United States, it can be explained only as a veto inspired by sordid commercial rivalry, since the North Americans are planning to establish a company similar to ours – although no doubt with greater capital backing.

The public campaign in support of Colombian interests did little to weaken American resolve. Secretary of State Frank Kellogg informed Charles Hilles, vice-chairman of the Republican National Committee, that SCADTA's incitement of anti-Americanism was further reason to deny it entry to Panama. The American minister in Bogotá, Samuel Piles, informed the department at the height of the press campaign: 'I heartily favor doing all we can consistently for Colombia but never through that company which I now regard as an absolute menace since it is viciously and publicly undertaking to incite a whole nation against us.' When SCADTA began stamping patriotic slogans on all airmail it carried, Piles' hostility increased. 'It is not Colombians who initiate attacks against us,' he wrote on 20 November, 'but foreigners seeking favors who incite them.' The American minister restricted his opposition to SCADTA, however. He recommended that some way be found to grant landing rights in Panama to a 'truly Colombian company.' 'I am more than anxious,' he noted, 'to promote not only a friendly feeling here, but to do everything I can to advance the welfare and happiness of this people ... We are in a fight,' Piles added, 'to counteract the open and insidious influences that are daily working to discredit us in these countries ... I am confident that ... nothing but ... persistent ... retaliation against such people will prove effective.'[11]

It is likely that American officials would have pursued a similar course even had SCADTA not attempted to incite anti-Americanism.[12] As chairman of the interdepartmental committee on aviation, Assistant Secretary of State Francis White was extremely influential in the articulation of a Latin American policy during both the Kellogg and Stimson years. His support for what he viewed as benevolent interventionism in Haiti, Cuba, and the Dominican Republic was consistent with the type of aviation diplomacy he advocated. On 19 December 1927 White outlined the basis of that policy:

These German interests have developed a net-work of lines over the Republic of Colombia so that they control aviation in that Republic. Germanic interests likewise are operating air lines in the Republic of Bolivia and in certain parts of Brazil. The French Parliament has just voted a large sum ... for rapid mail service [to Brazil] ... This service will be an advantage to European competitors over those of the United States unless we likewise can reduce time by carrying mail to South America.

The key to the situation is Panama, communication through Central America to there ... This work must be undertaken immediately ... if American interests are to be able to get on that field at all.[13]

The question of commercial aviation became one of the prominent topics at the Sixth International Conference of American States, which convened in Havana on 16 January 1928. In the committee on Commercial Air Communication a controversy developed between the United States and Colombia over an American-sponsored amendment to article 31 of the projected convention on Commercial Aviation drafted by the Inter-American Commercial Aviation Commission in May 1927.[14] The secretary of state stressed to the American delegates the importance of revising the convention in a manner guaranteed to protect the position of the United States in the Caribbean.[15] The department's proposed wording of article 31 was as follows:

The right of any of the contracting States to enter into any convention or special agreement with any other State or States concerning international aerial navigation is recognized, so long as such convention or special agreement shall not impair the rights or obligations of any of the States party to this Convention, acquired or imposed herein; provided however that prohibited areas within their respective territories, and regulations pertaining thereto, may be agreed upon by two or more States for military reasons or in the interest of public safety. Such agreements, and all regulations pursuant thereto, shall be subject to the same conditions as those set forth in Article 5 of this Convention with respect to prohibited areas within the territory of a particular State.[16]

The amendment was conspicuously designed to enable the United States to acquire special privileges with Central American countries – as in the Canal Zone and Guantánamo.[17]

The United States assured the Colombian delegates that it had no intention of discriminating against SCADTA's operations in the Caribbean. Nevertheless, the American delegation refused to apply the final convention to aircraft used for state functions, such as airmail service; this meant the effective exclusion of SCADTA from the protection of the convention. Some months later Francis White described for Henry Stimson the American objectives at the Havana Conference in terms which underlined the meaningless nature of the assurances given to the Colombians in 1928. Von Bauer, he informed Stimson, continually urged the Colombian delegates to oppose the American position on commercial aviation. 'It was necessary,' White observed, 'to speak very plainly to the Colombian delegates and tell them that unless those provisions (in the Convention unfavorable to U.S. interests in Panama) were eliminated the United States would sign the Convention with reservation.'[18]

Under this pressure Olaya was able to achieve no more than a slight rephrasing of Henry Fletcher's amendment, which became article 30 in the final document. The clauses delineating the basis of the Colombian-American compromise did not weaken the effectiveness of the convention from the American perspective.

These regulations shall in no case prevent the establishment and operation of practicable inter-American aerial lines and terminals. These regulations shall guarantee equality of treatment of the aircraft of each and every one of the contracting states and shall be subject to the same conditions as are set forth in Article 5 of this Convention with respect to prohibited areas within the territory of a particular state.[19]

There was small justification for *El Tiempo*'s interpretation of the events at Havana as a partial Colombian victory. A more accurate indication of the future trend of inter-American aviation was Charles Lindbergh's timely flight to Havana during the conference and to Cartagena and Bogotá on 27 January; in both countries he received a hero's welcome.[20]

Following the Havana Conference, the United States intensified its efforts to extend air service into Latin America. In July 1928 the government granted an airmail contract, under the provisions of the Foreign Air Mail Act of 2 March, to Pan American Airways from Key West to the Panama Canal. This was only one stage in an expansion which officials hoped would soon extend down both coasts of South America.[21] SCADTA continued, however, to dominate Colombian aviation and to hold the key to through routes to Ecuador, Peru, and Chile. When the company sent representatives to Guayaquil and Quito to obtain landing rights from the Ecuadorean government, the State Department moved quickly to prevent the Colombian company from blocking Pan American Airways.[22] The Americans were particularly vulnerable in Ecuador early in 1928 because President Ayora resented the failure of the United States to recognize his regime following the coup d'état of 9 July 1925. In July 1928 the Ecuadorean government issued a contract to SCADTA for coastal mail service from Buenaventura to Guayaquil. 'It is known to the legation,' the American minister in Quito, G.A. Bading, observed, 'that the German minister here has been exceedingly active in advocating the Scadta Company contract.' Significantly, on 14 August, the United States granted *de jure* recognition to the Ayora government.[23]

Undeterred by American opposition, SCADTA continued to press for concessions throughout Central America. In Honduras the representative of Pan American found that the local press identified Pan American with the United Fruit

Company, and he was consequently unable to obtain an airmail contract. Both he and the State Department blamed 'German' interests for agitating against the United States. When a similar problem arose in Cuba in July 1928, Francis White outlined the American position:

We are most anxious here to have American aviation as prominent as possible in the Caribbean region and for that reason this Department did everything possible to favor the bill that was enacted by Congress at its last session authorizing the Post Office Department to give subventions for the carrying of mails in the Caribbean region. The Pan American Airways is a hundred percent American owned and managed company.[24]

SCADTA also obtained permission from the Republic of Panama to establish a temporary base for its hydroplanes near Porto Bello (about twenty miles from the canal's Atlantic entrance) to conduct an aerial survey of the Colombian-Panamanian border for the Colombian government. The United States War Department immediately protested. 'From every viewpoint,' Dwight Davis wrote the secretary of state, 'the establishment of this base at Porto Bello is objectionable and should be prevented.' The Department of War conceded the innocent nature of the survey, but recommended firstly that the American government offer to perform the service for Panama, and secondly that all airports in Panamanian territory be placed under joint United States-Panamanian control with no independent commercial bases. The result was the creation in 1929 of a Joint Aviation Board with complete control over the movement of aircraft and establishment of airfields in the Republic of Panama. The members of the Aviation Board were to be appointed by the president of Panama, three on the designation of the United States.[25]

The American government was particularly concerned that SCADTA would come under the control of Lufthansa and thus give the larger German company a foothold in the Caribbean. A vice-president of Pan American, John Hambleton, in September 1928 informed Francis White that he was under the impression SCADTA had recently received capital support from Lufthansa. 'The Company's policy has changed considerably,' Hambleton noted, 'and I feel they will attempt to expand as rapidly as possible throughout South America and that we can expect very little cooperation from them in the immediate future.'[26] Disturbed by the implications of German financing, White instructed the American chargé in Berlin to observe the activities of the company's representatives and to assist Pan American officials in their efforts to purchase a controlling interest in the Colombian enterprise.[27] Pan American's overtures remained unreciprocated for the moment, however, and the American government was obliged to implement a more direct policy.

On 23 February 1929, Secretary of State Kellogg and the Colombian minister in Washington, Enrique Olaya Herrera, signed an agreement providing for reciprocal landing privileges on the coasts of Colombia and the United States and the right to fly over Colombian territory, the United States, and the Canal Zone.[28] The Kellogg-Olaya agreement was evidence of the American determination to open the west coast of South America to Pan American service. For Pan American to bid for U.S. airmail contracts in this area, it had to obtain the right to operate across intervening territory, previously blocked by SCADTA's monopoly. To obtain a Chilean contract for Pan American the State Department was willing to concede permission to Colombian planes to land in American territory; but, confident that they could now control aviation in the caribbean, American officials considered the concession a minor one.[29] In fact Francis White argued that the Colombian-American exchange of notes had 'regularized' the situation in the Isthmus.[30] On 2 March, little more than a week after the conclusion of the Kellogg-Olaya agreement, the Post Office Department granted the airmail contract for Panama-Chile service to Pan American-Grace Airways, Pan American's operating partner in Peru and Chile.

A delay in implementing the Chilean service, occasioned by a dispute over the granting of the Post Office contract, enabled SCADTA to expand its Ecuadorean line and to extend its service to the port of Paita in Peru by June of 1929 – developments that disturbed the State Department. As Francis White observed to the secretary of state: 'If this German company gets into Peru it will then easily link up with the German companies already operating in Bolivia, and perhaps will be able to extend its services on to Buenos Aires and to Chile.'[31]

The resistance of SCADTA and other non-American lines to Pan American expansion led the State Department to redefine its policy toward private airlines. The department had consistently lent unofficial support to Pan American Airways, but with the encouragement of the Post Office Department it now debated the feasibility of granting diplomatic assistance to companies holding U.S. international airmail contracts; in Latin America this meant giving official sanction to the near-monopoly operations of Pan American and Pan American-Grace Airways. White was very sympathetic to the Post Office's request. For strategic reasons in the Caribbean, he argued, it was essential for U.S. mail to be on American carriers. Since the French and German governments were active in Latin American aviation, the United States needed to provide equal support to its own nationals. 'If the United States,' White suggested to the secretary of state on 6 July 1929, 'keeps hands off and lets American companies fight one another indiscriminately for concessions in Latin America, all Americans are apt to lose out.' He conceded that the announcement of such a policy would invite criticism but thought this was a light burden to carry in defense of American interests.[32] When

Stimson raised the issue at a Cabinet session on 12 July 1929, President Hoover was reluctant to support a policy which would encourage monopoly conditions, but he approved the recommendation. The State Department promptly instructed heads of mission in Latin America to give full diplomatic support to Pan American Airways.[33]

The loosening of SCADTA's grip on domestic aviation in Colombia promised to be a more delicate operation than blocking the company's international expansion. In 1929 Juan Trippe developed a new line in Colombia to compete with SCADTA, but the Sociedad Anónima Colombo-Americana de Aviacíon experienced little success, primarily because Pan American failed to take sufficient interest in local aviation developments. Although the American legation in Bogotá gave enthusiastic support to the new enterprise in its efforts to obtain operating rights, Pan American officials appeared to consider the line more useful as a nuisance to von Bauer.[34]

The State Department remained the main antagonist of the Colombian company. White suggested to Caffery that in the light of the deterioration of SCADTA's operating equipment, limiting American sources of capital would make the company more inclined to accept financial control. 'If he [von Bauer] can now get funds from the United States,' the assistant secretary commented, 'he will ... be again in a good strategic position to cause American companies a good deal of difficulty. I am, therefore, not in favor of giving him American capital to do so. If he will sell out to an American company ... a big thorn will be removed in the development of our air lines to South America.'[35] Significantly, the poor state of SCADTA's equipment in 1929 casts doubts on the State Department's earlier contention that Lufthansa was financing the Colombian company.

Well aware of SCADTA's financial difficulties, Trippe attempted to force a 'showdown' with von Bauer. Several times the latter had tested Pan American's willingness to purchase the Colombian line, but on each occasion he had halted short of a definite commitment. Late in November 1929 Pan American sent a representative to Bogotá with instructions either to purchase SCADTA directly or to obtain an airmail contract for the Pan American subsidiary from the Colombian government.[36] The American initiative led to an operating agreement between the two companies, but once again the elusive von Bauer retained his control.

In the international context, Pan American and SCADTA concluded an agreement in October 1929 coordinating their airmail routes on the west coast of South America. Under the provisions of the agreement Pan American transferred to SCADTA all mail destined for Colombia at Buenaventura, and SCADTA transferred to Pan American-Grace Airways mail destined for Peru. Trippe considered the October agreement, supplemented by cooperation at Colón and Barranquilla early in 1930, as 'one of the first steps toward a settlement of the international rivalry for supremacy in South American air transportation.'[37]

It was not until 1931 that the protracted negotiations between SCADTA and Pan American resulted in the financial takeover of the Colombian company. SCADTA's need for capital and its inability to compete with Pan American outside Colombia facilitated the transfer of 84% of the stock to the American company. The acquisition of SCADTA was given little publicity at the time; the absence of publicity, plus the fact that there was no immediate management change, meant that even some Colombian officials were unaware of the American takeover. Nevertheless, the few Colombian newspapers which took note of the negotiations between the companies responded favorably.[38]

The State Department recognized the value of not effecting a management reorganization of the company at that time, although it anticipated that within a few years SCADTA would be entirely Americanized.[39] It was this failure to implement Americanization which led to subsequent difficulties.

Pan American had little intention to work through SCADTA in Colombia. After concluding the financial arrangement with SCADTA it established another subsidiary, the Urabá, Medellín, and Central Airways, Inc. (UMCA). Pan American provided the technical personnel, and its representative in Colombia, Allan Winslow, was made president. In mid-1932 UMCA inaugurated Colombian airmail service between Colón and Medellín.[40]

The conflict with Peru over the control of Leticia added a new dimension to Colombian aviation. The government placed SCADTA under the direction of the Ministry of War and began to expand its air power to meet the Peruvian challenge. It expanded in part by increasing the number of German flyers with the Colombian army. The diversion of most of SCADTA's personnel and equipment for military purposes necessitated an expansion of the commercial fleet, making Colombia an attractive market for American, British, and German enterprise.

The Americans had to overcome an initial European advantage. SCADTA's manager, Hermann Kuehl, was government adviser on military aviation in 1932; Herbert Boy, a German national, one of SCADTA's most distinguished pilots and a colonel in the Colombian army, became inspector-in-chief of the Ministry of War's air branch, and in 1933 headed a Colombian delegation to Europe to place aircraft orders. There were technical factors as well which favored the European suppliers. American planes hastily purchased for the early fighting around Leticia proved decidedly inferior to SCADTA's Junkers and the British planes used by Peru, and Joaquím Samper Herrera, a representative in Colombia of the Curtiss-Wright Export Corporation, indicated that aircraft were more readily available in Europe than in the United States. As early as 1929 the United States military attaché in Paris recommended that the United States should make every effort to impress a then touring Colombian military mission in order to prevent Germany from further strengthening its foothold.[41]

Although the United States government was not anxious to stimulate armaments sales to Latin America, it was concerned with the strategic implications of allowing European suppliers to monopolize the market. In addition, American manufacturers had long been attracted by the potential of Latin America as a market for aviation equipment and viewed the hostilities between Colombia and Peru as an opportunity to establish contacts.[42] The Curtiss Aeroplane and Motor Co., Inc., for example, despatched to Bogotá one of its vice-presidents, James P. Strong, who was a recently retired U.S. navy commander, to strengthen the American position.

Prior to his arrival in Bogotá and while still with the Navy Department, Strong had worked closely with the Colombian consul general in New York to facilitate Colombian armaments purchases and prepare a Colombian defense plan. After retirement, Strong proved a valuable asset to private industry, joining Curtiss-Wright and locating in Bogotá. In late 1933 he also obtained a position in the Colombian Ministry of War as assessor for aircraft purchases. He impressed on Olaya the advantages of placing aircraft orders in the United States and gradually undermined SCADTA's influence, with the result that in March 1934, Olaya instructed Boy in London that to maintain unity of type and prompt delivery he had decided to cancel European orders.[43]

Strong's fortunes shortly met with a sharp reversal, however. Personal friction with the American legation and his aggressiveness in obtaining contracts for American companies alienated his Colombian associates, and the Colombian government dismissed him.[44]

The Strong incident, however, did little to divert Colombia from American sources of supply. This was at least in part due to the cumulative effect of training Colombian aviators in the United States. They tended to return to Colombia impressed with American technology and ideas and passed this sentiment along to their fellow officers.[45] In the later 1930s, the United States reinforced this orientation of the Colombian military by sending elaborate military missions to Colombia and other sensitive areas of Latin America.

Between the Leticia conflict and the second world war, SCADTA's popularity in Colombia gradually declined, preparing the way for its ultimate takeover by Pan American and the Colombian government. There are a number of reasons for the deterioration in what was a highly productive and mutually rewarding relationship between the company and Colombian society. The ascendancy of Hitler and his turn toward militarism had an unfortunate impact on SCADTA. Although the record of the company's relationship to the German government remains extremely vague, it is apparent that there was some pressure on the company from

Berlin. The charter members of SCADTA, men like Peter von Bauer, found themselves in sensitive positions. Von Bauer was an Austrian Jew, and what cooperation he did provide Berlin likely derived from his fear that his Austrian properties would be confiscated. When that took place, von Bauer immediately obtained Colombian citizenship. Some of the German pilots and technicians employed by SCADTA, however, had very definite Nazi sympathies, which created considerable friction in Colombia. In addition, the immigration of German Jews late in the decade seems to have stimulated some general anti-German sentiment, although this is difficult to evaluate with any precision.[46]

A tragic accident in 1935 involving SCADTA and SACO (Servicio Aéreo Colombiano) aircraft at the Medellín airport further undermined the company's public support. This was the first major commercial airline crash in Colombia; it had a decidedly unsettling impact, in part because among the people who died in the flaming wreckage on the runway were Ernesto Samper Mendoza, a noted Colombian aviator and a member of one of the nation's elite families, and Carlos Gardel, a still-idolized Argentine singer and master of the tango. Although the cause of the crash was uncertain, SCADTA, as the foreign enterprise, bore the brunt of the public outcry. President López exchanged sharp notes with the company and spoke openly of nationalizing civil aviation.[47]

By 1938 State Department and military officials were convinced that greater supervision of SCADTA's activities was essential to American security. Before Alfonso López left office, the Colombian Council of State approved a five million peso credit from German interests, part of the credit to be allocated for the purchase of aircraft and hangars from Germany. This transaction was much to the annoyance of American officials and Bethlehem Steel, which had submitted a lower tender for the hangar construction and had offered to provide long-term credit to finance the operation. Yet President López turned to German interests only after receiving assurances that American engineers would be used and that substitute parts and equipment were available in the United States. This would appear to be an instance where American neutrality laws restricting sales of munitions abroad forced Colombia to turn to European interests.[48] This development of course intensified American efforts to use Pan American financial control of SCADTA to undermine German influence. When Trippe informed the State Department that von Bauer was under pressure from Berlin to regain the stock held by Pan American, the department urged Trippe to assume more positive direction of SCADTA's operations.[49]

Although Colombians continued to maintain respect for SCADTA, President Santos provided essential assistance to the State Department in eliminating the company's German personnel. Santos was concerned only that the action not become a public issue. 'President Santos,' Spruille Braden commented on 31 December 1939, 'does not want to be embarrassed by enquiry but only to be told a *fait accompli*.'[50] In his message to Congress in July 1939 the Colombian president referred briefly to the necessity of assuming greater national direction of the aviation industry and recommended the establishment of a national airline absorbing both SCADTA and SACO.[51]

Legislation passed late in the López administration provided the vehicle for the elimination of SCADTA. Law 89 of 1938 required 51% Colombian ownership, either private or government, of aviation companies operating in Colombia. It was a potential instrument of economic nationalism and had been designed as such by the López government; but under his successor it functioned as a two-edged weapon, serving as the basis for the establishment of Avianca (Aerovías Nacionales de Colombia) and allowing the Colombian government to eliminate SCADTA in the interest of hemispheric security.[52]

To the State Department the proposed creation of Avianca was a mixed blessing. The reorganization of Colombian aviation promised to remove SCADTA from the field, but it would also reduce Pan American influence; as a result there would be no guarantee that the Colombian government would carry out the elimination of former SCADTA officials and personnel in accordance with United States objectives. Immediately prior to the final organizational meeting of Avianca, the State Department wired Braden that it opposed the creation of a Colombian company in which Pan American Airways did not possess ultimate control.[53] In the compromise solution devised during the spring of 1940 Pan American retained financial control, the Colombian government was given an option to purchase 40% of the stock, and an additional 20% of the stock was reserved for Colombian nationals.[54]

Before the creation of Avianca on 8 June 1940, the Colombian government, under pressure from the United States and with the cooperation of Pan American, first neutralized the German pilots by requiring all aircraft to have Colombian military copilots; then, in a swift tactical maneuver, Pan American dismissed German personnel and moved in Colombians and Americans. As Spruille Braden informed Laurence Duggan and Herbert Feis, the joint action successfully eliminated the strategic threat which SCADTA posed for the Panama Canal and ended the company's commercial rivalry with Pan American on the West coast of South America. Chief of Staff George Marshall portrayed Colombian cooperation as 'a source of deep gratification.'[55]

An analysis of Colombian-United States aviation relations demonstrates the continuity of American policy between the world wars. It indicates the primacy of strategic factors and the secondary role of commercial considerations in shaping the response of the United States to the initial predominance of European-affiliated airlines in Latin America. The United States pursued, understandably, a closed door objective in keeping with its traditional sphere of influence policy in the Western Hemisphere. In the process, there evolved a unique relationship between the United States government and Pan American Airways, which after 1929 received full diplomatic support from American officials in establishing a monopoly over inter-American commercial aviation. By the time the United States entered the second world war, it had at its disposal a potent economic and strategic weapon.

This chapter is reprinted with revisions from *The Journal of Interamerican Studies and World Affairs*, vol. 14, no. 3 (August 1972): 297–324, by permission of the Publisher, Sage Publications, Inc.

8

In retrospect

This discussion of the relations between the United States and Colombia between the world wars is intended as a case study of the development and operation of the Good Neighbor policy in Latin America. The articulation and implementation of United States policy in Latin America generally and Colombia specifically was a multidimensional phenomenon, and attempts to apply convenient labels to the diplomatic maneuvers of these years may tend to obscure their inherent complexity; yet there is a need to consider the dominant strains in that policy and the manner in which the Colombian instance reflects the operation of American diplomacy in a broader context.

The several aspects of Colombian-American relations on which this study concentrates indicate that the formal trappings of the Good Neighbor – nonintervention; the Trade Agreements program; Export-Import Bank loans; the Foreign Bondholders' Protective Council – were measures designed to stabilize the political and economic environment in Latin America for United States interests. American policy, when defined in this general fashion, was largely successful in the short-run achievement of its objectives in Colombia. It promoted political stability in Colombia; it shifted Colombian political support away from a nationalistic stance on resource development and foreign investment, especially in the petroleum industry; it fashioned a Colombian commercial policy more in line with a closed door objective, thereby undercutting 'foreign,' especially German, competition in the Colombian marketplace; it delayed a moratorium on the Colombian debt and subsequently effected a debt settlement in line with American interests. In addition, the State Department managed to mitigate the effects of the unfavorable public image of the United Fruit Company and to prolong its dominance over the Colombian banana industry. Finally, United States diplomacy shaped the political and economic environment in which American aviation interests gained ascendancy in Colombia as well as in Central America and on the west coast of South America.

To suggest that these policy objectives, based largely on a neo-mercantilist understanding of the American place in international relations, were successful in the short term of course begs criticism. Yet to argue that the policy was successful is to level neither praise nor condemnation at that policy. Certainly the Good Neighbor was not as negative as some of its recent critics would have us believe.[1] It may have been designed to stem the tide of Latin American nationalism. But this in itself suggests a definite commitment on the part of American policymakers to the idea that the American route to 'modernization' was in the best interest of all concerned, including the developing nations.[2] That this route may have led in the long run to an intensification of nationalistic hostility to the American presence is not in itself evidence that New Deal diplomacy failed to comprehend the importance of nationalism in relations with the Third World. We have all, moreover, perhaps too loosely used such terms as *development* and *underdevelopment* without demonstrating the extent to which alternative courses of action were practicable and the extent to which the American presence actually retarded 'development.'

From the perspective of the United States in the years before the second world war the Good Neighbor was certainly successful in promoting hemispheric solidarity and interdependence in both a strategic and an economic sense. That the American path to development involved policies which benefited American interests at the expense of Colombian does not negate the success of the policy; it rather confirms it. Foreign policy is by definition intended to protect the national interest. The United States perceived American hegemony in Latin America, within a wider context of the open door, as essential to the national interest, and it used its economic and political power to ensure that predominance in the hemisphere. That the policies of Hoover and Roosevelt now appear anachronistic does not negate their effectiveness at the time; deteriorating relations with Latin America in the post-1945 period are as much a commentary upon the inadequacies of recent policies as on those of the Good Neighbor, though it may have been weak, its inception selfish, and its rewards restrictive.

The use of economic rather than military pressure indicated a temporary policy preference rather than a renunciation per se of the right to intervene to protect American interests. Differing interpretations and responses within the State Department to J. Reuben Clark's effort to sever the connection between the Roosevelt Corollary with its acceptance of military force, and the Monroe Doctrine were evidence that, especially in the early years of the depression, the Hoover and Roosevelt administrations were not prepared to forfeit the right to use one of their tactical diplomatic weapons.[3] The fact remains, however, that there was a pronounced tendency in the Hoover-Roosevelt years to eschew military intervention and to concentrate on other means to achieve the objectives of American policy.

Although the quest for a more effective, less abrasive policy toward Latin

America did not originate in the Hoover or Roosevelt administrations, the impact of the depression following the panic of 1929 tended to emphasize the immediacy of the problem. Like the policy-makers in the 1890s, those of the late 1920s and 1930s viewed solutions to domestic, social, economic, and political disequilibrium in terms of continued productivity and increased consumption. Foreign markets and sources of raw materials were perceived as essential to the realization of this objective, and Latin America had long been envisaged as one of the most promising of markets and suppliers. Evidence suggests that there was a prevalent belief in government circles and in internationalist-oriented business organizations, such as the American Manufacturers' Export Association and the National Foreign Trade Council, that increased reciprocity with Latin American countries was a prerequisite to the continued access of American products to Latin American markets.[4] Hoover's willingness to sign the protectionist Smoot-Hawley tariff has obscured the fact that the president and his secretary of commerce, Robert Lamont, shared the conviction that more flexible tariff procedures were vital to an expansion of the United States's commercial frontiers. Even such staunch protectionists within the Hoover administration as Under Secretary of State William Castle Jr saw protectionism as only one aspect of a commercial policy oriented toward market expansion. Hoover nevertheless continued to support the nationalist segment of business opinion in tariff matters, particularly where agricultural products were involved, but he did work toward an increase in presidential initiative in tariff policies and greater powers for the U.S. Tariff Commission.[5] The concept of reciprocity was not systematically applied, however, until the inauguration of the Hull-Roosevelt program during the New Deal.

If American policy-makers were not entirely prepared to compromise on domestic protectionism, they clearly attempted to counteract protectionism abroad. American officials were determined to cushion the negative impact of Colombian tariff policies on American exports. Neither American nor Colombian officials were satisfied with the existing commercial relations between the two countries, the United States because it sought a more liberal Colombian tariff schedule and Colombia because it sought greater security for coffee exports and more protection for its industry from American products.

The negotiations leading to a commercial agreement were arduous and prolonged, leading first in 1933 to the conclusion of a trade treaty which was not ratified and two years later to a trade agreement under the provisions of the 1934 Reciprocal Trade Agreements Act. During the negotiations, American officials indicated little willingness to yield to Colombian desires to protect infant industries, little comprehension of the general problems which beset the Colombian economy after 1929, and relatively little insight into the long-range economic interests of the two countries. The United States was not alone in its myopia, of course. Colombians continued to look to the coffee industry for their salvation, not a surprising tendency in a period of depression when the economy's traditional source of foreign exchange was threatened. The protection of coffee was not surprising, but it was perhaps lamentable given the desire of the emergent manufacturing sector to gain a competitive advantage over imported commodities.

That the interwar years produced no departure from this pattern was reflected in the Colombian position at the 1945 Chapultepec Conference of American States, where it urged strongly that continued liberal access of United States products to Latin American markets ought to be accomplished in a manner which would facilitate domestic economic growth through industrialization.[6] Herbert Hoover appears to have anticipated this problem in the 1920s when he stressed the need for productive loans and investments to increase productivity in Latin American countries and to provide a more permanent prosperity within which American expansion could occur. Franklin Roosevelt, on the other hand, did not comprehend Hoover's position and articulated a substantially more paternalistic 'give them a share' philosophy, an approach which denied the existence of fundamental differences between the Colombian and American political economies.[7] It was in part because the Roosevelt phase of the Good Neighbor policy failed to adhere to the thrust of the Hoover years that it ultimately failed to realize the intent of its rhetoric.

Just as the interwar years witnessed a sustained effort on the part of the United States to augment its commercial relations with Colombia, so they saw continued interest in private investment, at least until the post-1929 depression brought a want of confidence. In the case of indirect investments such as Colombian government bonds, interest reached a peak in the mid-1920s and then rapidly declined as investors became aware of the dangerous over-expansion of public works projects. The diplomacy surrounding Colombian-American financial relations absorbed the energies of bankers, investors, and government officials throughout the two decades. The United States managed to discourage somewhat private American investment in Colombian bonds in the late 1920s but failed to prevent Colombian default on its foreign bonded debt during the Olaya administration. Even a partial settlement of the dispute was delayed until the pressures of international conflict after 1939 introduced new strategic and commercial urgency to the discussions. The 1940 settlement was accompanied by the advent of the Export-Import Bank into Colombian-American economic relations and marked a departure from the traditionally private investment of previous decades.[8]

The State Department assumed an equally prominent role in determining the course of negotiations between Colombian authorities and United States-based firms operating in Colombia, three of the most prominent instances of which were examined in this study. American officials viewed the protection of American enterprise as of economic, strategic, and political significance, such an emphasis being logically derived from a foreign policy which placed high priority upon the defense of the principle of free enterprise at home and abroad. This emphasis was especially pronounced in the case of the petroleum industry, which was one of the most important areas attracting foreign capital and one of the focal points of international rivalry in these years.[9] For its part, the State Department was anxious to direct Colombian policy away from either the course of the Mexican revolution toward nationalization of natural resource production, or the less significant example of Bolivia's takeover of Standard Oil in 1937. The virtual monopoly which American petroleum interests acquired in the industry in Colombia owed a good deal to effective diplomacy as well as to Colombian shortage of capital, technology, and political leverage. Certainly the negotiations relating to petroleum and aviation served to highlight the strong sphere-of-interest orientation of the Good Neighbor policy and the absence of more than a tactical departure from traditional diplomacy in Latin America.

In the case of the United Fruit Company, although the State Department used its good offices to protect the enterprise from what the department viewed as unreasonable challenges from the host government, it tended to be less concerned and less satisfied with the often antagonistic policies of United's management. With trade competition keen, with American investment under frequent challenge, and with a growing ideological threat from extreme left and right in the 1930s, American officials were not prepared to allow the Boston-based firm to jeopardize the American presence in the country and strategic interests in the Caribbean perimeter. Since much of the thrust of the Good Neighbor policy was related to image creation, irresponsible behavior by American firms abroad was not to be endured without protest.

In terms of the Colombian experience, what was remarkable in the political and diplomatic debates occasioned by the American presence was not the strength of the opposition to the United States but the degree of consensus among Colombian officials on questions related to the United States and to foreign investment and enterprise. There were certainly distinctions between the two major parties on foreign policy issues, although conflict tended to be more intense in the 1920s and 1930s than subsequently. The vision which President Marco Fidel Suárez (1918–21) articulated of the United States as a 'Polar Star' and an example to be emulated represented an extreme pro-American position; yet there has been little rejection of the American presence from within the Colombian mainstream. In the second half of the 1920s both Liberals and Conservatives questioned the degree of direct and indirect American investment and the extent to which Colombia was economically dependent upon the United States. Nevertheless, even one of the leading Liberal critics of the United States, Alfonso López, once installed in the presidency, did relatively little to mitigate United States influence or to reduce economic dependency. The primary ideological challenge to the United States came from the right, from Conservatives such as Laureano Gómez, who, opportunistic as his stance may have been, saw more to be emulated in fascist Italy or in Ghandi's vision of India than in the United States.[10] The challenge arose as well from the Socialist and Communist left, which organized Colombian workers in the oil fields, on banana plantations, and on the docks. In Colombia, the issue of different routes to modernization, which was implicit in the debates over foreign loans and investment, trade policy, agricultural development, and aviation, never fully matured into the confrontation situation characteristic of the conflict between the industrialized nations and the developing world since 1945. There has been a persistent preoccupation with development-related issues since 1945, but in terms of its foreign policy Colombia has consistently supported the institutional structure of the inter-American system, although it has also been instrumental in establishing such sub-regional organizations as the Latin American Free Trade Association and the Andean Group. Colombia has been distinctly pro-American in the Cold War era, even though it has actively encouraged trade with the Soviet bloc countries and has softened its position on Cuba since the original rupture of relations in 1961.[11]

The years between the first and second world wars proved to be pivotal ones in determining the direction of Colombian relations with the United States. The period opened with the legacy of the loss of Panama still fresh in Colombian memory. The official reconciliation between Colombia and the United States embodied in the Thomson-Urrutia Treaty (1921), the indemnity payment of twenty-five million dollars, and the prosperity of the 1920s softened the bitter legacy until economic depression and instability intervened. For the ten years between 1927 and 1937 American officials feared that Colombia might pursue more nationalistic goals, that it would close its doors to American investment in key sectors of the economy, nationalize foreign enterprise already in operation, curtail American imports, and threaten American security in the Caribbean. Weak as its economic and political position may have been, those options were open to Colombian society but were not selected by the elite groups which dominated the political economy. The interwar years ended as they had begun, with a major international war and with a Colombian administration under Eduardo Santos which brought an end to the domestic reform program of Alfonso López and reaffirmed its loyalty to the dual principles of free enterprise and hemispheric solidarity under United States hegemony.

Notes

INTRODUCTION

1 Robert Seidel 'Progressive Pan Americanism: Development and United States Policy toward South America, 1906-1931' (PHD dissertation, Cornell University 1973) is an excellent account from this perspective.
2 Joseph Tulchin *The Aftermath of War* (New York 1971) 241
3 Robert F. Smith *The United States and Revolutionary Nationalism in Mexico, 1916-1932* (Chicago 1972); Bryce Wood *The Making of the Good Neighbor Policy* (New York 1961) 13-47, 299
4 Seidel 'Progressive Pan Americanism' and 'American Reformers Abroad: The Kemmerer Missions in Latin America, 1923-1931' *Journal of American History* 32 (June 1972): 520-45
5 Wood *Good Neighbor Policy* 124; G.S. Mount 'American Imperialism in Panama' (PHD dissertation, University of Toronto 1969)
6 Robert Ferrell 'Repudiation of a Repudiation' *Journal of American History* 51 (March 1965): 669-73; Frank Kellogg MSS, A.K 30, box 2, Colombian Treaty (Minnesota Historical Society); L. Ethan Ellis *Frank Kellogg and American Foreign Relations, 1925-1929* (New Brunswick, New Jersey 1961)
7 Assistant Secretary of State Francis White to Jefferson Caffery (American minister to Colombia), 31 March 1930; White to William R. Castle Jr, 25 May 1932 and 22 June 1929 (Francis White MSS: correspondence, RG 59)
8 For a discussion of Hoover's foreign policies as Secretary of Commerce see Joseph Brandes *Herbert Hoover and Economic Diplomacy* (Pittsburgh 1962) and Joan Hoff Wilson *American Business and United States Foreign Policy 1920-1933* (Lexington 1971)

9 *The State Papers and Other Public Writings of Herbert Hoover* ed. William A. Myers 1: 27-31; Alexander DeConde *Herbert Hoover's Latin American Policy* (Stanford 1951) 59-60; Herbert Hoover *The Memoirs of Herbert Hoover* 2: *The Cabinet and the Presidency 1920-1933* (New York 1952) 333

10 N. Gordon Levin *Woodrow Wilson and World Politics: America's Response to War and Revolution* (New York 1968)

11 Joan Hoff Wilson *Herbert Hoover, Forgotten Progressive* (Boston 1975)

12 Carl Parrini *Heir to Empire: United States Economic Diplomacy, 1916-1923* (Pittsburgh 1969)

13 Among the most perceptive analyses of business-government relations in the domestic context are Robert Wiebe *Businessmen and Reform* (Cambridge, Massachusetts 1962); Gabriel Kolko *The Triumph of Conservatism* (New York 1963); James Weinstein *The Corporate Ideal in the Liberal State* (Boston 1968); Murray Rothbard 'Herbert Hoover and the Myth of Laissez Faire' in Ronald Radosh and Murray Rothbard, eds. *A New History of Leviathan* (New York 1972) and 'The Hoover Myth' *Studies on the Left* 6, 4 (Summer 1966); Ellis Hawley *The New Deal and the Problem of Monopoly* (New Brunswick, New Jersey 1966).

14 DeConde *Hoover's Latin American Policy* 123

15 Wood *Good Neighbor Policy* 7, 132-3. On the Roosevelt philosophy among the most thorough works are James M. Burns *Roosevelt: The Lion and The Fox* (New York 1956); D. Fusfield *The Economic Thought of Franklin D. Roosevelt* (New York 1956); William E. Leuchtenberg *Franklin D. Roosevelt and the New Deal* (New York 1963); B.J. Bernstein 'The New Deal: The Conservative Achievements of Liberal Reform' in B.J. Bernstein, ed. *Towards a New Past* (New York 1968) 263-88.

16 The phrase is that of J. Lloyd Mecham in *A Survey of United States-Latin American Relations* (Boston 1965) 123. On Cuba, see the very thorough study by Irwin Gellman *Roosevelt and Batista* (Albuquerque 1973) and the more revisionist Robert F. Smith *The United States and Cuba: Business and Diplomacy, 1917-1960* (New York 1960).

17 David Green *The Containment of Latin America* (Chicago 1971). See as well Lloyd Gardner *Economic Aspects of New Deal Diplomacy* (Madison, Wisconsin 1964) and William A. Williams *The Tragedy of American Diplomacy* (New York 1959). One of the most outspoken critics of economic nationalism as practiced abroad was Assistant Secretary of State Francis B. Sayre. Note his article 'The Menace of Economic Nationalism' *Proceedings of the Academy of Political Science* 14 (January 1935): 206-14.

18 Stimson MSS: Union League Club folder, box 486, Yale University Library. Note Stimson's article 'Bases of American Foreign Policy During the Last Four Years' *Foreign Affairs* (April 1933) 383-96.

19 On the importance of American subsidiaries to foreign policy see Williams *Tragedy of American Diplomacy* 152.

20 The only survey treatment of Colombian-American relations is E. Taylor Parks *Colombia and the United States, 1765-1934* (Durham, North Carolina 1935). See also J. Fred Rippy *The Capitalists and Colombia* (New York 1931).

21 This portrait is drawn largely from the detailed reports of the US Military and Naval Attachés, RG 165, 10568-M-6/1, 2277-M-14/5, 2391-85/1, 26/0-66/ 132; RG 38, C-10-H 17883; and from W.P. McGreevey *Statistical Series on the Colombian Economy* (mimeograph, Department of Geography, University of California, Berkeley 1964) table 1A.

22 BPAU 63 (1929): 1023; 67 (1933): 566

23 US Bureau of Foreign and Domestic Commerce 'The Foreign Trade of Colombia' *Commerce Reports* (8 April 1939) 330-3

24 BPAU 65 (1931): 1069

25 Colombian domestic history in the 1920s and 1930s has received little attention. See Diego Montaña Cuéllar *Colombia: país formal y país real* (Buenos Aires 1963); David Bushnell *Eduardo Santos and the Good Neighbor, 1938-1942* (Gainesville 1967); V.L. Fluharty *Dance of the Millions: Military Rule and the Social Revolution in Colombia* (Pittsburgh 1957); Miguel Urrutia *The Development of the Colombian Labor Movement* (New Haven and London 1969).

26 W. Stewart 'Ratification of the Thomson-Urrutia Treaty' *Southwest Political and Social Science Quarterly* 10 (March 1930): 416-28

27 See below, chapter 5.

28 See below, chapters 6 and 7.

29 Olaya is most deserving of a biography. This sketch is drawn largely from Jesús María Henao and Gerardo Arrubla *A History of Colombia* translated and edited by J. Fred Rippy (Chapel Hill 1938) 540-8; 'Colombia's President, A Liberal Statesman' *New York Times* 23 February 1930, 10:1; *El Tiempo* 30 January 1930; M. Monsalve Martínez *Colombia: posesiones presidenciales, 1810-1954* (Bogotá 1954). There is a brief discussion below on pages 63-4 of Olaya's position during the 1930 elections.

30 Urrutia *Colombian Labor Movement* 123

31 Eduardo Zuleta Angel *El Presidente López* (Medellín 1966) passim. The Mercantile Bank of Colombia was purchased by the Royal Bank of Canada. See G.S. Mount 'Canadian Investment in Colombia' *Canadian Journal of Latin American Studies* 1 (1976): 50-1.

32 Urrutia *Colombian Labor Movement* 70-80

33 Ibid. 120; Zuleta *El Presidente López* 74ff; Fluharty *Dance of the Millions* 49-59

CHAPTER 1

1 Robert Beyer 'The Colombian Coffee Industry: Origins and Major Trends, 1740-1940' (PHD dissertation, University of Minnesota 1947) table 4, appendix

2 Stewart 'Ratification of the Thomson-Urrutia Treaty' *Southwest Political and Social Science Quarterly* 10 (March 1930): 416-28; E. Taylor Parks *Colombia and the United States, 1765-1934* (Durham, North Carolina 1935); Paolo Coletta 'William Jennings Bryan and the United States-Colombian Impasse, 1903-1921' HAHR 48: (November 1967): 486-501

3 Frank Kellogg MSS: A.K30, box 5, Correspondence 1915-19; A.K30, box 2: Diplomatic Correspondence and Documents Relative to a Settlement of Differences with Colombia, submitted to the Committee on Foreign Relations, U.S. Senate, 63rd Congress, 3rd Session, 1915 (Minnesota Historical Society). Barrett's statement is on p. 77.

4 7 December 1920, Kellogg MSS: A.K30, box 6: Correspondence 1920

5 Pan American Advertising Association, bulletin No. 5, Columbus Memorial Library, Pan American Union

6 Donnelly to William Cooper, 19 February 1930, RG151: 434

7 Alexander DeConde *Herbert Hoover's Latin American Policy* (Stanford 1951) 11, 75 ff

8 Hoover to the chairman of the Wyoming State Hoover-Curtis Committee, 20 October 1932. Hoover assured his supporters that he believed 'in a protective tariff ... on all products of the farm, the ranch and the mine.' (Presidential File, PPF 664 Tariff, Hoover MSS, West Branch, Iowa).

9 Herbert Hoover *The Memoirs of Herbert Hoover* 2: *The Cabinet and the Presidency 1920-1933* (New York 1952) 294; Hoover MSS, Presidential File, Subject File: Tariff Commission, 21 August to 28 September 1929

10 Hoover *Memoirs* 2: 294-9; Joan Hoff Wilson *American Business and United States Foreign Policy 1920-1933* (Lexington 1971); Thomas W. Lamont to SC, 26 November 1936, TWL MSS, file 140-4, Baker Library, Harvard; Stimson to Hoover, 8 June 1930, *Foreign Relations* 1930, 1: 998. For a list of nations which protested the Smoot-Hawley legislation see CR 71 Cong. 2 sess., 1930: 10784 ff. See also Hoover MSS, Presidential File, PPF 664 Tariff.

11 *New York Times* 19 April 1929

12 TWL MSS, file 154-30, National Foreign Trade Council File; *New York Times* 28 and 29 May 1931

13 William R. Castle Jr MSS, addresses and speeches, January 1932, January 1933, 7 December 1938; 'What will Revive Trade' *New York Herald Tribune* 19 May 1935. Note also the general correspondence in the Castle papers

between Castle and Frank Kellogg; it reveals the protectionist orientation of both men.

14 Colombian exports to the United States increased in value from $74,100,000 in the first nine months of 1928 to $76,200,000 in the same period of 1929, while U.S. exports to Colombia declined from $41,500,000 to $39,400,000 in the same period (U.S. Tariff Commission *An Analysis of Trade between Colombia and the United States* [1933]; see as well *Duties Levied in Foreign Countries on Agricultural Commodities from the United States* completed by the U.S. Tariff Commission in 1929; both reports are in the Hoover MSS, PSF Tariff Commission, 24 June to 14 July 1929).

15 *El Tiempo* 16 and 21 June 1930

16 Luis Ospina Vásquez *Indústria y Protección en Colombia, 1810-1930* (Medellín 1955) 458-9

17 Caffery to SS, 29 August 1930, RG 59 621.003/92

18 RG 59 621.003/95; U.S. Department of Commerce *Commerce Reports* 26 January 1931, 250

19 RG 59 621.003/96. Note the protests of American exporters of rice and grains about the Colombian situation: American Rice Growers' Cooperative Association, Houston, 25 November 1931; Federal Farm Board, 28 November 1931 (621.113 CP/23); Millers' National Federation, Washington, 27 June 1932 (621.113 CP/26).

20 To provide more effective machinery for the direction of Colombian commercial policy, the Colombian Congress had created a National Economic Council composed of representatives of public and private organizations, including the major agricultural and industrial associations (*Diario Oficial* 17 February 1931). Caffery to SS, 25 February 1931, RG 59 821.5123/33; see also 621.003/127.

21 RG 59 621.003/120, /131. *Commerce Reports* 18 May 1931; see *Diario Oficial* 22 May 1931, for law 62 of 14 May 1931. For the discussion of the petroleum question see chapter 5 below.

22 *Diario Oficial* 24 September 1931. From 1922 to 1926, the value of U.S. exports of agricultural machinery increased from $1,537,000 to $4,179,000 (*Commerce Reports* 22 August 1927).

23 Luxury items included silk textiles and apparel, automobiles exceeding $1,000 in value, watches, precious and semi-precious stones, pianos, phonographs, radios, cigars and cigarettes, perfumes, playing cards, and liquors (BPAU 66 (1932): 732; *Commerce Reports* 12 October 1931, 112; Caffery to SS, 15 December 1931, 621.003/176).

24 See the document entitled *Substantial Tariff Revisions in Latin America*, Hoover MSS. Executive Departments, Commerce, Foreign Tariff, 1931; see

as well *El Tiempo* 1 October 1931. The most detailed analyses of the impact of the Colombian tariff changes on domestic production and American imports are the Commercial Attaché Reports in the files of the BFDC, RG 151.

25 *New York Times* 29 September 1929, 8:3

26 *Foreign Relations* 1929, 2:885

27 Colombia, Ministerio de Relaciones Exteriores *Memoria de 1928* 50. John L. Merrill, who was at that time president of the Chamber, was also the president of All-America Cables, Inc. See Colombia, Departamento Administrativa Nacional de Estadística, *Anuario General* (Bogotá, 1941) 38-9. The statistics on the coffee industry are from W.P. McGreevey *Statistical Series on the Colombian Economy* (Department of Geography, Berkeley 1964) table 2D.

28 BPAU 64 (1930): 1160, 1051-2; Castle MSS, Houghton Library, Harvard: H. Freeman Matthews to Castle, 6 June 1927, Correspondence 1920-33, Colombia; *New York Times* 4 June 1930, 11; Caffery to SS, 30 March 1933, RG 59 611.213/13

29 Dawson to SS, 22 May 1933, RG 59 611.213/15; *New York Times* 24 April 1933, 9:2. Caffery left Bogotá on 20 May.

30 During 1933 the total value of American commerce with Colombia was, for the first time since 1914, below that of Great Britain. The U.S. share of Latin American trade fell from the 72% of 1929 to 64%. See George Coleman 'The Good Neighbor Policy of Franklin D. Roosevelt, with Special Reference to Three Inter-American Conferences, 1933-1938' (PHD dissertation, University of Iowa, 1951) 162-3.

31 Lloyd Gardner *Economic Aspects of New Deal Diplomacy* (Madison, Wisconsin 1964) viii. Individuals who provided continuity between the two administrations were, among others, Herbert Feis, Henry Stimson, William Phillips, Stanley Hornbeck, and H. Freeman Matthews.

32 Ibid. 18; *New York Times* 23 October 1928; U.S. Department of State *Opening Address to the Inter-American Conference for the Maintenance of Peace* Conference Series no. 33 (Washington 1937) 249

33 *New York Times* 16 September 1936, 21:2

34 U.S. Department of State 'Trade and Domestic Prosperity' Address of the Secretary of State Before the National Foreign Trade Council, Commercial Policy Series no. 31, (Washington 1934) 10

35 RG 59 611.2131/30, /24, /34; *Foreign Relations* 1933, 5: 218-19

36 This document is contained in RG 59 611.2131/19½.

37 There is a copy of the NFTC report in RG 59 611.2131/23; 80% of Colombia's total exports went to the United States. The Latin American average was close to 75%.

38 Ibid. 17

39 RG 59 611.2131/31
40 Charles Taussig MSS, box 31, 7 July 1933, FDR Library, Hyde Park
41 RG 59 611.2131/19
42 *New York Times* 13 July 1933, 1:2
43 Taussig MSS, General File, U.S. Government 1
44 RG 59 611.0031 Committee for Reciprocity Information/198
45 William Dawson to the acting secretary, 19 August 1933, RG 59 611.2131/45
46 August 22 1933, RG 59 611.2131/61; /67
47 *El Espectador* 24 August 1933
48 Ibid. 5 August 1933
49 Dawson to SS, 15 August 1933, RG 59 611.2131/71. For a brief discussion
   of the cotton textile industry see W.P. McGreevey *An Economic History of
   Colombia 1845-1930* (Cambridge 1971) 199.
50 *Tea and Coffee Trade Journal* 38 (January 1920): 50. Useful material on the
   role of foreign banking in Colombian commerce is in EWK MSS, Colombia
   1923 and 1930. See as well RG 43, International High Commission *Report
   on Colombian Trade and Finance* and RG 59 821.61333/110.
51 George Faust 'Economic Relations of the United States and Colombia, 1920-
   1940' (PHD dissertation, University of Chicago 1946) 14
52 See as well *El Espectador* 5 August 1933, and Dawson to SS, 29 August 1933,
   RG 59 611.2131/77
53 RG 59 611.2131/88. The dependence of the Colombian coffee industry on
   the United States was emphasized in an Associated Coffee Industries memorandum forwarded to the department in mid-September. The memorandum
   argued that the currently low price of Colombian coffee on the American
   market was the result of the competitive practices of the coffee roasting
   industry, which had been using larger quantities of cheaper grades of coffee
   because of the decline in purchasing power in the United States (ibid.
   /89½).
54 Ibid. /88, /78
55 Ibid. /36; for other lobbyists see ibid. /19, /85, /31, /44½, 356, 363, 368,
   /62, /89½. The activity of the bondholders is discussed more fully in chapters
   3 and 4 below.
56 RG 59 821.51/1711
57 RG 59 611.2131/49, /51, /65, /62; O.J. Abell to William Phillips, 21 August
   1933 ibid. /66
58 Ibid. /78A
59 Ibid. /99
60 *El Espectador* 9 September 1933
61 Ibid. 5 September 1933

62 Memorandum by Wallace McClure, 2 November 1933, RG 59 611.2131/109; memorandum, December 1934, Division of Foreign Tariffs, RG 40:95112
63 RG 59 611.2131/116A, /136. See chapter 5 below.
64 RG 59 611.2131/135
65 *El Diario Nacional* 28 November 1933; *El País*, the Conservative Bogotá paper owned by Laureano Gómez, was consistently in opposition to the treaty through the week preceding its adoption.
66 Sheldon Whitehouse to SS, 12 December 1933, RG 59 611.2131/151, /154; *El Espectador* 20 December 1933; FO 371 A/3891/51/11
67 *Foreign Relations* 1933, 2:246-7
68 Gulf Pacific Mail Line to Sumner Welles, 1 March 1934, RG 59 621.133 CP/77, /67, /73
69 *Seventh International Conference of American States, Minutes and Antecedents, Ninth Committee* (Montevideo 1933) 91-2. A later ambassador to Colombia, Spruille Braden, defended the American departure from the gold standard in a major speech before the conference (Braden *Diplomats and Demagogues* [New Rochelle, New York 1971] 99-100).
70 Ibid. 101-3
71 Hull MSS, box 35, folder 67, Library of Congress

CHAPTER 2

1 William Phillips diary 7: 889, 976, 996; 3: 85-91 (Houghton Library); George Peek and William Crowther *Why Quit Our Own?* (New York 1936) 40
2 William Phillips to Hull, 12 December 1933 *Foreign Relations* 1933, 1: 930; Peek to Francis B. Sayre, 15 December 1933, Ibid. 1933, 1: 930-1, and Sayre to Peek, 18 December 1933, Ibid. 930-3. See also George Peek *Proposed Foreign Trade Administration* Hull MSS, box 35, folder 67, Library of Congress.
3 Charles Taussig MSS, box 38: Cuba, box 29. For State Department opposition to Peek see the unsigned memorandum dated 8 January 1934, Hull MSS, box 35, folder 68; Hull to Jesse Jones, Henry Wallace, and Daniel Roper, 31 January 1934, ibid. folder 70; Daniel C. Roper to Hull, 1 February 1934, ibid. box 36, folder 71. Secretary of Agriculture Henry Wallace was, of course, strongly in favor of Hull's position by 1934; witness his popular pamphlet of that year, *America Must Choose*. For a brief discussion of the influence of Wallace on Republicans such as Henry Stimson, see William E. Leuchtenburg *Franklin D. Roosevelt and the New Deal* (New York 1963) 204.
4 Francis B. Sayre to Roosevelt, 9 January 1934, Hull MSS, box 85, folder 384

5 Memorandum on White House conversation, 19 February 1934, ibid.
6 CR 73 Cong., 2 sess., 1934, 3644
7 Republican Congressman Everett Dirksen of Illinois argued that 'foreign trade can help us very little, and for that little we are willing, if we pass this bill, to invite [foreign producers] to send manufactured goods into our markets and further aggravate conditions' (ibid. 5765).
8 Ibid. 8265-8 and Roosevelt MSS, OF 567, Hyde Park, New York. Leuchtenburg's comment in *Franklin D. Roosevelt and the New Deal* that there was 'strenuous' opposition from business interests is an oversimplification (see 204-5).
9 The U.S. share of world trade fell from 13.83% in 1929 to 10.92% in 1932 (BPAU 68 [1934]: 780-1).
10 U.S. Congress, House, Committee on Ways and Means *Reciprocal Trade Agreements, Hearings* 73 Cong., 2 sess., 8-14 March 1934, 84301; CR 73 Cong., 2 sess., 1934, 5808
11 U.S. Congress, Senate, Committee on Finance, *Hearings*, HR 8687 *An Act to Amend the Tariff Act of 1930* 26 April - 1 May 1934, 76
12 In his testimony before the committee Robert L. O'Brien, chairman of the U.S. Tariff Commission and a Republican, was harshly critical of the effectiveness of the flexible tariff provisions of the 1922 and 1930 Tariff Acts: 'I regard the term, applied to our present law, as an extreme joke' (*Hearings* 144). Former Secretary of State Stimson spoke out in favor of the Trade Agreements Bill (CR 73 Cong., 2 sess., 1934, 4074).
13 CR 73 Cong., 2 sess., 1934, 9222, 9340, 9341, 9592, 9594
14 Ibid. 7748, 7756, 9340
15 Ibid. 9342, 9475, 9591. Arthur Vandenburg of Michigan took a similar stand against the bill (9805, 9338, 9589).
16 Ibid. 9588-9, 9593, 10395; Lamont to Robert Doughton, 19 April 1943, TWL MSS 127-5, 1943, Baker Library, Harvard
17 William Allen 'Cordell Hull and the Defense of the Trade Agreements Program, 1933-1940' in Alexander DeConde, ed. *Isolation and Security* (Durham, North Carolina 1957) 117. For the 1890 reciprocity provision see W. La Feber *The New Empire* 112-23. For an expression of business sentiment favorable to increased government support see Virgil Jordan 'The Imperialism Ahead' JABA (August 1934) 23-5, 40.
18 Peek to Roosevelt, 23 May 1934, Roosevelt MSS, PSF Peek
19 Hull MSS, box 36, folder 75
20 Department of State memorandum, 26 May 1934, RG 59 611.2131/196
21 Luckett-Wake Tobacco Company to Hull, 13 June 1934, ibid. /190, /197
22 William Phillips to S. Walter Washington, 24 August 1934, ibid. /205B. By

August of 1934 there had been a change of government in Colombia as the Liberal Alfonso López replaced Olaya Herrera. López was considered anti-American by business opinion, and he rapidly inaugurated a Colombian reform program modelled on Mexico and the New Deal. *La revolución en marcha*, as the López program became known, made frequent overtures to the left in Colombia and in so doing inevitably became embroiled with American interests. Nevertheless, the influence of Olaya, who held the minister of foreign relations post for part of the administration, had a continued moderating effect on relations with the United States (Department of State *Press Releases* 8 September 1934, 160-3).

23 RG 59 611.0031 Committee for Reciprocity Information /69. A number of the letters to the committee complained of European competition for the Colombian market and in other parts of South America.

24 *New York Times* 9 September 1934, 8:5; 7 October 1934, 15:5.

25 RG 59 611.2131/266

26 The full report of 9 October 1934 is contained in ibid. /277. This was certainly not 'the first assault on Hull's trade program by ... Peek,' as Irwin Gellman suggests in 'Prelude to Reciprocity: The Abortive United States-Colombian Treaty of 1933' *Historian* 32 (November 1969): 65.

27 Peek to Sayre, 7 December 1934, RG 59 611.2131/260. In a letter of December 6 to Henry Grady, the chairman of the Trade Agreements Committee, James Edwards of Peek's office argued that there were few, if any, indications that the Colombian government had liberated the blocked exchange of U.S. nationals originating prior to September 1931. He believed that the Colombian announcement that the final 20% would be liberated by 15 February 1935 was simply an effort to expedite the American acceptance of the trade agreement (Roosevelt MSS, PPF 313 Colombia). When Peek submitted his resignation a year later, it was as a result of his growing alienation from administration policy (Hull MSS, box 37, folder 81 and Leuchtenburg *Franklin D. Roosevelt and the New Deal* 214-15). Financial problems are discussed below.

28 Hull to Roosevelt, 28 November 1934 and Francis Sayre to Roosevelt, 28 November 1934, Roosevelt MSS, PSF

29 John Dickinson, assistant secretary of commerce, to Hull, 17 December 1934, Hull MSS, box 37, folder 81

30 Henry Chalmers memorandum to Murchison, Department of Commerce, 13 December 1943, RG 40: 95112

31 *New York Times* 17 February 1935, 18:2; W. Gephart, St Louis Chamber of Commerce, to Hull, 9 February 1934, RG 59 611.2131/174

32 Roosevelt MSS, PPF 313 Colombia; Herbert Feis to Francis Sayre and Sumner Welles, 11 July 1935, RG 59 611.2131/313½

33 Feis memorandum, 23 January 1935, RG 59 611.2131/282½, /193
34 S. Walter Washington to SS, 24 September 1934, ibid. /218. Colombian press activity directed toward the agreement was much lighter during the fall of 1934 than it had been in 1933. Nevertheless, pressure groups which had been active in 1933 continued to lobby while the Committee for Reciprocity Information concluded the public hearings on the agreement in Washington. One of the few editorials which expressed concern over the influence of the American bondholders' groups on the hearings was in *El Espectador* 13 October 1934.
35 The most complete account of the Leticia settlement is Bryce Wood *The United States and Latin American Wars 1932-1942* (New York and London 1966).
36 There is a copy of this draft of the agreement in RG 59 611.2131/257. The provision on foreign exchange control read in part: 'With reference to the matter of foreign exchange control, the Government of the United States proposes that there be included in a separate exchange of notes, to be entered into concurrently with the proposed trade agreement, provisions ... designed ... to protect the interests of the two countries.'
37 S. Walter Washington to SS, 26 December 1934 *Foreign Relations* 1934, 5: 82-3
38 Donald R. Heath, treaty division memorandum, 24 December 1934, RG 59 611.2131/272
39 S. Walter Washington to SS, 17 January 1935, ibid. /279
40 Washingtpn to SS, 23 January 1935, ibid. /283, /288
41 Hull to Washington, 24 January 1935, ibid. /283
42 Washington to SS, 13 February 1935, ibid. /292, /293, /296. Olaya became minister of foreign relations to placate Peru in view of the refusal of the Colombian Congress to approve the Rio Pact. His preoccupation with issues other than the American agreement was, therefore, a genuine reason for failing to deal promptly with the trade pact. In fact, Olaya accepted the ministry on the understanding that President López would refrain from molesting foreign companies and devote greater attention to consideration of the trade agreement with the United States (Washington to SS, 5 February 1935, ibid. /290).
43 *Foreign Relations* 1935, 4: 437
44 Ibid. 431-7
45 RG 59 611.2131/309
46 Heath memorandum, ibid. /310. On 4 February 1935, an editorial in *El Tiempo* suggested that the drop in coffee prices following the conclusion of the American agreement with Brazil necessitated a rapid development of the European markets for Colombian coffee, particularly with countries such as

England and Germany that enjoyed very favorable balances of trade with Colombia. See Robert Seidel 'Progressive Pan Americanism: Development and United States Policy toward South America, 1906-1931' (PHD dissertation, Cornell University 1973) 420-83.

47 *El Espectador* 1 July 1935

48 Sumner Welles to Francis Sayre, 18 July 1935, RG 59 611.2131/320½; Feis desired that Colombia be encouraged to follow a more 'scrupulous' commercial policy (ibid. /313½).

49 *El Heraldo Industrial* 25 August 1935

50 U.S. Minister William Dawson to SS, 17 September 1935, RG 59 821.2131/342 *New York Times* 10 October 1935, 14:1; 11 October 1935, 24:2. There is a memorandum on the Colombian concessions in RG 40:95112.

51 Dawson to SS, 12 October 1935, RG 611.2131/363; *El Espectador* 10 October 1935; *El Tiempo* 15 and 16 October 1935

52 *La Prensa* 1 and 8 November 1935

53 *El Colombiano* itself tended to be favorable to American interests on certain issues. On 1 December 1935, for example, it carried a lengthy article on the benefits which Westinghouse had brought to Medellín since its establishment there in 1931.

54 *El Colombiano* 2 November 1935

55 Ibid. 10 November 1935; *El Tiempo* 8 November 1935

56 For the text of the Chamber Committee on the commercial agreement see *Anales de la Cámara de Representantes* no. 151, 28 January 1936. *El Espectador* 22 January 1936 contains a full summary. See also *El Tiempo* 29 January 1936 and 8 February 1936; *Diario del Pacífico* (Cali) 16 February 1936.

57 *El Tiempo* 12 February 1936; RG 59 611.2131/449, /382, /483; Colombia, *Anales del Senado* 16 March 1936, 2347-53

58 RG 59 611.2131/449, /501

59 Roosevelt's personal interest in combating German and Italian influence in Latin America seems to have come somewhat later. See Roosevelt to James Harvey Rogers, 13 December 1938, cited in Lloyd Gardner *Economic Aspects of New Deal Diplomacy* (Madison, Wisconsin 1964) 60.

60 U.S. *Commerce Reports* 8 April 1939, 331

61 For a discussion of the importance of Colombia to American security during the first world war see U.S. Department of State *The Lansing Papers, 1914-1920* (Washington 1938-40) 1: 514-15 and *Commerce Reports* 8 April 1939, 331. The reports of the U.S. naval and military attachés in Colombia underline the close relationship between commercial and strategic considerations (RG 38 and RG 165).

62 William Castle to Francis White, 27 September 1927, RG 59 821.15/41; Hoover *Memoirs* 2: 210 (curiously Hoover did not include Colombia in his itinerary).

63 Alton Frye *Germany and the Western Hemisphere, 1933-1941* (New Haven 1967) 218

64 Ibid. 30

65 Ambassador to Mexico Josephus Daniels wrote to Hull on 8 November 1933 that the commercial attaché in Mexico City believed firmly that 'Japan is making a drive to get the business of Latin America' (Hull MSS, box 35, folder 65).

66 Colombia, Ministerio de Relaciones Exteriores *Memoria de 1933* 226; RG 151, Commercial Attaché Reports, Bogotá, 20 September 1934. In 1934 Japan's total exports to South American countries were 250% greater than her purchases from the same area. Japanese exports increased from 1.1% of total Latin American purchases in 1929 to 4.8% in 1934. See the analysis of the Colombian trade situation in relation to Japan in U.S. Tariff Commission *Recent Developments in the Foreign Trade of Japan* (Washington 1926) 60-1.

67 *El Espectador* 17 May 1935; *El Diario Nacional* 21 May 1935; *New York Times* 18 May 1935, 25:4; *El Tiempo* 17 May and 24 June 1935

68 *El Tiempo* 18 September 1935; *El Heraldo Industrial* 17 August 1935; *El Espectador* 20 March 1935.

69 RG 59 621.9431/15

70 Department of State to Dawson, 1 June 1935, RG 59 621.6217/5A. According to a *New York Times* article (23 June 1935, 9:1), the National Foreign Trade Council had expressed concern over the use of compensation marks. Brazil at that time had an agreement with Germany permitting registered marks to be accepted in payment for up to 65% of the value of goods purchased by Germany.

71 Dawson to SS, 3 June 1935, RG 59 621.6217/16

72 Dawson to SS, 19 June 1935, RG 59 821.5151/285; Hull to Dawson, 1 July 1935, ibid. /289. After speaking with Olaya, Dawson reported that the minister of public works had decided to grant the contract to the American company (RG 59 621.6217/23).

73 RG 59 621.6231/6

74 RG 59 621.6231/9. The full text of the agreement is found in *El Tiempo* 5 November 1935.

75 H.J. Trueblood 'Trade Rivalries in Latin America' *Foreign Policy Reports* 13 (15 September 1937): 161

76 *Commerce Reports* 19 March 1938, 276. The strongest press support for continued trade with Germany came from the Conservative *El Siglo*; see, for

example, the editorial of 22 May 1937 following the conclusion of a trade agreement between the two countries the previous day, which continued the compensation agreement.

77 *New York Times* 1 September 1935, 9:4. Grace Beckett 'Effect of the Reciprocal Trade Agreements Upon the Foreign Trade of the United States' *Quarterly Journal of Economics* 55 (November 1940): 80-94 demonstrates that American trade with agreement countries in 1937 showed a 65.8% increase over the 1934-5 period; total trade with non-agreement countries increased only 44.3% in that year.

78 Although this chapter does not attempt to cover this aspect of the Colombian economy, there does not seem to have been any dislocation of domestic industry following the conclusion of the agreement with the United States. Certainly American goods poured into Colombia in greater quantities once the agreement went into effect, but available statistics do not indicate any decline in sales for Colombian products in the summer of 1936. Ministry of Finance data indicated a marked increase in production for some commodities in the period following the implementation of the new tariff schedules. Furthermore, the Colombian government continued to publicize its economic policy as one of nationalism and, in fact, moved in 1937-8 to raise duties on a number of items not covered by the agreement with the United States. See *Mundo al Día* 31 October 1936; *Commerce Reports* 4 July 1936, 516 and 21 May 1938, 464; Ministerio de Indústria *Memoria de 1938* 3: 17.

79 RG 59 611.2131/534, /536; Ministerio de Relaciones Exteriores *Memoria de 1936* i-xlvii

80 The full report is contained in RG 59 611.2131/540; *Commerce Reports* 12 September 1936, 725.

81 RG 59 611.2131/545. The British minister was less convinced than were American representatives that the trade agreement was responsible for the improvement in trade with Colombia. In his annual report for 1936, he commented: 'It is too early to reach any definite conclusions ... but it would appear that such increase as has taken place has been the result of the normal rise now taking place all over the world' (PRO, Foreign Office File 371).

82 Henry Wallace, proposed press release, Roosevelt MSS, PSF Agriculture

83 Daniel Roper, 26 November 1937, ibid. PPF Commerce

84 Unless otherwise indicated, the source for the following statistics is the analysis of Colombian trade in *Commerce Reports* 8 April 1939, 330-3.

85 RG 59 611.2131/540. The value of the peso was relatively stable at $.56 to $.57 in 1935-7.

86 Although banana exports to the United States rose by 25% from 1935 through 1937, the value was less than in 1935.

87 Ministerio de Indústria *Memoria de 1938* 3: 49. The second world war had
the effect of increasing Colombian dependence on the American market for
its exports; see the table in David Bushnell *Eduardo Santos and the Good
Neighbor, 1938-1942* (Gainesville 1967) 121.
88 *Commerce Reports* 12 February 1938, 144. Colombia was not typical of
South American countries in this respect. Some studies indicate that the non-
trade agreement countries in Latin America were better customers for American exports than were the ten trade agreement countries. In the 1932-8
period, the value of exports to the latter group of countries increased only
141%, in contrast to a 164% increase to the former countries (U.S. Tariff
Commission *The Foreign Trade of Latin America* part 1, report no. 146,
second series (Washington 1942) 37-41).
89 Dawson to SS, 4 October 1937, RG 59 611.2131/557. American concern for
German activities increased in 1938 and through the war years. See Daniel
Roper's memorandum of 1 March 1938 to Roosevelt, Roosevelt MSS, OF 614.

CHAPTER 3

1 See Carl Parrini *Heir to Empire: United States Economic Diplomacy, 1916-
1923* (Pittsburgh 1969) and Joseph Tulchin *The Aftermath of War* (New
York 1971). The general trend from 1920 to 1931 was the export of large
amounts of long-term capital, reaching a peak in 1928; see Charles Darling-
ton Jr 'United States Foreign Trade' JABA (April 1934) 28-30.
2 See V.L. Fluharty *Dance of the Millions: Military Rule and the Social Revolution in Colombia* (Pittsburgh 1957). *El Espectador* used the expression on
4 January 1929.
3 The most thorough discussion of this view is in Robert Seidel 'Progressive
Pan Americanism: Development and United States Policy toward South
America, 1906-1931' PHD dissertation, Cornell University 1973).
4 L.V. Chandler *American Monetary Policy, 1928-1941* (New York 1971)
5 U.S. Department of Commerce, *Commerce Reports* 19 September 1927,
762-8; Institute of International Finance *Bulletin* no. 53 (8 July 1932) 6.
The peso was $.975 at this time.
6 PRO, FO 371 A/3193/11; E. Taylor Parks *Colombia and the United States,
1765-1934* (Durham, North Carolina 1935) 472; BPAU 64 (1930): 1160
7 U.S. Department of Commerce *American Underwriting of Foreign Securities
in 1928* (Washington 1929) 1-9
8 Chester Lloyd Jones 'Loan Controls in the Caribbean' HAHR 14 (1934):
159-60
9 EWK MSS, Colombia 1923, Princeton University Library; Robert Seidel

'American Reformers Abroad: The Kemmerer Missions in South America, 1923-1931' *Journal of Economic History* 32 (June 1972): 520-45; RG 59 821.51A/4

10 Seidel 'American Reformers Abroad' and *Leyes presentadas al gobierno Colombiano por la misión financiera Norte Americana* (Bogotá Editorial Cromos 1923)

11 *Report on Colombian Banking* (1920) I-127, V passim, contained in RG 43, The International High Commission

12 FO 371 A 3192/3192/11

13 D. Joslin *A Century of Banking in Latin America* (London 1963) 241

14 FO 371 A/3192/3192/11; RG 59 821.51/410; Colombia, *Anales del Senado* 11 June 1928

15 The best discussion of loan policy is in Seidel 'Progressive Pan Americanism' 500-79. See the testimony of Thomas Lamont, Otto Kahn of Kuhn, Loeb & Co., and Charles Mitchell of the National City Company in U.S. Senate *Sale of Foreign Bonds ... Hearings Before the Committee on Finance Pursuant to S. Res. 19* 72 Cong., 1 sess., 18 December 1931 to 10 February 1932, part I; *Foreign Relations* 1922 1: 557-8; Betty Glad *Charles Evans Hughes and the Illusions of Innocence* (Urbana and London 1966) 304-13; Joan Hoff Wilson *American Business and United States Foreign Policy 1920-1933* (Lexington 1971) 101-22.

16 Hoover *Memoirs* 2: 87; Herbert Feis *The Diplomacy of the Dollar: First Era, 1910-1932* (Baltimore 1950) 8-9; Parrini *Heir to Empire* 172-212; Joseph Brandes *Herbert Hoover and Economic Diplomacy* (Pittsburgh 1962) x, 192

17 See, for example, Julius Klein to General Palmer Pierce, 3 May 1930, RG 40: 86681; Klein to W.M. McCormick, 6 May 1929, RG 151: 640 General. The phrase is Robert F. Smith's. The positive attitude of American bankers to productive loans is reflected in Emmet Harris 'Latin America Waits for Money' JABA (November 1929) 489, 535.

18 Lamont address, 2 May 1927, TWL MSS, Baker Library, Harvard, 149-23 International Chamber of Commerce; Jones's letter of 17 October 1927, RG 151: 640 Colombia; Jones to Lamont, 13 July 1929, RG 151: General, memorandum entitled 'The Foreign Loan Policy of the United States.' Note the very favorable press response to Lamont's address in *The American Banker* 12 May 1927 and letter of 2 June 1927 from the managing editor to Lamont, TWL MSS 149-23. This file contains a number of letters from members of the American banking community expressing agreement with Lamont's views.

19 *New York Times* 26 March 1928, 34.1; 24 March 1928, 25:5; 21 March 1928, 37:4; David Bushnell *Eduardo Santos and the Good Neighbor, 1938-42* (Gainesville 1967) 68-9. *El Tiempo* and *Mundo al Día* early in 1928 expressed

concern that unchecked foreign loans would lead to the type of political controls which had characterized American relations with the Caribbean countries.

20 S.W. Morgan to Francis White, 15 September 1928, RG 59 821.51/419, /420; Morgan to Henry Stimson, 27 October 1928, ibid. /446

21 *Foreign Relations* 1927, 1: 312-13

22 James C. Corliss *Latin American Budgets* part 3 *Colombia and Venezuela* Department of Commerce Circular no. 305 (a copy is contained in RG 151: 640 Colombia).

23 RG 59 821.51/420; J. Fred Rippy *The Capitalists and Colombia* (New York 1931) 152-76; Samuel H. Piles U.S. Minister to Colombia, for the SS, 12 June 1928, ibid. /410. Law 88 of 1923 became effective 1 June 1928.

24 RG 151: 640 Colombia. The reference to Olaya's visit is from Morgan's note of October 27 to Stimson, above note 20.

25 H. Freeman Matthews to SS, 8 November 1928, RG 59 821.51/453

26 A copy of this letter is contained in ibid. /447.

27 Edmund Monson to Foreign Office, 13 November 1928, FO 371 A/8471/5072/11. The question of the Barco concession and the petroleum industry receives full attention in chapter 5 below.

28 RG 151: 640 Colombia.

29 See note of Grosvenor M. Jones dated 15 November 1928, RG 151: 640 Colombia; EWK MSS, Colombia 1930, Memorandum on Laws Governing Revenue.

30 Letter dated 6 February 1929, RG 151: 640 Colombia

31 Morgan memorandum, 30 November 1928, RG 59 821.51/451; Monson to Chamberlain, 23 January 1929, FO 371 A/1125/368/11

32 Monson to Chamberlain, 23 January 1929, ibid.

33 The National Council for Transportation and Communication was created by executive decree in February 1929. It included five technical experts – three foreigners and two Colombians. The American member was Edwin James (BPAU 63 [1929]: 721).

34 R.L. Craigie, minutes on Monson's despatch, dated 20 February 1929, FO 371 A/1125/368/11

35 J.G. Lomax, British vice-consul at Bogotá to the Foreign Office, 5 December 1928, FO 371 A/365/365/11; Caffery to SS, 29 April 1929, RG 59 821.51/503. The *New York Times*, 17 July 1929, 26:2, commented that the 'inflow of foreign capital has largely stopped.'

36 Chandler *American Monetary Policy* 26, 36, 84; Milton Friedman and Anna Schwartz *A Monetary History of the United States* (Princeton 1963) 360-1, 370; Frank Costigliola 'Anglo-American Rivalry in the 1920's' (paper

read before the Organization of American Historians, Denver, April 1974) 14-15

37 FO 371 A/8560/268/11, A/297/297/11
38 *New York Times* 31 December 1928, 6:4; there is a more complete survey of the 1930 election in Jesús María Henao and Gerardo Arrubla *A History of Colombia* translated and edited by J. Fred Rippy (Chapel Hill 1938) 540-3; Fluharty *Dance of the Millions* 43-5.
39 *El Tiempo* 30 January 1930; *New York Times* 27 January 1930, 7:4
40 Matthews to Feis and White, 7 March 1932, RG 59 821.51/1354.
41 *New York Times* 17 March 1930, 8:5
42 Ibid. 21 April 1930, 5:1; interview of the author with H.F. Matthews, 27 November 1970 in Washington, DC
43 Klein to Lewis Strauss, one of Hoover's long-time business associates, 23 May and 2 July 1930, RG 40: 86818; EWK MSS, Letter Files: Colombia, Pyke Johnson, National Automobile Chamber of Commerce, to Roy Chapin, 24 July 1930
44 *New York Times* 13 January 1932, 1:5; 16:1; testimony of Victor Schoepperle, vice-president, National City Bank, Senate Finance Committee *Hearings* (1931-2) 1623-81
45 *New York Times* 8 June 1930, 4:1. Howard M. Jefferson, a former official of the Federal Reserve Bank, New York, to Kemmerer, 29 March 1930, EWK MSS, Letter Files: Colombia
46 EWK MSS, Colombia 1930
47 Ibid.; Kemmerer diary, especially entries for 13 and 19 September and 16 October 1930. See also Kemmerer's address 'Currency Stabilization in Latin America' Fourth Pan American Commercial Conference *Proceedings* (Washington, 5-13 October 1931) 1: 24-30.
48 RG 59 821.51A Kemmerer Commission
49 White to Caffery, 27 October 1930, Francis White MSS, RG 59
50 Donald Barnhart 'Colombian Transport and the Reforms of 1931: An Evaluation' HAHR 37 (February 1958): 1-25; *New York Times* 14 December 1930, 5:5
51 *Diario Oficial* 25 September 1931, 23; testimony of Victor Schoepperle before the Senate Finance Committee *Hearings* 12 January 1932, 1623-81. See also Stimson to Caffery, 16 March 1931 *Foreign Relations* 1931, 2: 29-30.
52 Caffery to SS, 17 March 1931, RG 59 821.51/872
53 Ibid.
54 White MSS: Correspondence File. Rublee considered himself 'the real representative for Colombia in the United States.' See the memoir of George Rublee, OHC 262-3.

55 RG 59 821.51/933
56 Caffery to SS, 19 June 1931, RG 59 821.51/980; Stimson to Caffery, 22 June 1931, ibid. /982A; Caffery to William Castle, Jr, 1 July 1931, ibid. /998. There is a full discussion of the transaction in the Stimson diary, volume 16: 14 and 18 May and 1 June 1931. Feis's apprehensions materialized the following spring when Lancaster requested the department to pressure Colombia and Peru on their debts. In the Peruvian case Lancaster suggested American military protection for the Guggenheim interests; Stimson flatly rejected the request (Stimson diary, volume 21: 7 March 1932).
57 EWK MSS, Letter Files: Colombia, Howard M. Jefferson to Kemmerer, 2 January 1932
58 *Diario Oficial* 24 September 1931; Caffery to SS, 2 September 1931, RG 59 821.516/141; Institute of International Finance *Bulletin* no. 53, 8 July 1932 2. Petroleum development did little to assist the Colombian balance of payments. The Central Bank estimated that in 1931 only 20% of the value of petroleum exports returned to Colombia. See a memorandum of the British Treasury Department to the Foreign Office, 5 October 1938, FO 371 A/ 7223/67/11.
59 Caffery to SS, 10 September 1931 and attached note to H. Freeman Matthews, 16 September 1931, RG 59 821.516/143, /144; *New York Times* 16 September 1931, 9:2
60 Stimson to Caffery, 2 October 1931, RG 59 821.51/1100A; Caffery to SS, 4 October 1931, ibid. /1101; Stimson to Caffery, 6 October 1931, ibid. The financial crisis is discussed in Friedman and Schwartz *A Monetary History of the United States* 299-419 and Chandler *American Monetary Policy*.
61 John T. Madden et al. *America's Experience as a Creditor Nation* (New York 1937) 301, 112-13; J.U. Grissinger 'Olaya's Loan Fight: Colombian Presiden Stands Firm to Maintain His Country's Credit' *Barron's* (21 December 1931) 24; Dickson to the Foreign Office, 20 December 1931, FO 371 A/36/18/11; Institute of International Finance *Bulletin* no. 53, 8 July 1932, 13
62 Thomas Lamont to Everard Maynell, 30 July 1931, TWL MSS, series 2, 82-1, Argentina 1928-43.
63 CR 72 Cong., 1 sess. 213-14; U.S. Congress, Senate Finance Committee *Hearings on the Sale of Foreign Bonds in the United States* 72 Cong., 1 sess. 1931-2
64 Hoover *Presidential Press Releases* 27 June 1931
65 *New York Times* 2 January 1932, 1:6; Department of State *Review of Questions of Major Interest in the Relations of the United States with the Latin American Countries 1929-1933*, part 2; Senate Finance Committee *Hearings, passim.* Thomas Lamont's testimony was of primary importance

on the larger question of the status of American securities. His assurances that the American financial houses were solvent and that the amount of German short-term credits held by American banks had been exaggerated received an enthusiastic response from the press and New York Stock Exchange (*Hearings* 18 December 1931; TWL MSS, file 211-4, Senate Finance Committee). For petroleum see chapter 6.

66 White MSS: Barco Concession Folder; Senate Finance Committee *Hearings* 1681 ff; *New York Times* 15 January 1932, 1:5

67 Interview of the author with H. Freeman Matthews, 27 November 1970 in Washington. See also the Stimson diary entries for 9-16 January 1932, volume 20; RG 59 821.51/1579½; Senate Finance Committee *Hearings* part 3, 1700-2000; Department of State *Review of Questions* volume 2; Stimson diary, entry for 12 January 1932, volume 20; *New York Times* 21 January 1932, 15:1; see the editorial 'Colombia and Oil' ibid. 18 January 1932, 14:1. On 21 January 1932 President Olaya published an open letter in the *New York Times* (20:7) denying he had ever discussed the Barco concession with Andrew Mellon and confirming Stimson's testimony. See also George Rublee's letter to *The New Republic* 70 (17 February 1932); 21.

68 Dawson to SS, 16 January 1932, RG 59 821.8363 Barco/622; 27 January 1932, RG 59 711.21/907

69 The then left-wing Liberal and subsequent Colombian president Alberto Lleras Camargo wrote on the arrival of Hamilton Ward, former attorney general of New York, for a bird-hunting holiday on the Sabana of Bogotá: 'You have arrived in time. A few more days and you would have found all the birds of the country plucked by your countrymen' (*El Tiempo* 27 January 1932).

70 See *El Tiempo* and *El Colombiano* 5-15 April 1932; *New York Times* 13 April 1932, 24:2.

71 Guillermo A. Suro 'Financial Measures Taken in Colombia to Meet the Economic Crisis' BPAU 66 (1932): 819. For decree 711 see *Diario Oficial* 23 April 1932, 211.

72 Foreign Bondholders' Protective Council, *Annual Report 1935;* U.S. Securities and Exchange Commission *Report on the Study and Investigation of ... Protective and Re-organization Committees Pursuant to Section 211 of the Securities Exchange Act of 1934* part 5 (Washington, 14 May 1937) 496-9, 587

73 Caffery to SS, 26 July 1932, RG 59 821.516/300. Late in July a prominent group of Colombian businessmen formed a National Executive Committee of Debtors to Foreign Banks. At its first meeting the committee passed a resolution requesting Congress to modify Colombian banking laws to ensure

the primacy of national over foreign financial institutions and urged the retirement of all deposits in foreign banks (RG 151: Reports of commercial attachés, R. Macgowan to SC, 30 July 1932).

74 Macgowan to SC, 30 July 1932; Caffery to SS, 1 August 1932, RG 59 821. 516/303; 1 September 1932, ibid./318; 15 September 1932, ibid./350; E.C. Wilson memorandum, ibid./329. Dever moved easily in Colombian social circles. In 1928 he had married the daughter of Abadía's foreign minister.

75 Bryce Wood *The United States and Latin American Wars, 1932-1942* (New York and London 1966) 169-255

76 Fluharty *Dance of the Millions* 45; *New York Times* 22 September 1932, 8:4

77 *New York Times* 27 November 1932, 29:4; Acting SS to Dawson, 12 June 1933, RG 59 821.51/1658A; *New York Times* 13 November 1933, 10:4; Pan American Union 'Latin American Dollar Debts' *Commercial Pan America* (June 1935)

78 Lamont to Herbert Hoover, 5 May 1927, TWL MSS 149-23. See the table in Tulchin *Aftermath of War* 176 showing the profits of American bankers on Latin American loans, 1920-30.

79 Comments by Garrard Winston, National City Bank, at the 1932 meeting of the Investment Bankers' Association (EWK MSS, Foreign Investments, Foreign Bondholders' File)

CHAPTER 4

1 Robert Lamont to Thomas Lamont, 18 January 1930 and reply of 5 February 1930, TWL MSS 102-20, Baker Library, Harvard

2 By the end of 1935, 85% of Latin American dollar bonds were in default, compared with 52% of European and 3% of Canadian (United Nations, Department of Economic and Social Affairs *Foreign Capital in Latin America* [New York 1955] 3-15). See the table overleaf, adapted from the *New York American*, which shows the relative importance of the Colombian bonds.

3 See the Committee Report of 6 June 1924 to Charles Sabin, chairman of the Foreign Securities Committee, Investment Bankers' Association, TWL MSS 100-12, Investment Bankers Association of America. See also the comments of Garrard Winston to the association, October 1932, EWK MSS, Foreign Investments File, Princeton University.

4 Hull to Franklin Roosevelt, 9 November 1933, Roosevelt MSS, OF 567, Hyde Park, New York

5 U.S. Securities and Exchange Commission *Report on the Study and Investigation of the Work, Activities, Personnel, and Functions of Protective and Reorganization Committees, Part V, Protective Committees and Agencies for*

190 Notes to pages 74-6

Country	Amount issued $000	Approx. outstanding $000	Approx. market value 1931 low $000	% of par
Argentina	420,418	389,414	122,035	31.4
Bolivia	68,653	59,293	4,521	7.7
Brazil	414,130	350,745	63,035	18.1
Chile	296,112	282,935	33,947	12.0
Colombia	170,335	154,385	28,781	18.7
Peru	94,500	90,950	5,152	6.8
Uruguay	67,757	59,490	14,272	21.0
Total	1,531,906	1,396,185	272,743	

Holders of Defaulted Foreign Bonds (Washington 1937) passim. See also
New York Times 10 November 1932, 31:2 and 12 November 1932, 30:1.

6 Press release of the Colombian consul-general in New York *New York Times*
15 November 1932, 33:1; see the report of the American consul in Barranquilla for 14 February 1933, RG 59 821.51/1575; *La Prensa* (Barranquilla)
10 February 1933.

7 Cited in Herbert Feis *The Diplomacy of the Dollar: First Era, 1910-1932*
(Baltimore 1950) 14. Roosevelt had himself been anxious to facilitate
American investment abroad as a way to 'put to sound protective uses a
part of the surplus wealth of our nation.' Witness his involvement (along
with Edwin Kemmerer) in the abortive attempt in the mid-twenties to create
a Federal International Investment Trust (Frank Freidel *Franklin Delano
Roosevelt: The Ordeal* [Boston 1954] 146; Hoover *Memoirs* 3:245). For the
Pecora investigation see U.S. Senate Banking Committee *Stock Exchange
Practices* Senate Report 1455, 73 Cong., 2 sess., 1934.

8 Herbert Feis *1933: Characters in Crisis* (Boston 1966) 268

9 Securities and Exchange Commission *Report* part 5, 62; also Correspondence Files, Foreign Investments, EWK MSS

10 SEC *Report* part 5, 63 and passim

11 Feis *1933* 266

12 Assistant Secretary of State William Phillips memorandum, 17 May 1933,
RG 59 800.51/806

13 William E. Leuchtenburg *Franklin D. Roosevelt and the New Deal* (New
York 1963) 59-60

14 Securities and Exchange Commission *Report* part 5, 71-3

15 Feis *1933* 274; see also his memorandum of 15 March 1933 to Cordell Hull,
RG 59 800.51/788.

16 Owen to Bundy, 6 February 1933 and Bundy to Owen, 21 February 1933, RG 59 821.51/1569
17 Matthews memorandum, 27 April 1933, RG 59 821.51/1653; memorandum, 9 May, ibid/1634; Feis memorandum, 15 March, 1933, ibid./1602
18 Matthews to Edwin C. Wilson, Department of State, 8 June 1933, ibid./1664
19 Francis White wrote to Jefferson Caffery on 11 January 1933 with respect to López: 'I found him very narrow-minded; in fact a small town politician, always looking at some little political advantage and not ... at the problem in a broad, statesmanlike way.' In his reply of 18 January, Caffery agreed. See Francis White MSS: Correspondence, RG 59.
20 William Dawson to Phillips, 19 June 1933 and SS to Dawson, 24 June 1933, RG 59 821.51/1665
21 Stevens to Roosevelt, 28 July 1933; cited in Edgar B. Nixon, ed. *Franklin D. Roosevelt and Foreign Affairs* (Cambridge, Massachusetts 1969) 1: 334-6
22 Ibid. 338
23 Stevens to Roosevelt, 5 August 1933 cited in ibid. 348
24 Roosevelt MSS, OF 4194
25 Nixon, *Roosevelt and Foreign Affairs* 1: 379-80
26 Feis to Hull, 15 September 1933, ibid. 396-7
27 Roosevelt to Steiver, 6 November 1933, ibid. 463. See Parrini *Heir to Empire: United States Economic Diplomacy, 1916-1923* (Pittsburgh 1969) for a discussion of state capitalism in the Wilson and Harding years.
28 Securities and Exchange Commission *Report* 80-5; Nixon *Roosevelt and Foreign Affairs* 1: 404n; *New York Times* 19 December 1933, 3:1
29 *El Tiempo* 28 October 1933; RG 59 821.51/1723; also, RG 151: 640 Colombia
30 Hull to Dawson, 31 October 1933, RG 59 821.51/1722; British commercial secretary, T.J. Anderson, to the Foreign Office, 31 October 1933, FO 371 A/8947/52/11
31 *El Tiempo* had been one of the first advocates of a suspension of payment on the foreign debt: *El Tiempo* 10 and 13 January 1932, 9 March 1934, and 26 October 1933; Colombia *Memoria de Hacienda* (1934) 74; Dawson to SS, 5 November 1933, RG 59 821.51/1728, 11 November 1933, ibid./1734, 13 November 1933, ibid./1735; Dawson to Phillips, 14 November 1933, ibid./ 1736, /1746; *Diario Oficial* 5 December 1933, 521; RG 59 821.51/1744, /1784, /1748
32 U.S. Minister Sheldon Whitehouse to William Phillips, 5 December 1933, RG 59 821.51/1757
33 U.S. Tariff Commission *The Foreign Trade of Latin America* part 2 section 5 *Colombia* (Washington 1940) 13; Institute of International Finance *Bulletin* no. 98 (New York, 7 March 1938) 14; RG 59 821.51/1748, /1857

34 RG 59 821.51/1769
35 Johnson introduced the bill in late 1933 but it was dropped after objections from the State Department. On 11 January 1934 it reappeared on the Senate calendar and was quickly passed. Approval by the House of Representatives followed on 4 April. See U.S. *Congressional Record* 73 Cong., 2 sess., 1934, 441, 6167; Whitney Shepardson and William Scroggs *The United States in World Affairs, 1934-5* (New York and London 1935) 68-100; *New York Times* 25 March 1934, 9:6; Ellis Hawley *The New Deal and the Problem of Monopoly* (New Brunswick, New Jersey 1966).
36 V.L. Fluharty *Dance of the Millions: Military Rule and the Social Revolution in Colombia* (Pittsburgh 1957) 43-66; Miguel Urrutia *The Development of the Colombian Labor Movement* (New Haven and London 1969) passim
37 Eduardo Zuleta Angel *El Presidente López* (Medellín 1960) passim
38 *El Tiempo* 31 May 1928; *Seventh International Conference of American States, Minutes and Antecedents, Ninth Committee* (Montevideo 1933) 90-103; Diego Montaña Cuéllar *Colombia: país formal y país real* (Buenos Aires 1963) 148
39 Sheldon Whitehouse to SS, 19 June 1934, RG 59 821.51/832; BPAU 69 (1935): 860-4. The official American reaction to López is implicit in the contrast between the welcome accorded the president-elect in June 1934 and that accorded Olaya in 1930. In 1934, the White House staff thought it was 'too bad the President should be bothered with this visit in the last few days before his departure' on a cruise (James Dunn to Marvin McIntyre, 15 June 1934, Roosevelt MSS, PPF 313 Colombia).
40 Securities and Exchange Commission *Report* 378-9; Foreign Bondholders' Protective Council *Annual Report 1934* 95; ibid. *1935* 107
41 Spencer R. Dickson (British minister in Bogotá) to R.L. Craigie, 4 December 1934, FO 371 A/10465/34/11; Fluharty *Dance of the Millions* 58
42 T.J. Anderson to Sir Samuel Hoare, 23 July 1935, FO 371 A/6942/162/11; Whitehouse to SS, 3 January 1935, RG 59 821.51/1879
43 Landis to Cordell Hull, 15 October 1935, RG 59 821.51/1942; E.C. Wilson memorandum, 12 October 1935, ibid./1945; Laurence Duggan memorandum, 22 November 1935, ibid./823; W. Phillips diary, 11 and 17 April 1935, volume 7
44 For a State Department summary of the investigation see RG 59 821.51/2013, memorandum dated 1 May 1936; William Dawson to SS, 28 December 1935, ibid./1967; for the Colombian reaction see *El Tiempo* 28 December 1935.
45 Securities and Exchange Commission *Report* 583 ff; Department of State memorandum, RG 59 821.51/2082 to /2090; *El Tiempo* 4, 5, and 6 March 1937

46 Feis *1933* 267; Duggan memorandum, 14 August 1936, RG 59 821.51/2037; Dawson to SS, 25 October 1936, ibid./2046
47 Cordell Hull to Harold Dodds, president of Yale University, 10 February 1937, RG 59 821.51/2075A
48 Dawson to SS, 17 May 1937, ibid./2113
49 Ibid./2137, /2140; *El Tiempo* 13 and 21 September 1937; Fluharty *Dance of the Millions* 58-61
50 Lleras's comment is cited in the Institute of International Finance *Bulletin* no. 98 (New York, 7 March 1938) 3. See also Braden to SS, 18 May 1939, RG 59 821.51/2320, /2141
51 RG 59 821.51/2178. For an excellent analysis of the Colombian economy see the report prepared by James Wright, third secretary of the American legation, ibid./2190.
52 David Bushnell *Eduardo Santos and the Good Neighbor, 1938-42* (Gainesville 1967) 77-8
53 Roosevelt MSS, OF 212. Morgenthau took a similar position with respect to the Mexican expropriation of foreign petroleum property. See David Green *The Containment of Latin America* (Chicago 1971) 31.
54 Roosevelt MSS, PSF Welles; see Welles to Roosevelt, 20 November 1939
55 Henry Morgenthau Jr diaries, volume 187: 324, FDR Library
56 FO 371 A/8841/67/11
57 Bushnell *Eduardo Santos* 72
58 Welles to Roosevelt, 20 November 1939, Roosevelt MSS, PSF II, Department Correspondence, State Department; Morgenthau diaries, volume 224: 185-7; see also Hanes memorandum, 27 November 1939, Morgenthau diaries, volume 224:304.
59 Morgenthau diaries, volume 226: 410. See also Joseph P. Cotton Jr's memorandum to Morgenthau, 16 December 1939, diaries, volume 230: 19-29.
60 Gabriel Turbay, Colombian ambassador to the United States, to Morgenthau, 6 February 1940 *Foreign Relations* 1940, 5: 695-6, 702, 708-18; D.W. Bell, under secretary of the Treasury, memorandum, 6 July 1940, Morgenthau diaries, volume 280: 67-70
61 *Foreign Relations* 1940, 5: 708-18
62 Morgenthau diaries, volume 343: 282 ff. There is a very good summary of the negotiations in J.M. Blum *From the Morgenthau Diaries* 1: *Years of Urgency, 1938-1940* (Boston 1965): 55-8.

CHAPTER 5

1 Inter-American High Commission *Colombia: Financial and Economic Conditions* (Washington, October 1921) I-17, box 1052, RG 43. See Joseph Tulchin

The Aftermath of War (New York 1971) and the reports of the military attaché, RG 165, 2655-M-112/1-15 for the strategic implication of petroleum.

2 On the Mexican situation see E. David Cronon *Josephus Daniels in Mexico* (Madison, Wisconsin 1960); David Green *The Containment of Latin America* (Chicago 1971); Eugene P. Trani 'The Harding Administration and Recognition of Mexico' *Ohio History* 75 (Spring-Summer 1966): 137-48; Robert F. Smith *The United States and Revolutionary Nationalism in Mexico, 1916-1932* (Chicago 1972).

3 The Andian National Corporation was formed in 1919 by James W. Flanagan, Jersey Standard's representative in Colombia. To strengthen the 'Canadian' image of the company several prominent Canadians, among them Sir Herbert Holt, president of the Royal Bank of Canada, were nominated to the Board of Directors. Flanagan himself retained control and in 1925 was elected to the presidency. Although the company was ostensibly Canadian it was controlled by the International Petroleum Company through Cordillera Investments, a wholly owned subsidiary of IPC. See Harvey O'Connor *World Crisis in Oil* (New York 1962), 233-44; George Gibb and Evelyn Knowlton *A History of Standard Oil: The Resurgent Years, 1911-1927* (New York 1956) 359-409; H.M. Larson et al. *New Horizons, 1927-1950* (New York 1971), 113-17.

4 For a description of Tropical's early history, see Gibb and Knowlton *History of Standard Oil; Fortune* 22 (January 1941): 72 ff; Alfonso Ordóñez *Historical Resumé of the Tropical Oil Company's Concession* (1928) contained in the records of ESSO Inter-America, Inc., Coral Gables, Florida

5 Department of State memorandum, 12 September 1928, RG 59 821.6363 Barco/200½. In 1936 the Texas Corporation purchased the South American Gulf Oil Company from Mellon interests and transferred one-half of the stock to the Socony-Vacuum Oil Co., Inc. (ibid. Barco/660).

6 Department of State 'Review of Questions of Major Interest in the Relations of the United States with the Latin American Countries, 1933.' Mr Matthews repeated this assertion in an interview with the author on 27 November 1970.

7 Diego Montaña Cuéllar *Colombia: país formal y país real* (Buenos Aires 1963) 114 ff. See also BPAU 49 (July-December 1919): 325.

8 Cf Adelberto Pinelo *The Multinational Corporation as a Force in Latin American Politics: A Case Study of IPC in Peru* (New York 1973).

9 RG 59 821.6363/322. The term *nationalism* appears more appropriate than particularism here because it conveys the fact that Montalvo's appeal was broad rather than sectarian and regional.

10 *Foreign Relations* 1928, 2: 588-603; *Diario Oficial* 28 January 1928

11 J. Fred Rippy *The Capitalists and Colombia* (New York 1931) 140; British Record Office, FO 371 A/7483/143/11

12 Interviews with ESSO Inter-America officials L.P. Maier, 23 March 1971 and Lionel Charlesworth, 22 March 1971
13 For a discussion of these negotiations see Edmund Monson, British Minister, to the Foreign Office, 29 March 1928, FO 371 A/3003/143/11
14 Kellogg to Samuel Piles, 29 June 1927, RG 59 821.6363/310, /339, /348
15 Piles to SS, 10 December 1927, ibid. /352
16 FO 371 A/3003/143/11. The fact that in 1927 the net production for Tropical's fields was the highest of all Jersey's foreign operations is an indication of the relative importance of Colombia to Standard Oil at this time. See Gibb and Knowlton *History of Standard Oil*, 373-4.
17 Edmund Monson to the Foreign Office, 29 March 1928, FO 371 A/3003/ 143/11. See also Samuel Piles to SS, 17 August 1928, RG 59 821.6363/322.
18 The main spokesman for the Gulf interests at this juncture was Francis B. Loomis, who had been Theodore Roosevelt's assistant secretary of state at the time of the Panama Revolution. Kellogg to Piles, 12 January 1928, RG 59 821.6363 Barco/65; ibid./359A; *Foreign Relations* 1928, 2: 588-9.
19 *Foreign Relations* 1928, 2: 588-9 (emphasis added); for the Dulles visit see RG 59 821.6363 Barco/72.
20 1 February 1928; see also the interview with Montalvo, 24 February 1928.
21 3 March 1928. There was some speculation at the time that the Abadía government moved toward a more nationalistic stand on the petroleum question at that juncture partly to broaden its political appeal. Were this the intention, the *Claridad* position early in 1928 would indicate that the ploy was at least momentarily successful. See *New York Times* 4 March 1928, 22:2.
22 *El Debate* 21 February 1928 and Samuel Piles to SS, 15 August 1928, RG 59 821.6363/458
23 *Foreign Relations* 1928, 2: 613-14
24 Ibid. 593
25 Ibid. 594
26 Piles to SS, 19 May 1928, *Foreign Relations* 1928, 2:594
27 *Foreign Relations* 1928, 2: 595
28 Interview with H. Freeman Matthews, November 1970
29 Stabler's correspondence with the Department of State and some of his communications with the Gulf Oil Company may be found in the Francis White MSS: Official Correspondence Files, RG 59.
30 Piles to SS, 15 August 1928, RG 59 821.6363/458; *Foreign Relations* 1928, 2: 596; FO 371 A/7483/143/11. For press comments on Montalvo see editorials in *El Tiempo* 11 July 1928, and *Universidad*, a left-wing journal edited by Germán Arciniegas, 21 July 1928.
31 W.B. Heroy to the Bureau of Foreign and Domestic Commerce, 5 July 1928; bureau memorandum, 11 July 1928, RG 59 821.6363/422

32 Acting secretary of state, William Castle Jr to Piles, 3 July 1928, RG 59
821.6363 Barco/105; Piles to SS, 5 July 1928, ibid. Barco/106. For the
public reaction to Stabler's mission see the editorials in *El Tiempo* 30 June
1928 and *El Espectador* 29 June 1928. Carlos Uribe's protests that he had
no knowledge of Stabler's intentions are in *Anales del Senado* 13 August
1928. For Stabler's personal account of his Colombian reception see his
memorandum dated 15 July 1928, RG 59 821.6363 Barco/152.

33 RG 59 821.6363 Barco/116

34 SS to the American legation, 27 July 1928, ibid/119

35 *Diario Oficial* 17 August 1928, 396 ff. See also *El Tiempo* 5 August 1928,
which praised the government for its stand.

36 Piles to SS, 5 August 1928 *Foreign Relations* 1928, 2: 623-4; FO 371 A 7331/
2073/11, 27 September 1928

37 The left-wing journal *Universidad* urged on 18 August that the nation had to
honor its contractual obligations while exercising caution in negotiating with
foreign companies.

38 22 August 1928; see *El Espectador* for the same day and RG 59 821.6363/
450.

39 H. Freeman Matthews to Francis White, 5 May 1930, RG 59 821.6363
Tropical Oil/14

40 *Foreign Relations* 1928, 2: 596-7

41 For a discussion of the Committee reports see *El Tiempo* and *El Espectador*
for 1 October 1928; *Foreign Relations* 1928, 2: 597-602; Jefferson Caffery,
American minister in Bogotá, to SS, 16 December 1928, RG 59 821.6363/
554; Matthews's memorandum to White, 5 May 1930, note 39 above; memorandum by Thomas W. Palmer, Tropical Oil, 4 November 1928, Tropical
Oil Company Contract, File no. 1-2, records of ESSO Inter-America, Inc.

42 This summary is based on minutes prepared by the British Foreign Office,
15 November 1928, FO 371 A/7483/143/11.

43 See Wilson's letter dated 24 September 1928 to the director of Anglo-Persian
in FO 371 A/7326/143/11.

44 Ibid.

45 Matthews to SS, 21 September 1928, RG 59 821.6363 Barco/170; Edmund
Monson to the Foreign Office, 27 September 1928, FO 371 A/7331/2073/11;
New York Times 23 September 1928, 18:4

46 See *Anales de la Cámara de Representantes, suplemente* 15 May 1929; FO
371 A/7331/2073/11; the *El Tiempo* article was headlined 'The Intervention
of the White House on Behalf of the Barco Concession.'

47 RG 59 821.6363 Barco/172; Grant Smith to SS, 24 September 1928, ibid.

48 Matthews to SS, 25 September 1928, ibid. Barco/182

49 Ibid. Barco/185. For the views of Francis White and Jefferson Caffery, Piles's replacement in Bogotá, see ibid. Barco/188. Matthews's view was shared by the British minister. See FO 371 A/7331/11.

50 See above, chapter 3.

51 Tropical Oil Company Contract, File no. 1-2, records of ESSO Inter-America, Inc.

52 Department of State *Register* (Washington 1936) 42; Daniels to Hull, 10 July 1934, box 750, Daniels Papers, Library of Congress. For a more favorable view of Caffery in his Cuban period, see S.M. Sternbach, a New York businessman, to Roosevelt, 22 May 1936, Roosevelt MSS, Official File 884, FDR Library, Hyde Park.

53 Heroy to SS, RG 59 821.6363/538

54 The director of Anglo-Persian to the British under-secretary of state, 4 January 1929, FO 371 A/167/167/11

55 On the Mexican connection see the editorial in the Conservative *El Diario Nacional* 14 November 1928 entitled 'The Politics of Petroleum.' See also Heroy to SS, 2 November 1928, RG 59 821.6363/563, and despatches of 15 April, 1929, ibid./606; 25 April, ibid./611; 28 September, ibid./723.

56 Colombia *Boletín de Minas y Petróleos* April 1929, 1, no. 4

57 See, for example, *El Tiempo* 30 May 1929 'The Case of Mr. Foster Bain.' For Bain's views see *Boletín de Minas* May 1929, 1, no. 5.

58 See R. Ogarrio to Samuel Haskell, both of the Texas company, 10 September 1929, RG 59 821.6363/722; Caffery to SS, 30 August 1929, ibid./701; 28 May 1929, ibid./643. For the American legislation see Harold F. Williamson et al. *The American Petroleum Industry: The Age of Energy 1899-1959* (Evanston 1963) 38.

59 Monson to the Foreign Office, 10 August 1929, FO 371 A/5931/167/11

60 The best summary of the legislation is contained in a Foreign Office memorandum dated 19 September 1929, FO 371 A/5931/167/11. See also a memorandum prepared by the Richmond Petroleum Co. dated 28 August 1929 in RG 59 821.6363/731.

61 *New York Times* 11 October 1929, 7:5, 5 September 1929, 34:4

62 Caffery to SS, 19 November 1929, RG 59 821.6363/762 and 17 April 1929, ibid. Barco/245

63 *New York Times* 18 November 1929, 5:1

64 See Matthews to SS, 27 October 1928, RG 59 821.6363 Barco/219; Caffery to SS, 12 March 1930, ibid. Barco/268 and 13 March 1930, ibid. Barco/269.

65 *New York Times* 14 April 1930, 14:2

66 RG 59 821.6363 AN2/15. *El Espectador* strongly disagreed with the contention of foreign oil representatives that the laws were unworkable; see the

editorial on 11 March 1930. Montalvo pointed to the contract with the Unión
Colombiana de Petróleos as evidence of the viability of the legislation. See his
comments in Ministerio de Industrias y Trabajo *Memoria* (Bogotá 1930) 41
67 H. Freeman Matthews memorandum to Francis White, 16 May 1930, RG 59
821.6363 Barco/278; also ibid. Barco/277. For the developments on the
Barco case, which had been referred to the Colombian courts, see Caffery to
SS, 12 December 1928, ibid. Barco/229, 17 April 1929, ibid. Barco/245.
Although it is beyond the focus of this chapter, Andrew Mellon's alleged
relationship with Olaya during the Barco negotiations was one of the pieces
of evidence introduced against him in 1932 before the House Judiciary
Committee. Hoover, of course, shortly removed Mellon from his treasury
post and appointed him Ambassador to the Court of St James. See *New
York Times* 15 January 1932, 2:1.
68 Matthews memorandum to White, 3 June 1930, RG 59 821.6363 Barco/279
69 Ibid. AN 2/24; 821.6363 Tropical Oil/9, /13. Because of his significant involvement in Colombian petroleum, Metzger deserves some comment. A
highly cultured and talented man, Metzger is still considered by many of his
associates to be 'the best man ever associated with the company.' During his
years in Colombia in the late twenties and early thirties he demonstrated a
keen awareness of the problems of foreign enterprise in the country, considerable facility to function within Colombian society, and a willingness to
operate with respect for the sensitivities of that society (interview with
J.K. Oldfield, 24 March 1971, Coral Gables, Florida).
70 Memoir of George Rublee, OHC 229 (hereafter cited as Rublee memoir)
71 Francis White to Rublee, 23 May 1930, RG 59 821.6363/848a; White to
Caffery, 1 August 1930, White MSS: Correspondence File; Rublee memoir,
OHC 245
72 RG 59 821.6363 Barco/282; Caffery to SS, 10 September 1930, ibid. Barco/
398
73 Caffery to SS, 17 September 1930, ibid. Barco/399; 14 October 1930, ibid.
Barco/404; 22 September 1930, ibid./901; *Foreign Relations* 1931, 2: 3-5.
74 RG 59 821.6363/916
75 Rublee later commented: 'I was going to advise a government in regard to
matters I knew nothing about' (Rublee memoir, OHC 246). For Colombian
reservations see the magazine *Cromos* 1 November 1930 and *La Nación*
17 December 1930.
76 Caffery to SS, 11 November 1930, RG 59 821.6363/964; *Foreign Relations*
1931, 2: 8
77 Félix Mendoza and Benjamín Alvarado *La industria del petróleo en Colombia*
(Bogotá 1939) 77-87; BPAU 65 (1931): 642-3

78 See the memorandum of the British Commercial Secretary in Bogotá, 31 December 1930, FO 371 A/981/65/11; Rublee memoir, OHC 251-2; author's interview with E.J. Reeves, ESSO Inter-America, 22 March 1971, *New York Times* 16 February 1931, 31:4; *Foreign Relations* 1931, 2: 11-13
79 *Foreign Relations* 1931, 2: 11-13
80 Memorandum of 31 December 1930, FO 371 A/981/65/11. A good case could also be made for the petroleum companies' objections to both Bain and Rublee for their isolation from field operating conditions in Colombia, and this was especially true of Rublee. A retired president of the Andian National Corporation and the International Petroleum Company, L.P. Maier, informed the author in an interview on 23 March 1971 that the companies had been unsuccessful in their efforts to have Rublee consider local conditions.
81 Caffery to SS, 4 November 1930, RG 59 821.6363 Barco/407; letter of 8 January 1931 from American Maracaibo to Stimson, ibid. Barco/413; Matthews to White, 12 January 1931, ibid. Barco/416; *Foreign Relations* 1931, 2: 18-19; Rublee memoir, OHC 254
82 *Foreign Relations* 1931, 2: 19-20; RG 59 821.6363 Barco/429, /430
83 *Foreign Relations* 1931, 2: 20-1
84 Ibid. 21-2
85 Caffery to SS, 14 March 1931, RG 59 821.6363 Barco/477
86 *Foreign Relations* 1931, 2: 25. On 5 March, Stimson cabled 'heartiest congratulations' to the American minister and Rublee. See RG 59 821.6363 Barco/464; Caffery to SS, 20 March 1931, ibid. Barco/482. Also see the memorandum on the Barco Concession in the records of ESSO Inter-America, 30 May 1935, file no. 1-1.
87 Caffery to SS, 13 March 1931, RG 59 821.6363 Barco/476; *New York Times* 1 March 1931, 32:2. For the contract itself see Colombia, Congreso *Anales del Senado* 11 March 1931 and *Anales de la Cámara de Representantes* no. 259 and no. 260, 11 May 1931, 2017-23; Ministerio de Industrias y Trabajo *Contrato Chaux-Folsom y documentos relacionados con esta negociación* (Bogotá 1931). Stimson was sufficiently pleased with Rublee's work in Colombia and Mexico that on the death of Jospeh Cotton in February he considered Rublee for a departmental appointment. Senator Reed of Pennsylvania successfully pressed for the appointment of William R. Castle Jr as under secretary of state (Rublee memoir, OHC 256-7). Stimson also believed that Rublee had 'serious limitations' for an assistant secretary. See his letter of 11 February 1931 to Felix Frankfurter (Stimson MSS, box 107).
88 Ricardo Rendón, one of Bogotá's leading cartoonists, portrayed Olaya as the frontier medicine man attempting to 'sell' the Catatumbo contract as the

instant tonic for Colombian financial ills. See *El Tiempo* 10 April 1931; *New York Times* 17 June 1931, 16:6.

89 See the following articles and editorials in *El Tiempo*: 12 March 1930 'All Guarantees Are Contained in the Contract with Gulf Oil'; 21 March 1931, an unfavorable article by the former consul in New York, Carlos Arbeláez Urdaneta; 28 March 1931 'Catatumbo Petroleum and Nationalist Politics'; 9 April 1931; 24 June 1931.

90 *El Espectador* 6 May, 10 June, and 5 August 1931; *Mundo al Día* 17 June 1931

91 See editorial of 7 February 1929 for *El Nuevo Tiempo*'s earlier attitude. The reference to the relationship between the paper's editorial position and Olaya's use of patronage is from RG 59 821.6363 Barco/492. See also *New York Times* 29 July 1931, 9:4.

92 *La Defensa* 13 April 1931 'The Nation in Peril'; 20 April 1931 'The Obedient Congress'

93 RG 59 821.6363 Barco/480; Caffery to SS, 28 March 1931, ibid. Barco/489

94 Caffery to SS, 30 March 1931, ibid. Barco/490; Caffery to SS, 30 March 1931, ibid. Barco/502; 2 April 1931, ibid. Barco/503; *El Nuevo Tiempo* 23 May 1931. One of the most active senators in his opposition to the Chaux-Folsom contract was Aníbal Cardoso Gaitán; Cardoso had been the principal attorney for the Department of Mines and Petroleum in the Ministry of Industries from 1927 until 1931, when he resigned to run for office. Cardoso was an excellent example of the type of 'patriot of deep convictions' who advocated greater national control over the industry. See *El Tiempo* 29 June 1931; Caffery to SS, 1 July 1931, RG 59 821.6363 Barco/608. The reference to Cardoso's patriotism is Caffery's.

95 RG 59 821.6363 Barco/592, /605; *New York Times* 17 June 1931, 16:6; *Anales de la Cámara de Representantes* 4 July 1931, no. 311, 2435 for law 80 of 1931

96 Chaux's comment is related by Caffery in a dispatch of 19 September 1932, RG 59 821.6363 Barco/643; for a brief discussion of Gulf's relations with the government later in the decade see David Bushnell *Eduardo Santos and the Good Neighbor, 1938-1942* (Gainesville 1967) 96-9.

97 RG 59 821.6363 Barco/510; Caffery to SS, 2 June 1931, ibid. Barco/587

98 See Raymond Vernon *Sovereignty at Bay: The Multinational Spread of U.S. Enterprises* (New York 1971).

99 See Edward A. Shaffer *The Oil Import Program of the United States* (New York 1968) 4-12. Mark Requa's statement can be found in the U.S. Fuel Administration *Final Report* (Washington 1921) 272. There is a copy of the 1929 report of the Federal Oil Conservation Board in the Hoover MSS, Presidential File, Subject File: Oil Matters 1929.

100 Gerald Nash *United States Oil Policy* (Pittsburgh 1968) 98-112
101 Ibid. 106. For the efforts to pass legislation in 1930 and 1931 see CR 71
Cong., 2 sess. (22 March 1930) 5946; 71 Cong., 3 sess., (21 January, 30
January 1931) 2861, 3567. Wilbur expressed his opposition to a tariff in an
address of 16 January 1931 to the Governors' Conference on Oil. See Hoover
MSS, Presidential File, Subject File: Oil Matters 1929, Federal Oil Conservation Board. For the extent of the industry's pressure on Hoover see the tele-
grams from the independent producers in the Hoover MSS, Oil Matters 1929,
A folder.
102 Wilbur to Hiram Johnson, Hoover MSS, Presidential File, Subject File: Oil
Matters 1932-3. For the tariff bill see CR 72 Cong., 1 sess. (10 and 25
February, 14 and 25 March, 1932) 3721, 4731-4, 6044, 6825.
103 28 January 1931, Federal Oil Conservation Board File, Wilbur MSS
104 See Requa to C.J. Wrightsman, president of Wrightsman Petroleum Co.,
21 November 1931, Hoover MSS, Presidential File, Official File 496 Mark
Requa.
105 This letter is dated 3 December 1931, ibid.; see also F. Feiker, BFDC, to
Wilbur, 13 January 1932, Wilbur MSS, 1-D/223, Oil Tariff Folder
106 Herbert Hoover 3: 429 ff
107 Shaffer *Oil Import Program* 9; Nash *United States Oil Policy* 128-57; there
is an excellent account of the oil problems of the Roosevelt administration
in Harold Ickes *The Secret Diary of Harold L. Ickes: The First Thousand
Days 1933-1936* (New York 1953) *passim.* See also Herbert Feis *Petroleum
and American Foreign Policy* (Palo Alto, California 1944) 17.
108 Caffery to SS, 17 March 1931, RG 59 821.6363 Barco/484. The Colombian
chargé in Washington, José M. Coronado, called on Stimson to discuss the
effects of a U.S. petroleum embargo on the Colombian economy. Coronado
pointed out that any reduction in Colombia's revenues would seriously
hamper her ability to meet foreign obligations (Stimson MSS, Memorandum
of Conversations part 2, dated 19 February 1931, box 497).
109 Caffery to SS, 15 April 1931, RG 59 821.6363 Tropical Oil/47
110 Stimson to Caffery, 19 June 1931, ibid. Tropical Oil/51
111 Caffery to SS, 23 July 1932, RG 59 611.213/3
112 Ministerio de Industrias *Memoria* (Bogotá 1935) 309
113 Caffery to SS, 20 March 1933, RG 59 821.6363 Tropical Oil/105; *El Espectador* 10 and 16 August 1933; *El Tiempo* 12 November 1933; *Anales de la
Cámara de Representantes* 16 November 1933; *El Tiempo* 14 November
1933
114 Whitehouse to SS, 24 April 1934, RG 59 821.6363 Tropical Oil/115. On
8 June, Sumner Welles instructed the American ambassador in London to

observe the activities of the Colombian mission to seek financing in Europe (ibid. Tropical Oil/117).

115 *Annual Report* of the British legation for 1936, dated 18 January 1937, FO 371; see also Whitehouse to SS, 17 May 1934, RG 59 821.6363 Tropical Oil/116.

116 *New York Times* 23 June 1934, 20:2

117 *El Tiempo* 10 September 1934. See also the report of British Foreign Office official Spencer R. Dickson to Sir John Simon, Foreign Office, 20 September 1934, FO 371 A/7500/5930/11.

118 RG 59 821.6363 Tropical Oil/119

119 Washington to SS, 10 December 1934, ibid. Tropical/120

120 RG 59 821.51/1862

121 Washington to SS, 8 April 1935, RG 59 821.6363 Tropical/121

122 Ibid.; Washington to SS, 12 April 1935, ibid. Tropical Oil/122

123 Washington to SS, 26 April 1935, ibid. AN2/88

124 The American minister, William Dawson, to SS, 21 November 1935, ibid. Tropical Oil/127

125 See *El Tiempo* 17 January 1936 for the membership of the committee. For the committee's report see ibid. 19 January 1936; *Anales de la Cámara de Representantes* no. 148, 24 January 1936; Dawson to SS, 26 January 1936, RG 59 821.6363 AN2/91.

126 *El Tiempo* 29 January 1936

127 M. Paske-Smith to the Foreign Office, 17 August 1936, FO 371 A/7014/1081/11. For the original outline of the bill see the *Exposición de motivos* published in *El Tiempo* 28 August 1936. See also Paske-Smith to the Foreign Office, 9 December 1935, FO 371 A/10160/1081/11.

128 Paske-Smith to the Foreign Office, 9 December 1935, FO 371 A/10160/1081/11.

129 This summary is based largely on an analysis of law 160 by W.W. Waring of Tropical Oil, February 1937, Petroleum Legislation binder, records of ESSO Inter-America, Inc. See also Paske-Smith, 9 December 1935. FO 371 A/10160/1081/11; Colombia *Leyes de 1936* (2nd ed., Bogotá 1950) 389-99.

130 Mendoza and Alvarado *La industria del petróleo en Colombia* 206-7

131 Memorandum by Eduardo Esguerra Seranno, Petroleum Legislation binder, records of ESSO Inter-America, Inc. Author's interview of 23 March 1971 with L.P. Maier (in 1936 vice-president of Andian National Corporation). Petroleum Legislation binder, records of ESSO Inter-America, Inc.

132 Duggan memorandum, 29 December 1937, RG 59 821.6363 Barco/671; Austin T. Foster to Cordell Hull, 4 January 1938, ibid. Barco/670

133 William Dawson to SS, 18 January and 19 October 1937, ibid./1246, /1253

134 Memorandum of 21 July 1942, O.C. Wheeler, geological department of the International Petroleum Company, records of ESSO Inter-America, Inc.

135 See RG 59 821.6363/1290. For a more complete analysis of the Mexican situation see: Cronon *Josephus Daniels in Mexico*; Bryce Wood *The Making of the Good Neighbor Policy* (New York 1961) 203-59. The Only American company not nationalized by Mexico in 1938 was Gulf Oil.

136 The best treatment of the Santos period is Bushnell *Eduardo Santos*, but Spruille Braden *Diplomats and Demagogues* (New Rochelle, New York 1971) is enlightening.

137 For a comparative view see Karl Gabriel 'The Gains to the Local Economy From the Foreign-Owned Primary Export Industry: The Case of Oil in Venezuela' (PHD dissertation, Harvard Graduate School of Business Administration 1967).

138 Vernon *Sovereignty at Bay* 173 ff

139 Colombia, Ministerio de Hacienda y Crédito Público *Memoria* (1930) 12-13; EWK MSS, Colombia 1930, Report on Departmental Revenues. In 1929 the national government paid 45% of its Tropical Oil royalty to the Department of Santander (RG 165, 2655-M-111/1).

140 Bank for International Settlements *Ninth Annual Report* (Basle 1939) 35

141 Colombia, Departmento Administrativa Nacional de Estadística *Anuario* (1938) 44; Larson *New Horizons* 819, 375 ff

142 Military Attaché Report, 1929, RG 165, 265-M-111/1

CHAPTER 6

1 Note for example *El Espectador*'s editorial of 27 May 1926 attacking the United Fruit monopoly. See also chargé Jefferson Patterson to SS, 2 June 1926, RG 59 821.6156/46

2 Shortly after he assumed office President Hoover urged representatives of the American Federation of Labor to take an active interest in Latin American unions. 'I have the impression,' he wrote Peter J. Brady, a New York labor official, 'that something useful might be accomplished if the American Federation of Labor would attempt to stimulate the organization of the conservative forces of labor in those areas' (Hoover to Brady, 11 June 1929, Hoover MSS, Foreign Affairs: General Subjects, Latin American Republics 1929). See as well the work of Ronald Radosh *American Labor and United States Foreign Policy* (Toronto 1969) 348-71.

3 The early history of the United Fruit Company in Colombia is told lucidly in Charles Kepner and Jay Soothill *The Banana Empire* (New York 1935) and *Social Aspects of the Banana Industry* (New York 1936). See also

Stacy May and Galo Plaza *The United Fruit Company in Latin America* (New York 1958).

4 Colombia *Revista de Industrias* (January 1929) 240. In 1955 the company owned or controlled 18% of Colombian banana acreage (May and Plaza *The United Fruit Company* 175).

5 Lawrence Cotie, vice-consul at Santa Marta, to SS, 19 January 1928, RG 59 821.00/630. See also Cotie's comments on United Fruit's relationship with Colombian politicians, 12 April 1928, RG 59 821.6165/60.

6 George H. Faust 'Economic Relations of the United States and Colombia, 1920-1940' (PHD dissertation, University of Chicago 1946) 22

7 *Diario Oficial* 1 July 1931. The most thorough treatment of Colombian labor is Miguel Urrutia *The Development of the Colombian Labor Movement* (New Haven and London 1969). I am particularly grateful for Dr Urrutia's assistance. See also Robert J. Alexander *Organized Labor in Latin America* (New York 1965); Victor Alba *Politics and the Labor Movement in Latin America* (Stanford 1968).

8 Alexander *Organized Labor* 132-4; Urrutia *Colombian Labor Movement* 69-83

9 Alexander *Organized Labor* 245-6; Urrutia *Colombian Labor Movement* 101-6

10 Law 21 of 1920 provided for compulsory collective bargaining, but it stipulated that, in addition to being Colombian citizens, workers' representatives had to have been in the employ of the company for a minimum period of six months (Kepner *Social Aspects of the Banana Industry* 181-9).

11 RG 59 821.504/24. The American military attaché viewed the strike as an isolated incident, not a communist offensive (report of 21 January 1929, RG 165, 2657-M-214/3).

12 Kepner *Banana Empire* 326; Urrutia *Colombian Labor Movement*, 105-6. Other strike leaders were Raúl Eduardo Mahecha (also active in the oil fields), Tomás Uribe Márquez, José G. Russo, Manuel López Camargo, José F. Lozano, and José Montenegro. The military attaché portrayed Mahecha as an unprincipled opportunist (RG 165, 2657-M-214½).

13 RG 59 821.504/25. The best press coverage of these events is in *El Diario Nacional*, a left-wing Liberal-Socialist daily of Bogotá (15 and 22 November 1928); also see *Vanguardia Obrera* 10 November 1928.

14 Ministro de Industrias 'Informe rendido ... sobre el movimiento obrero ocurrido en el Departamento del Magdalena' *Memoria de 1928-1929* 172-209

15 Caffery to SS, 3 December 1928, RG 59 821.5045/36

16 FO 371, E. Monson to the Foreign Office, 17 December 1928, despatch no. 122; *New York Times* 6 December 1928, 1:4; Kepner *Banana Empire* 327

17 Caffery to SS, 27 December 1928, RG 59 821.00GC/9

18 Kepner *Banana Empire* 328; Caffery to SS, 11 December 1928, RG 59 821.5045/40

19 Kepner *Banana Empire* 328; RG 84: Santa Marta, 850.4; RG 59 821.5045/34, /35. On 13 December Howard F. Diehl became vice-consul in charge of the Santa Marta office.

20 Caffery to SS, 5 December 1928, RG 59 821.5045/24

21 Monson to the Foreign Office, 17 December 1928. See also Urrutia *Colombian Labor Movement* 105-6. Contemporary accounts should be used with extreme caution: Alberto Castrillón *120 Día bajo el terror militar; o la huelga en las bananeras* (Bogotá 1929); Carlos Cortés Vargas *Los sucesos de la bananeras* (Bogotá 1929); *New York Times* 6 December 1928, 1:4. See also Howard F. Diehl to SS, 4 April 1929, RG 59 821.5045/58.

22 See also *El Diario Nacional* 24 December 1928. The *New York Times* referred to Cotie's request for intervention on 6 December 1928 (2:2), but it was not until 24 December that the Colombian press printed the news, and then it was reported to have originated with the Cuban press RG 59 821. 5045/48).

23 There is a perceptive sketch of Gaitán in Urrutia *Colombian Labor Movement* 106-9. See also J. Fred Rippy *The Capitalists and Colombia* (New York 1931) 187; Antonio García *Gaitán y el problema de la Revolución Colombiana* (Bogotá 1955) 256-7.

24 Caffery to SS, 2 September 1929, RG 59 821.00 Amnesty; ibid./678; *El Espectador* 17, 20, 23, and 25 July 1929, 4 and 5 September 1929

25 Urrutia *Colombian Labor Movement* 105-9; *El Espectador* 19 July 1929, 5 and 7 September 1929

26 *New York Times* 30 October 1929, 14:3, 15 November 1929, 10:5; *Gaitán* (Bogotá, 1968) 39; RG 59 821.5045/106

27 Kepner *Social Aspects of the Banana Industry* 192 *Banana Empire* 312

28 Lawrence Cotie to SS, 9 March 1928 and 21 August 1928, RG 59 821.6156/ 63; Kepner *Banana Empire* 70; May and Plaza *United Fruit* 17

29 Kepner *Banana Empire* 287-93

30 *El Tiempo* 18 June 1930; *El Espectador* 17 June 1930. See Calderón's interview in *El Espectador* 15 June 1930. The American vice-consul in Santa Marta, Benjamin Muse, thought Bradshaw was mistaken in his assessment of the minister of industry's actions; (RG 59 821.6156/78).

31 Ministro de Industrias *Memoria* 1931 2: 212-18; Kepner *Banana Empire* 288-9. See Bradshaw's exchange with Chaux in Ministro de Industrias *Memoria* 1931, 2: 218. Caffery commented on 10 September: 'I am not at all sure Mr. Bradshaw knows how to adopt a conciliatory attitude when Colombians are concerned' (RG 59 821.6156/87, /92).

32 RG 59 821.6156/83. See also Matthews' memorandum of 29 July 1930, ibid. /79.
33 Also see *El Nuevo Tiempo* 14 September 1930; RG 59 821.5045/27.
34 The British minister in Bogotá analyzed the dispute in reports of 2 and 13 October 1930 (FO 371 A/7138/761/11). For the favorable press reaction to the Colombian government's attempted mediation, see *Mundo al Día* 16 September 1930: *El Espectador* 16 September 1930; *El Tiempo* 17 September 1930. See also RG 59 821.6156/86; Caffery to SS, 27 September 1930, ibid./103; ibid./100; *El Espectador* 23 September 1930; *El Tiempo* 28 September 1930.
35 Caffery to SS, 27 September 1930, RG 59 821.6156/103, /111
36 ibid./107, /109. For the dissolution of the cooperative see *El Espectador* 7 November 1930 and RG 59 821.6156/119. Matthews commented late in the year: 'It is partly due to the good offices of the Legation that the company still exercises control' (memorandum of 17 December 1930, ibid./129).
37 Colombia *Informe de la comisión nombrada para estudiar el conflicto surgido entre la United Fruit Company y la Cooperativa Bananera Colombiana* (Bogotá 1930); *El Tiempo* 16 November 1930
38 Colombia *Informe*; see also RG 59 821.6156/121, /154.
39 RG 59 821.6156/123; Matthews's memorandum of 17 December 1930, ibid./129; *New York Times* 8 December 1930, 8:3, 16 December 15:3. The tax was raised to three cents the following year, and the United Fruit Company was assured that it would be given the same rights as any future companies. Law 30 was signed on 24 February 1931. See *New York Times* 21 December 1931, 8:4; EWK MSS, 1930 Memorandum on Proposal to Place an Export Tax on Bananas.
40 Caffery to SS, 15 July 1931, RG 59 821.6156/135; Kepner *Social Aspects of the Banana Industry* 213; British Foreign Office memorandum, 15 February 1938, FO 371 A/1096/67/11; Colombia, Departmento Administrativo Nacional de Estadística *Anuario General de Estadística* 1938, 112. The Colombian peso in 1937 was $.56 U.S.
41 RG 59 821.6156/135
42 Orme Wilson, assistant chief, division of Latin American affairs, memorandum of a conversation with Commander Lammers, 18 July 1931, RG 59 821.5045/133; also L.H. Woolsey, *United Fruit*, to Wilson, 17 and 20 July 1931, RG 80, EF 17/P8-1 (310717)
43 RG 59 821.6156/139. For the details of the settlement see *New York Times* 2 August 1931, 18:3; *El Tiempo* 11 August 1931; Kepner *Social Aspects of the Banana Industry* 196; RG 59 821.6156/158. See also the report of the vice-consul in Santa Marta, T.M. Fisher, 31 July ibid./143.

44 H.W. Carlson, vice-consul, Barranquilla *Current Wages in the Republic of Colombia* 10 February 1933, RG 59 821.504/62; T.M. Fisher, 12 December 1931, RG 84: Santa Marta, 850.4. See also the letter from the United Fruit Company to Fisher, 16 November 1931, RG 84: Santa Marta, 850.4, and the memorandum of H.F. Matthews, 5 April 1932, RG 59 821.6156/167.
45 RG 59 821.6156/156; Caffery to SS, 9 December 1932, ibid./193
46 Ibid./193
47 Caffery to SS, 11 October 1932, ibid./191; *Moody's Industrials* (1936) 2514. For the background of the dispute see RG 59 821.77/523-/530 and 821.6156/52, /53; Luis B. Ortiz C. 'El Ferrocarril de Santa Marta y las compañías Imperialistas: La United Fruit Company y the Santa Marta Railway Co., Ltd.' *Acción Liberal* (December 1937) 41-53. For the loan negotiations see *New York Times* 10 March 1932, 33:4. Also see *Historia de las leyes, Legislatura de 1931* 27 (Bogotá 1940): 219ff.
48 *Foreign Relations* 1928, 2: 635-7; RG 59 321.1154 United Fruit Company/14
49 *Diario Oficial* 20 February 1933: also see Caffery to SS, 24 February 1933, RG 59 821.6165/196.
50 William Dawson to SS, 17 June 1935, RG 59 711.21/924
51 Chargé S.W. Washington to SS, 17 December 1934, RG 59 821.5045/149; 29 December 1934, ibid./149; *El Tiempo* 15 December 1934; *El Diario Nacional* 13 December 1934; Ministro de Industrias, *Memoria* 1938 1: 140-204; J.V. Garcés Navas 'La Administración López y la Industria Bananera del Magdalena' *Acción Liberal* (August 1938)
52 Washington to SS, 3 January 1935, RG 59 821.6156/204
53 *El Tiempo* 30 October 1934; *Anales de la Cámara de Representantes* 21 December 1934; Ministro de Industrias *Memoria* 1934, 1: 141-4
54 Law 149 is discussed in chapter 5 in relation to the petroleum industry. See *Anales de la Cámara de Representantes* 21 November 1936; Dawson to SS, 20 October 1936, RG 59 821.504/82, /84.
55 For law 1 of 22 January 1937 see Colombia *Leyes* (January-June 1937) 4; Ministro de Industrias, *Memoria* 1938, 1: 147; *New York Times* 29 January 1937, 3:4; RG 59 821.6156/208, /210, /211. For comment on the constitutional and agrarian reforms of the López administration see V.L. Fluharty *Dance of the Millions: Military Rule and the Social Revolution in Colombia* (Pittsburgh 1957) 51-7; A. Hirschman *Journeys Toward Progress* (New York 1963) 93-158; C.W. Anderson *Politics and Economic Reform in Latin America* (Toronto and London 1967) 210-11.
56 RG 821.6156/211
57 Ibid.; ibid./214, /215, /216, /217; *Anales del Senado* 17 March 1937

58 Dawson to SS, 19 April 1937; SS to the American minister, 20 April 1937, RG 59 821.6156/218; Duggan to G.H. Butler (division of American Republics), 27 August 1937, ibid./231

59 *Anales del Senado* 26 August 1937; Dawson to SS, 27 August 1937, RG 59 821.6156/230. López pressed on with the legislation in spite of the fact that his brother-in-law, the manager of the Bank of Colombia, attempted to convince him that the measure had little support and should be abandoned.

60 *El Tiempo* 13 September 1937; RG 59 821.6156/230

61 Dawson to SS, 30 October 1937, RG 59 821.6156/240; *Anales del Senado* 29 October 1937

62 RG 59 821.6156/245; Colombia *Leyes* (July-December 1937) 95-6; Ministro de Industrias, *Memoria* 1938, 2: 147

63 RG 59 321.1121 Bennett, George /37; American chargé Winthrop S. Greene to SS, 1 February 1938, RG 59 821.5156/255

64 Chargé Winthrop S. Greene to SS, 18 February 1938, RG 59 821.6156/256. See also Feis's memorandum of a conversation with the chairman of the board of United Fruit, 5 May 1938, RG 59 810.612/2.

65 Greene to SS, 6 October 1938, RG 59 821.6156/262; Spruille Braden, American ambassador, to SS, 21 and 29 September 1939, ibid./267, /268

66 Cited in Greene to SS, 25 March 1938, RG 59 321.1121 Bennett/37. The debate on the Carreño investigation and the labor problems in the banana zone early in 1938 are reported fully in the Colombian press. The Conservative papers *El Siglo* and *El Deber* were largely pro-Carreño and critical of the Liberal government, as was the right-wing Liberal daily of Bogotá, *La Razón*. See *El Siglo* 23 March 1938; *El Deber* 12 March and 21 April 1938; *La Razón*, 24 and 28 March 1938. Also see *El Espectador* 5, 7, 11, 14, and 26 March 1938; *El Tiempo* 23 March 1938. David Bushnell *Eduardo Santos and the Good Neighbor 1938-1942* (Gainesville 1967) 89-90 has a lucid account of the Carreño investigation and negotiations during Santos' presidency. Carreño defends his interests in *Explicaciones de un ex-Ministro de Estado* (Bogotá 1938).

67 Bushnell *Eduardo Santos* 87-95; Spruille Braden *Diplomats and Demagogues* (New Rochelle, New York 1971)

CHAPTER 7

1 F.D. McCann Jr 'Aviation Diplomacy: The United States and Brazil, 1939-1941' *Inter-American Economic Affairs* 21 (Spring 1968): 35-50; W.P. Newton 'International Aviation Rivalry in Latin America, 1919-1927' *Journal of Inter-American Studies* 7: (July 1965), 345-56; Stetson Conn and Byron

Fairchild *The United States Army in World War II: The Western Hemisphere* 1 *The Framework of Hemisphere Defense* (Washington 1960): William A. Burden *The Struggle for Airways in Latin America* (New York 1943). Professor Newton has also completed a monograph on aviation diplomacy concentrating on the period before 1931.

2 There is a wealth of material in the military records and naval and army intelligence documenting this attitude toward German interests in the hemisphere. For example, see the report of the military attaché in Costa Rica, 21 April 1939, RG 165, 2538-21/35; D.L. Stone, commander in the Canal Zone, 30 March 1939, RG 165, 2538-21/30; E.R. McCale, assistant chief of staff, G-2, to Stone, 10 April 1939, RG 165, 2538-21/29; Joseph Grew, acting secretary of state to the secretary of war, 28 August 1925, RG 165, 2538-21/18.

3 SCADTA was formed in 1919 by a group of prominent German-Colombians in Barranquilla. For its early history see Newton 'International Aviation Rivalry' and Herbert Boy (one of Scadta's leading pilots and operations manager when he resigned in 1940) *Una Historia con alas* (2nd ed., Bogotá 1963). See also Matthew Josephson *Empire of the Air: Juan Trippe and the Struggle for World Airways* (New York 1944). Professor Newton's soon to be published study 'The Perilous Skies' deals extensively with the diplomatic role of Charles Lindbergh mentioned briefly in this chapter. I am grateful to J.C. Leslie of the Pan American Airways history project for allowing me to read a yet unpublished manuscript.

4 *El Porvenir* (Cartagena) 20 November 1927; Newton 'International Aviation Rivalry' 354

5 See the memorandum of J. Butler Wright (assistant secretary of state), 6 December 1926, RG 59 821.796 Sca 2/106. It is interesting that at this juncture the American minister in Bogotá, Samuel Piles, was impressed with the sincerity of SCADTA's president (Piles to SS, 23 April 1927, ibid. Sca 2/109).

6 Davis to SS, 14 August 1925 and Joseph Grew, acting secretary of state, to Davis, 28 August 1925, RG 59 821.796 Sca 2/35

7 Francis White's memorandum of a conversation with the Colombian minister, Enrique Olaya Herrera, 26 September 1927, Francis White MSS, RG 59

8 John Baxter, the editor of *The Panama American*, was responsible for much of the business agitation; see his editorial for 19 November 1927. Also see American chargé in Panama, John F. Martin, to SS, 19 November 1927, RG 59 821.796 Sca 2/134. At the invitation of Aeromarítima's manager, Bogotá business interests met in the company's offices and subsequently cabled James H. Furay, a vice-president of United Press, in the hope of obtaining American press support for the Colombian petition. Shortly thereafter the

Bogotá Chamber of Commerce wrote to the Colombian foreign minister suggesting strong government support (Piles to SS, 23 November 1927, ibid. Sca 2/131 and *El Tiempo* 28 November 1927).

9 *El Tiempo* 23 November 1927

10 See also *El Diario Nacional*'s editorial of 23 November 1927, 'In Defense of Colombian Aviation'; *El Debate* 23 November 1927; *Diario del Comercio* (Cartagena) 23 November 1927.

11 Kellogg to Hilles, 29 November 1927, RG 59 821.796 Sca 2/130; Piles to SS, 30 November 1927, ibid. Sca/135, 28 November 1927, ibid. Sca 2/143. The SCADTA manager, Hermann Kuehl, was unable to convince Piles that the company considered itself Colombian and that it had no intention to expand beyond Colón.

12 SS to Piles, 29 November 1927, RG 59 821.796 Sca 2/133; memorandum of a conversation between White and Olaya Herrera, 28 November 1927, ibid. Sca 2/160; White memorandum, 30 December 1927, ibid. Sca 2/149

13 White MSS. For White's defence of intervention see *New York Times* 18 May 1930, 1:6. It is significant that when Franklin Roosevelt came to office White was appointed minister to Czechoslovakia as part of the general Good Neighbor facelift given the department after 1933 (Roosevelt MSS, OF 501).

14 See BPAU 61 (August 1927): 751-8 for the convention completed during the Washington Aviation Conference of May 1927.

15 *Foreign Relations* 1928, 1: 534-85

16 Ibid. 549; also Colombia *Informe del Ministro de Relaciones Exteriores* (Bogotá 1928) 199-205

17 *New York Times* 25 January 1928, 3:1

18 Memorandum to Stimson, 25 April 1929, White MSS

19 *Foreign Relations* 1928, 1: 593; *New York Times* 27 January 1928, 4:5; 8 February 1928, 4:3; *Sixth International Conference of American States, Final Act; Motions, Agreements, Resolutions, and Conventions* (Havana 1928); *Report of the Delegates of the United States of America to the Sixth International Conference of American States* (Washington 1928), especially 33-5

20 *El Tiempo* 1, 10, and 14 February 1928; BPAU 62 (April 1928): 333-50. For the satisfaction expressed by American officials over the results achieved in Havana see White's memorandum of 2 March 1928 to Dana G. Munro, Latin American Division, White MSS: Sixth International Conference of American States File, RG 59.

21 *New York Times* 11 July 1928, 12:1, 12 July 1928, 5:3

22 SS to the American legation (Quito), 15 June 1928, RG 59 821.796 Sca 2/165; American minister in Lima to SS, 14 June 1928 ibid. Sca 2/165.

A copy of the Lima report on aviation rivalry was sent to the postmaster general, Pan American Airways, and the departments of War, Commerce, and Navy.

23 Bading to SS, 6 July 1928, RG 59 821.796 Sca 2/176; *Foreign Relations* 1928, 2: 742

24 White to the counselor of the embassy in Havana, 12 July 1928, *Foreign Relations* 1928, 1: 786-8

25 Davis to SS, 21 July 1928, RG 59 821.796 Sca 2/171; the acting secretary of war, A. Summerall, to SS, 7 August 1928, ibid. Sca 2/178. The Department of the Navy also opposed the Panamanian agreement with SCADTA. See the acting secretary, R.H. Leigh, to SS, 6 August 1928, RG 59 821.796 Sca 2/177; 821.7961/35; the Panamanian foreign minister, J.D. Arosemena, to the American minister, 22 April 1929, *Foreign Relations* 1929, 3: 728-9.

26 Hambleton to White, 12 September 1928, White MSS: Pan American Airways File, box 14, RG 59

27 White to the American chargé in Berlin, 2 October 1928, RG 59 821.796 Sca 2/204A

28 Colombia, Ministro de Relaciones Exteriores *Memoria* (Bogotá 1929) 50-3

29 *Foreign Relations* 1929, 2: 879-80; *New York Times* 24 February 1929, 14:3; White Memorandum, 25 April 1929, White MSS. Prior to the conclusion of the agreement, SCADTA increased its advertising in the press and movie houses to ward off Pan American competition. See Jefferson Caffery to SS, 13 February 1929, RG 59 821.796 Sca 2/226.

30 White to Henry Stimson, 8 April 1929, box 502, Matters Pending in the Various Divisions, Stimson MSS, Yale University Library

31 White to SS, 25 April 1929, White MSS; *New York Times* 28 March 1929, 30:1, 18 April 1929, 2:5; von Bauer's letter to *El Porvenir* (Barranquilla) 27 June 1929; RG 59 821.796 Sca 2/266, /263; White to Stimson, 8 April 1929, box 502, Stimson MSS

32 White to Stimson, 6 July 1929, White MSS: Correspondence

33 *Foreign Relations* 1929, 1: 542 ff

34 See Wilcox's analysis of Colombian aviation in Caffery's despatch of 18 June 1929, RG 59 821.796/41; Caffery to SS, 18 July 1929, ibid. Sca 2/275.

35 White to Caffery, 26 October 1929, White MSS: Correspondence

36 White to Caffery, 14 November 1929, White MSS: Correspondence

37 *Foreign Relations* 1929, 1: 601; *New York Times* 3 March 1930, 10:4

38 See, for example, *Mundo al Día* 27 April 1931; RG 59 810.79611 Pan American Airways/1000, /1001.

39 See the memorandum of José M. Coronado, Colombian chargé in Washington, to SS, 19 March 1931, RG 59 821.796 Sca 2/314; H. Freeman Matthews,

assistant chief of the Latin American Division, memorandum, ibid. Sca 2/321; *Diario Oficial*, No. 21, 793, p. 818; Ministro de Relaciones Exteriores *Memoria* (Bogotá 1932) 75. See also Evan Young, State Department Official who joined Pan American in 1930, to Caffery, 31 January 1931, RG 59 821.796 Sca 2/314, /324.

40 Winslow to SS, 27 May 1932; Evan Young to Francis White, 11 September 1931; White to Young, 3 June 1932, White MSS: Official correspondence

41 Spencer R. Dickson, British minister in Bogotá, to the Foreign Office, 13 December 1932, FO 371 A/8758/1685/11; 18 December 1933, FO 371 A/395/395/11. The best general account of the dispute is Bryce Wood *The United States and Latin American Wars, 1932-1942* (New York and London 1966) 169-255. There is a discussion of the German influence in RG 165, 2257-B-109/5, dated 19 April 1933. See also RG 165, 2538-34/9 and 2257-M-34/1 to /26.

42 Leighton Rogers of the Department of Commerce commented to Francis White, 28 September 1927, that 'the Department of Commerce feels that South America is our greatest field for the sale of aviation equipment' (White MSS).

43 Memorandum of the British legation in Bogotá, 7 January 1935, FO 371 A/1072/1072/11. Olaya expressed annoyance at SCADTA's excessive charges for equipment it turned over to the government. Late in 1933 the president questioned the American minister in Bogotá, William Dawson, on the possibility of Pan American assuming management responsibilities more commensurate with its financial interest in SCADTA. See Dawson to SS, 2 June 1933, RG 59 821.796 Sca 2/345 and 13 December 1933, ibid. Sca 2/351; *New York Times* 8 September 1934, 1:1; 11 September 1934, 10:3.

44 British commercial secretary in Bogotá, T.J. Anderson, to the Department of Overseas Trade, 18 June 1934, FO 371 A/5828/395/11

45 See, for example, RG 165, 2257-M-34/1-/26 (1929-30) and RG 407, AG 350.2 Colombia (1939).

46 See the report of the military attaché, Costa Rica, 23 March 1939, RG 165, 2538-21/27. There is a thorough discussion of SCADTA's strategic threat in RG 407, AG 335.11 Colombia. See, for example, General David Stone, Canal Zone, to the adjutant general, 4 September 1939; assistant chief of staff to chief of staff, 5 September 1939. On von Bauer, see RG 165, 2538-21/28, /32, /35. In mid-1939, ten of nineteen SCADTA pilots were recent German emigrés.

47 The details of this incident have been pieced together from Colombian newspaper accounts: *El Diario Nacional* 25 June 1935; *El Espectador* 20 and 24 June and 26 June through 3 July 1935; *Colombia Nacionalista* (a proto-

fascist organ of Medellín) 2 March and 27 through 30 June 1935. See also
Dawson to SS, 26 June 1935, RG 59 821.7965/2; 21 March 1936, ibid.
Sca 2/383.
48 See the documents in RG 38, C-11-B, 22418.
49 The United States also negotiated an agreement for a military mission to
Colombia in 1938. See David Bushnell *Eduardo Santos and the Good Neigh-
bor* (Gainesville 1967) 9-11; *El Tiempo* 27 November 1938; U.S. *Military
Mission Agreement between the United States of America and Colombia*
(Executive Agreement Series no. 141, Washington 1939). There is a full
treatment of the mission in RG 407, 21.0 68 Colombia. See also Winthrop S.
Greene to SS, 26 April 1938, RG 59 810.79611 Pan American Airways /1622;
Josephson *Empire of the Air* 157-8; Boy *Una Historia con alas* 239-42.
50 RG 59 821.796 Avianca /20. Fascinating and revealing as his personal account
is, Braden exaggerates the lack of concern in the United States for SCADTA's
activities (*Diplomats and Demagogues* 196-261).
51 *El Tiempo* 21 July 1939; Spruille Braden to SS, 26 July 1939, RG 59
821.796/108
52 Colombia *Leyes* (February-May 1938) 114-28. SCADTA officials had not
been averse to law 89 since they believed that national control promised to
operate in their favor against both Pan American and German influence. In
March 1939 von Bauer assured the American ambassador that as an Austrian
his political views were not the same as those held by the Germans and that
he would dismiss the few Nazi sympathizers in SCADTA's employ. See Braden
to SS, 30 March 1929, RG 59 821.796 Sca 2/408.
53 SS to Braden, 2 February 1940, *Foreign Relations* 1940, 5: 723-6
54 RG 59 821.796 Avianca/4; *Foreign Relations* 1940, 5: 730-3; Bushnell
Eduardo Santos 23; *El Tiempo* 9 June 1940
55 *Foreign Relations* 1940, 5: 729-30; Marshall to D.L. Stone, Canal zone,
16 September 1939, RG 165, 2538-21/43

CHAPTER 8

1 David Green 'The Cold War Comes to Latin America' in B.J. Bernstein, ed.
The Policies and Politics of the Truman Administration (Chicago 1970) 151
2 David Green *The Containment of Latin America* (Chicago 1971) ix
3 R. Ferrell 'Repudiation of a Repudiation' *Journal of American History* 51
(March 1965): 669-73
4 For an analysis of the variations in business opinion see Joan Hoff Wilson
American Business and United States Foreign Policy, 1920-1933 (Lexington
1971).

5 Ibid. 90-7
6 U.S. Department of State, Conference Series no. 85 *Report of the Delegation of the United States of America to the Inter-American Conference on Problems of War and Peace, Mexico City* (Washington 1946) 216-17
7 Green *Containment of Latin America* passim
8 For a comparison with the Argentine situation, see Joan Hoff Wilson, *American Business* 181.
9 Louis Fischer *Oil Imperialism: The International Struggle For Petroleum* (New York 1926)
10 Antonio García *Gaitán y el problema de la revolución Colombiana* (Bogotá 1955) 302-3; David Bushnell 'Colombia' in Harold Davis and Larman Wilson, eds. *Latin American Foreign Policies* (Baltimore and London 1975) 401-18
11 Bushnell 'Colombia'

Bibliographical essay

There is a wealth of archival material and secondary literature on which students of inter-American relations can draw. Some of the primary sources are relatively untouched; others, seemingly exhausted by earlier generations, bear fruit when stimulated by fresh ideas and questions. The published *Papers Relating to the Foreign Relations of the United States* provide a carefully edited record of American foreign relations and are an essential starting point before attempting the records of the Department of State, Record Group 59, National Archives. RG 59 also contains some special collections which bear examination. The *Review of Questions of Major Interest in the Relations of the United States with the Latin American Countries* is one of the best brief accounts of the policies of the Hoover administration. The papers of Francis White, Assistant Secretary of State 1927–33, are especially interesting for Colombian relations because of his close friendship with Jefferson Caffery, the most important American diplomat in Colombia between the first world war and the arrival of Spruille Braden in 1938. The Consular Post Reports, Record Group 84, contain the observations of U.S. consuls on the local Colombian scene; especially valuable are the reports for Santa Marta and Barranquilla.

Historians and others working in American foreign policy are aware of the inadequacy of sole reliance on State Department files. RG 43, Records of United States Participation in International Conferences, is a good index of official objectives in Latin America. The files of the Department of Commerce, RG 40, and the Bureau of Foreign and Domestic Commerce, RG 151, are indispensable tools for the study of commercial and economic policy.

Military and naval records have often not received their due from diplomatic historians. Excellent in many instances, they are uneven in quality for the interwar years, at least as they pertain to Colombia. Most complete are the military attaché reports, RG 165, and the central files of the Office of the Adjutant General,

RG 407. Less valuable for Colombia are the naval records: RG 80, Office of the Secretary of the Navy, and the recently opened RG 38, Office of Naval Intelligence, containing the reports of the naval attachés.

The papers of the British Foreign Office provide an excellent supplement to the American materials. Foreign Office correspondence relating to Colombia is in file 371. Reports of British representatives in Bogotá tend to be more thorough and more capably written than their American equivalents, and provide a basis for evaluating State Department interpretation of Colombian policies.

The papers of Frank Kellogg, secretary of state in the Coolidge administration, at the Minnesota Historical Society, are of marginal value for Colombian-American relations, except for the earlier debate over the Thomson-Urrutia Treaty. Kellogg was one of the anti-treaty senators, and his correspondence with several prominent figures, including Theodore Roosevelt, illuminates the attitude of key individuals in the protracted debate over the American role in Panamanian secession from Colombia.

The Hoover years still provide considerable latitude for research on inter-American relations. In primary materials, one might begin with W.S. Myers, ed. *The State Papers and Other Public Writings of Herbert Hoover* (2 vols. 1934) and Hoover's *Memoirs* (1952). The Herbert Hoover Presidential Library in West Branch, Iowa, holds several collections relevant to inter-American relations. The presidential papers contain, among other items, correspondence on commercial policy and on Hoover's good will tour as president-elect. The papers of Ray Lyman Wilbur, Hoover's secretary of the interior, are important for the petroleum industry. Wilbur's correspondence also reflects his interest and involvement in inter-American cultural relations. Since 1970 the papers of Under Secretary of State William R. Castle Jr have been open to researchers. The collection includes copies of Castle's numerous public addresses and publications as well as his correspondence.

The diary and papers of Henry L. Stimson in the Sterling Library, Yale, are a vital source for the Hoover years and substantially supplement Stimson and McGeorge Bundy *On Active Service in Peace and War* (1948). As Secretary of State Stimson adhered to Hoover's initiative in marking a path toward restoration of good relations with South and Central America. Diary entries touch on George Rublee's mission to Colombia as Olaya's adviser on petroleum matters, but Rublee's activities are more fully documented in the George Rublee Memoir, Oral History Collection, Columbia University.

Two collections are especially pertinent to United States foreign economic policy: the Thomas Lamont papers, Baker Library Harvard, and the Edwin Walter Kemmerer papers and diary, Princeton. The Lamont collection is indispensable for an understanding of business-government relations. The Kemmerer papers are among the most valuable single collection on Colombian financial history for 1929–32; the diary is interesting but less relevant.

Most valuable for the Roosevelt period are the materials in the Roosevelt Presidential Library, Hyde Park, New York, and the Manuscript Division of the Library of Congress. The presidential files contain correspondence of some interest to a study of the Good Neighbor policy and supplement the documents edited by E.B. Nixon *Franklin D. Roosevelt and Foreign Relations* (3 vols. 1969), the multivolume *Public Papers and Addresses of Franklin D. Roosevelt* (13 vols. 1938–50), edited by Samuel I. Rosenman, and the *Complete Presidential Press Conferences of Franklin D. Roosevelt* (1972). Also of interest are the papers of Charles Taussig, one of Roosevelt's economic advisers and president of the American Molasses Company, which had Caribbean interests. Especially important are the diaries, papers, and most-recently opened presidential diaries of Henry Morgenthau Jr, secretary of the treasury. This voluminous record is very useful for the financial relationship with Latin America, especially the settlement of the outstanding foreign debts and the extension of new loans during the war. John M. Blum has selected a very representative sampling of these papers in *From the Morgenthau Diaries*, especially volume 1, *Years of Urgency* (1965). Also valuable are the recently opened papers of Adolf Berle, although for Latin American affairs they are not relevant until 1936.

The papers of Cordell Hull and Josephus Daniels in the Library of Congress also trace the evolution of American policy after 1932. Because of Daniels's close personal relationship with Roosevelt, his suggestions on Latin American affairs, especially Mexico, carried considerable weight with the president, much to the chagrin of Hull. Hull's papers contain little of direct relevance to Colombian-American relations with the exception of the trade agreements program and the participation of Colombia at the inter-American conferences of the 1930s. Rather disappointing are the *Memoirs of Cordell Hull* (1948), which lack penetrating analysis and should be supplemented by Julius Pratt *Cordell Hull* (2 vols. 1964). Most revealing for the relationship between the State Department and other government departments is William Phillips's diary in the Houghton Library, Harvard, for the years in which he served as Roosevelt's under secretary of state. Also of value is Phillips's memoir in the Oral History Collection, Columbia University. His *Ventures in Diplomacy* (1952) is a distillation of the manuscript diary. Writings by other participants in the administration include Laurence Duggan *The Americas* (1949); Sumner Welles *The Time For Decision* (1944); Herbert Feis *1933: Characters in Crisis* (1966), which is also pertinent to the final stages of the Hoover administration; Spruille Braden *Diplomats and Demagogues* (1971); and Adolf Berle *Navigating the Rapids, 1918–1971*, edited by Beatrice B. Berle and Travis Jacobs (1973).

Business records are invaluable, yet often not accessible. Standard Oil and Pan American Airways, however, were interested and helpful, unlike the United Fruit Company. The surviving records of the Tropical Oil Co. are now housed in the archives of ESSO Inter-America Inc., Coral Gables, Florida. Much of a potentially valuable collection was unfortunately destroyed at the time Tropical Oil moved its offices from Toronto. Interviews with active and retired officials of the Standard Oil affiliate filled some of the gaps left by the absence of documents. Among those who graciously gave of their time and interest were L.P. Maier, retired director and president of the International Petroleum Company; C. Kirkpatrick, retired vice-president and director of ESSO Inter-America, Inc.; John K. Oldfield, general counsel, now retired, ESSO Inter-America; Lionel Charlesworth, retired head of the tax division, ESSO Inter-America, and in the 1940s comptroller of Colombian operations. In Bogotá, others contributed to the sections dealing with the petroleum industry and other aspects of Colombian history, including Miguel Urrutia Montoya, at the time of interview assessor for the Junta Monetaria and author of a useful history of Colombian labor; Janet Hermann de Tobón, at the time of conversations in 1970 counsellor for the Institute of International Education; and James W. Raisbeck, whose law firm has for a generation been involved in dealings between American enterprise and the Colombian government. In his youth, Raisbeck worked as an overseer with United Fruit in Central America, a position he left as soon as he could earn passage; he also worked briefly for Tropical Oil. Raisbeck remains a critic of American policy. In Washington, former State Department official H. Freeman Matthews contributed from his remarkable memory.

Colombian materials of an archival nature are not readily available. The Foreign Ministry archives were closed at the time I worked on this study. Nevertheless useful materials are available in Colombia. Both the Biblioteca Luis Angel-Arango and the Biblioteca Nacional contain excellent collections of contemporary newspapers and some government documents. Cautious as one must be in using the Colombian press, it provides an essential insight into the domestic political economy and social structure, especially since it contains more complete accounts of congressional debates than can be found elsewhere. Papers used ranged from the Bogotá dailies *El Tiempo, El Espectador, Gil Blás*, and *El Liberal* to their conservative counterparts: *El Siglo, El Nuevo Tiempo, La Razón*, and *El Debate*. Especially interesting were the smaller circulation, ideological papers: *Claridad* (Bogotá, Syndicalist), *Colombia Nacionalista* (Medellín, fascist-conservative), *Tierra* (Bogotá, Communist), and *Vox Populi* (Bucaramanga, Revolutionary Socialist). Outside Bogotá, the most influential papers seem to have been *La Nación, El Heraldo*, and *La Prensa* (Barranquilla); *La Patria* (Manizales); *El Deber, Vanguardia Liberal*, and *El Frente* (Bucaramanga); *El Colombiano* (Medellín); *Diario del Pacífico* and *El Relator* (Cali); and *El Fígaro* (Cartagena). Popular magazines such as *Cromos* and *El Gráfico* provide another perspective.

For the United States, the *New York Times* and the *Wall Street Journal* provide useful background material and opinion. They should be supplemented by more specialized periodicals: *Journal* of the American Bankers Association (after 1934, *Banking*), *The Economist, Barron's, Fortune, The Lamp* (Standard Oil), *Imperial Oil Review, The Nation, New Republic, Tea and Coffee Trade Journal,* and *The Bulletin of the Pan American Union.*

Government documents relevant to a study of inter-American relations are abundant for both countries. For the United States one will find useful the *Congressional Record*, reports of congressional committee hearings (see the notes for more detail), and various publications of government departments such as *Commerce Reports* and the State Department *Bulletin*; for Colombia, *Anales de la Cámara de Representantes, Anales del Senado, Diario Oficial*, publications of the Departamento Administrativo Nacional de Estadística (DANE), *Leyes*, and the memorials, reviews, and bulletins of the several government departments. The legislative library is useful for the reports of parliamentary committees. One can only hope that in the future Colombian officials will make their personal papers more accessible to researchers.

Among the general analyses of American foreign policy which cast light on Latin American diplomacy are the revisionist essays in William A. Williams, ed. *From Colony to Empire* (1972) and Walter LaFeber et al. *Creation of the American Empire* (1973). They might be read in conjunction with Williams's *Tragedy of American Diplomacy* (rev. ed. 1962) and 'Latin America: Laboratory for American Foreign Policy in the Nineteen-Twenties' *Inter-American Economic Affairs* 11 (Autumn 1957); Robert F. Smith 'American Foreign Relations, 1920–1942' in B.J. Bernstein, ed. *Towards a New Past* (1966). For a more conservative and excellent survey of the literature see Richard Abrams 'United States Intervention Abroad: The First Quarter Century' *American Historical Review* 79 (February 1974) and Richard Leopold 'The Emergence of America as a World Power; Some Second Thoughts' in John Braeman, et al. *Change and Continuity in Twentieth Century America* (1966).

Many of the better standard treatments of inter-American relations are now somewhat dated. Samuel F. Bemis *The Latin American Policy of the United States* (1943) is yet to be superseded; Arthur Whitaker *The United States and South America: The Northern Republics* (1948) and his 'From Dollar Diplomacy to the Good Neighbor Policy' *Inter-American Economic Affairs* 4 (Spring 1951) are important early works; J. Fred Rippy *Latin America and the Industrial Age* (1941) is perceptive and rich in detail; Dexter Perkins *Hands Off: A History of the Monroe Doctrine* (1941) is a one-volume distillation of this three-volume study. More recent works include N.A. Bailey *Latin America in World Politics* (1967), G. Connell-Smith *The Inter-American System* (1966), W.F. Callcott *The Western Hemisphere: Its Influence on United States Policies to the End of World War II* (1968), Alonzo Aguilar Monteverde *Pan Americanism: From Monroe to the Present* (1968), Hernán Ramírez Necochea *Los Estados Unidos y América Latina* (1967), J.L. Mecham *A Survey of United States-Latin American Relations* (1965), and *The United States and Inter-American Security* (1961).

Not entirely satisfactory on the inter-American conferences of the period are James B. Scott, ed. *The International Conferences of American States, 1889-1928* (1931) and *First Supplement, 1933-1940* (1940). They need to be supplemented by the proceedings of the conferences housed in the Pan American Union Library, State Department instructions to delegates, the records of the conferences in RG 43, National Archives, and the official reports of the various Latin American states. Useful unpublished materials include Richard Gannaway 'United States Representation at the Inter-American Conferences, 1889-1928' (PHD dissertation, University of South Carolina 1968), George Coleman 'The Good Neighbor Policy of Franklin D. Roosevelt with Specific Reference to Three Inter-American Conferences, 1933-1938' (PHD dissertation, University of Iowa 1951).

There is a growing body of more specialized literature on American policy in Latin America. Among the better studies for the pre-1930 period are Joseph S. Tulchin *Aftermath of War: World War I and United States Policy Toward Latin America* (1971) and Robert Seidel 'Progressive Pan Americanism: Development and United States Policy Toward Latin America, 1906-1931' (PHD dissertation, Cornell 1973). More general, but still useful for Latin America, are Betty Glad *Charles Evans Hughes and the Illusions of Innocence* (1966) and Dexter Perkins *Charles Evans Hughes and American Democratic Statesmanship* (1956). Hughes's *The Pathway of Peace* (1925) provides additional insight on Harding's secretary of state. Salvatore Prisco *John Barrett, Progressive Era Diplomat* (1973), touches on a neglected figure. Samuel G. Inman provides a critical contemporary view in *Problems of Pan Americanism* (1925) and 'Imperialistic America' *Atlantic Monthly* 134 (July 1924). The response to the article is discussed in Kenneth Woods ' "Imperialistic America": A Landmark in the Development of United States Policy Toward Latin America' *Inter-American Economic Affairs* 21 (Winter 1967).

The performance of President Coolidge and his secretary of state Frank Kellogg has received less attention. L. Ethan Ellis gives Kellogg perhaps better than his due in *Frank B. Kellogg and American Foreign Relations, 1925-1929* (1961) and *Republican Foreign Policy, 1921-1933* (1968). See as well J.C. Traphagen 'The Inter-American Diplomacy of Frank B. Kellogg' (PHD dissertation, University of Minnesota, 1956).

Our knowledge of the Hoover administration has expanded considerably in the past several years, as reflected in the bibliographical essay of Joan Hoff Wilson, *Herbert Hoover, Forgotten Progressive* (Boston 1975). A provocative recent interpretation is Ellis Hawley's 'Herbert Hoover, The Commerce Secretariat, and the Vision of an "Associative State," 1921-1928,' *Journal of American History* 61 (June 1974). Hawley supplements Joseph Brandes *Herbert Hoover and Economic Diplomacy: Department of Commerce Policy, 1921-1928* (1962). They might be read in conjunction with Craig Lloyd *Aggressive Introvert: Herbert Hoover and Public Relations Management, 1912-1933* (1973), Carl Degler 'The Ordeal of Herbert Hoover' *Yale Review* 52 (June 1963), M.N. Rothbard 'The Hoover Myth' in James Weinstein, ed. *For a New America: Essays in History and Politics from 'Studies on the Left'* (1970). Robert Ferrell *American Diplomacy in the Great Depression* (1957) tends to be sketchy, and W.S. Myers *The Foreign Policies of Herbert Hoover* (1940) is dated. Alexander DeConde provides the standard analysis of one area of Hoover's foreign policy in the still excellent *Herbert Hoover's Latin American Policy* (1951). Richard Current *Secretary Stimson, A Study in Statecraft* (1954) and Elting Morison *A Study of the Life and Times of Henry L. Stimson* (1960) both supplement Henry Stimson and McGeorge Bundy *On Active Service*. Ferrell skillfully untangles the story around the Clark memorandum in 'Repudiation of A Repudiation' *Journal of American History* 51 (March 1965).

The Roosevelt period retains its fascination. Among the early assessments of the Good Neighbor are E. David Cronon 'Interpreting the "New" Good Neighbor Policy; The Cuban Crisis of 1933' *Hispanic American Historical Review* 39 (November 1959), F.M. Cuevas Cancino *Roosevelt y la buena vecinidad* (1954), and E.O. Guerrant *Roosevelt's Good Neighbor Policy* (1950). Donald M. Dozer deals with the 1930 to 1960 period in *Are we Good Neighbors?* (1960). J. Heckey provides a different perspective in 'Blackmail, Mendicancy and Intervention: Latin America's Conception of the Good Neighbor Policy?' *Inter-American Economic Affairs* 12 (Summer 1958), as do Daniel Restrepo 'Panamericanismo e hispano-americanismo' *Revista Javeriana* 11 (April 1939) and José de la Vega *El buen vecino* (1944). Two influential contemporary statements on New Deal diplomacy are Sumner Welles *The Roosevelt Administration and its Dealings with the Republics of the Western Hemisphere* (Washington, Department of State Latin American Series no. 9 1935) and Adolf Berle 'Our Foreign Policy in Latin America' *Academy of Political Science Proceedings* 18 (May 1939).

The best of the general assessments of the Good Neighbor in the Hoover-Roosevelt period is Bryce Wood *The Making of The Good Neighbor Policy* (1961); it is conceptually weak, however, and should be read in conjunction with William A. Williams's treatment of the period in *The Tragedy of American Diplomacy*, Lloyd C. Gardner *Economic Aspects of New Deal Diplomacy* (1964), and David

Green *The Containment of Latin America* (1971). There are several useful studies which include discussions of the Good Neighbor period. Among them are Irwin F. Gelman *Roosevelt and Batista* (1973), Karl Schmitt *Mexico and the United States, 1821-1973* (1974), J.C. Carey *Peru and the United States, 1900-1962* (1964), H. Peterson *Argentina and the United States, 1810-1960* (1964), F.B. Pike *Chile and the United States* (1963), Sheldon Liss *Aspects of United States-Panamian Relations* (1967), Howard Cline *The United States and Mexico* (rev. ed. 1963), Dana Munro *The United States and the Caribbean Republics, 1921-1933* (1974), and Robert F. Smith *The United States and Cuba: Business and Diplomacy, 1917-1960* (1960).

There has been comparatively little attention to United States relations with Colombia in the twentieth century. E. Taylor Parks *Colombia and the United States, 1765-1934* (1935) is the only survey treatment. David Bushnell *Eduardo Santos and the Good Neighbor, 1938-1942* (1967) is the best single volume on the subject, even though it was intended to be suggestive rather than definitive. I.F. Gellman 'The Abortive Treaty that Succeeded: United States-Colombian Reciprocal Trade Policies, 1933-1936' (MA thesis, University of Maryland 1966) and his 'Prelude to Reciprocity' *The Historian* 32 (November 1969) are thorough but occasionally uncritical studies. My own dissertation, 'Good Neighbours in Depression: the United States and Colombia, 1928-1938' (University of Toronto 1972), is somewhat more sympathetic to a revisionist perspective. Two dated but nonetheless useful studies are J. Fred Rippy *The Capitalists and Colombia* (1931) and George Faust 'Economic Relations of the United States and Colombia, 1920-1940' (PHD dissertation, University of Chicago 1946). Rather sketchy are José Antonio Uribe, ed. *Ministerio de Relaciones Exteriores, anales diplomáticos y consulares de Colombia* (9 vols. 1900-59), Germán Cavelier *La Política internacional de Colombia* (4 vols. 1959-60), Eduardo Guzmán Esponda, ed. *Tratados y convenios de Colombia, 1919-1928* (1939), Alfonso López *La Política internacional* (1938), Raimundo Rivas *Historia Diplomática de Colombia, 1810-1934* (1961), Y.M. Yepes 'La Política internacional de Colombia y el Panamericanismo' *Revista Colombiana de Derecho Internacional* 1 (July 1947), Alberto Miramón 'Historia Diplomática,' vol. 17 in the *Historia extensa de Colombia*, which is being published under the auspices of the Colombian Academy of History.

Twentieth-century Colombian history remains largely unwritten, although there are several excellent analyses of the post-1945 years by social and political scientists. A standard history covering the period prior to 1930 is Jesús María Henao and Gerardo Arrubla *History of Colombia* translated and edited by J. Fred Rippy (1938), but is it being superseded by the volumes in the *Historia extensa* series. Antonio Cacua Prado *Historia del periodismo Colombiano* (1968) is a valuable research tool. Polemical and often unreliable is Diego Montaña Cuéllar *Col-*

ombia, país formal y país real (1963). V.L. Fluharty *Dance of the Millions: Military Rule and the Social Revolution in Colombia* (1957) is an overly uncritical assessment concentrating on the 1950s. Fernando Guillén Martínez *Raíz y Futuro de la revolución* (1963) and Saturnino Sepúlveda Niño *Las Elites Colombianas en crisis* (1970) present insightful analyses, as does Orlando Fals Borda *Subversion and Social Change in Colombia* (1969).

Economic historians have made the most striking contribution. See several works by William McGreevey: 'Recent Research on the Economic History of Latin America' *Latin American Research Review* 3 (1968), *A Bibliography of Latin American Economic History, 1760-1960* (1969), 'Quantitative Research in Latin American History of the Nineteenth and Twentieth Centuries' in Val Lorwin and J. Price, eds. *The Dimensions of the Past* (1972), *An Economic History of Colombia, 1845-1930* (1971), and *Statistical Series on the Colombian Economy* (1964). A. Hirschman *Journeys Toward Progress* (1963) contains material on Colombia. William Glade *The Latin American Economies* (1969) and Charles Anderson *Politics and Economic Change in Latin America* (1967) are also useful. Miguel Urrutia Montoya has written one of the best histories of Latin American labor in *The Development of the Colombian Labor Movement* (1969). Two recent studies of the Colombian economy bear examination: Enrique Caballero *Historia económica de Colombia* (1970) and Abel Cruz Santos *Economía y hacienda pública* (2 vols. 1965-6). Some pathbreaking work on nineteenth-century Colombian economic history is represented by Frank Safford 'Foreign and National Enterprise in Nineteenth Century Colombia' *Business History Review* 39 (Winter 1965), and his recent *The Ideal of the Practical: Colombia's Struggle to Form a Technical Elite* (Austin 1976).

Both contemporary and recent analysts have devoted considerable attention to United States commercial relations with Latin America. As an academic and for some time chief of the Bureau of Foreign and Domestic Commerce, Julius Klein's work was of substantial importance: 'Economic Rivalries in Latin America' *Foreign Affairs* 3 (December 1924) and 'The Key to Latin American Trade' *Nation* 128 (16 January 1929). As a State Department official, William S. Culbertson influenced the policies of the 1920s and 1930s: see his *International Economic Policies* (1925) and *Reciprocity: A National Policy for Foreign Trade* (1937). The most thorough analysis of American economic foreign policy in the 1920s is Joan Hoff Wilson *American Business and Foreign Policy, 1920-1933* (1969). For a survey of American tariff policies see Frank Taussig *The Tariff History of the United States* (1964 ed.). The *Proceedings* of the National Foreign Trade Council provide an essential source for the opinion of one segment of the business community, as do several of the council's publications. See, for example, the *Survey of the Financial and Trade Problems of Colombia in their Rela-*

tion to the United States (1933). Also useful in this respect is the *Journal* of the American Bankers' Association.

Several publications of the U.S. Tariff Commission are especially applicable to the Colombian instance: *An Analysis of Trade Between Colombia and the United States* (1933), *Duties Levied in Foreign Countries on Agricultural Commodities From the United States* (1929), and *An Economic Analysis of the Foreign Trade of the United States in Relation to the Tariff* (1933). J.M. Jones indicates the foreign response to the Smoot-Hawley Tariff in *Tariff Retaliation* (1934). *Commerce Reports*, published by the Department of Commerce, contain useful statistics, as does the Colombian counterpart, *Anuario general de estadística,* especially the *Comercio Exterior* series.

David Bushnell provides some of the background for Colombian tariff policies in 'Two Stages in Colombian Tariff Policy: The Radical Era and the Return to protection, 1861–1885' *Inter-American Economic Affairs* 9 (Spring 1956). The best economic history, Luis Ospina Vásquez *Indústria y protección en Colombia, 1810-1930* (1955), places Bushnell's analysis in a broader perspective. Robert Beyer 'The Colombian Coffee Industry' Origins and Major Trends' (Ph D dissertation, University of Minnesota, 1947) deals with a vital area of the modern Colombian economy. Arno Pearse *Colombia, With Special Reference to Cotton* (1927) indicates the strong interest of the British textile industry in developing Colombia as a source of supply.

There is now a substantial body of literature on Cordell Hull and the reciprocal trade agreements program. Among the most relevant of the general studies, other than those mentioned above, are: R. Buell *The Hull Trade Program and the American System* (1938), A.W. Schatz 'Cordell Hull and the Struggle for the Reciprocal Trade Agreements Program, 1932–1940' (PH D dissertation, University of Oregon 1965), James Pearson *The Reciprocal Trade Agreements Program: The Policy of the United States and Its effectiveness* (1942), H. Grady 'Reciprocal Trade Agreements as an Evolution in Tariff Policy' *Academy of Political Science Proceedings* 19 (May 1940), William Allen 'Cordell Hull and the Defense of the Trade Agreements Program, 1933-1940' in Alexander DeConde, ed. *Isolation and Security* (1957), 'The International Trade Philosophy of Cordell Hull, 1907–1933' *American Economic Review* 43 (March 1953), Grace Beckett 'Effect of the Reciprocal Trade Agreements on the Foreign Trade of the United States' *Quarterly Journal of Economics* 55 (November 1940). Too recent to have been considered here was Dick Steward *Trade and Hemisphere* (Colombia, Mo. 1975).

Conflicting contemporary analyses of the program are reflected in U.S. Department of State *International Trade and Domestic Prosperity* (an address by Cordell Hull before the National Foreign Trade Council) Political Series no. 3 (1934), *The Menace of Economic Nationalism* (an address by assistant secretary of state Francis B. Sayre before the American Academy of Political Science) Department of State Political Series no. 4 (1934), *The Reciprocal Trade Agreements Program* Commercial Policy Series no. 64 (1940), *Our Need for Foreign Trade* (an address by Cordell Hull before the National Foreign Council) Commercial Policy Series no. 26 (1936), Henry A. Wallace *America Must Choose* (1934), George Peek and William Crowther *Why Quit Our Own?* (1936), William Castle Jr 'The Critique of the Trade Agreements Program' *Annals of the American Academy of Political Science* (July 1938).

American commercial policy was only one aspect of foreign relations as they affected the Western Hemisphere. Alton Frye discusses another dimension in *Nazi Germany and the American Hemisphere* (1967). Contemporary accounts of European-American relations in South America include H. Trueblood 'Trade Rivalries in Latin America' *Foreign Policy Reports* 13 (15 September 1937), Carleton Beals 'Japan Tiptoes Around the Monroe Doctrine' *Current History* 49 (September 1938), Percy Bidwell 'Latin America, Germany and the Hull Program' *Foreign Affairs* 17 (January 1939), T. Bisson 'Japan's Trade Boom' *Foreign Policy Reports* 12 (15 March 1936). For German interest in Colombian trade see *Documents on German Foreign Policy, 1918-1945* series C, vol. 3; on Japan, the U.S. Tariff Commission report *Recent Developments in the Foreign Trade of Japan* (1936) is an indication of American concern over Japanese competition.

Substantial progress has been made in our knowledge of inter-American financial relations between the wars. Dated but still useful for the financial expansion of the 1920s are: James Angell *Financial Foreign Policy of the United States* (1933), W. Feuerlein and E. Hanson *Dollars in Latin America* (1941), Cleona Lewis *America's Stake in International Investments*, John T. Madden et al. *America's Experience as a Creditor Nation* (1937), Max Winkler *Investments of United States Capital in Latin America* (1929), 'Investments and the National Policy of the United States in Latin America' *American Economic Review: Supplement* 22 (March 1932); U.S. Department of Commerce *American Underwriting of Foreign Securities* (1929). Testimony before congressional committees is an especially valuable source for the relations between business and government. See, for example: Senate, Committee on Foreign Relations *Foreign Loans: Hearings before the subcommittee pursuant to S. Res. 22, relative to engaging responsibility of Government in financial arrangements between its citizens and sovereign foreign governments, February 25, 26, 1925;* Senate, Committee on Foreign Relations *Foreign Loans: Hearings ... pursuant to Cong. Res. 15 ... , January 25 to February 16, 1927; Senate Sale of Foreign Bonds ... Hearings before the Committee on Finance pursuant to S. Res. 19, December 18, 1931 to February 10, 1932.*

Robert Seidel's 'Progressive Pan Americanism' contains the most thorough discussion of official and business attitudes toward loan controls but should be read in conjunction with Carl Parrini *Heir to Empire* (1969), Joan Hoff Wilson *American Business and Foreign Policy* (1971), and Herbert Feis *The Diplomacy of the Dollar; First Era, 1919–1932* (1952). Contemporary accounts include George Edwards 'Government Control of Foreign Investments' *American Economic Review* 18 (December 1928), Morris Ernst 'Controlling Foreign Loans' *Nation* 134 (10 February 1932), C.L. Jones 'Loan Controls in the Caribbean' *Hispanic American Historical Review* 14 (May 1934), Allen Dulles 'The Protection of American Foreign Bondholders' *Foreign Affairs* 10 (April 1932), W.O. Scroggs 'The American Investments in Latin America' *Foreign Affairs* 10 (April 1932). The *Bulletin* of the Institute of International Finance and the *Journal* of the American Bankers' Association are also useful for the bond question.

Robert Seidel 'American Reformers Abroad: The Kemmerer Missions in South America, 1923–1931' *Journal of Economic History* 32 (June 1972) is a perceptive analysis of the work of one of the more influential economists of the period. Kemmerer expresses his views in 'Economic Advisory Work for Governments' *American Economic Review* 17 (March 1927) and in the results of his first mission to Colombia, *Leyes presentadas al gobierno Colombiano por la misión financiera Norteamericana* (1923). The following are useful for both the American perspective and the state of the Colombian economy: International High Commission 'Report on Colombian Banking' (unpublished, 1919–22) and James C. Corliss *Latin American Budgets* part 3: *Colombia and Venezuela* Department of Commerce Circular no. 305 (1928). Donald Barnhart 'Colombian Transport and the Reforms of 1931' *Hispanic American Historical Review* 37 (February 1958) deals with one of the most important and troubled areas of Colombian public spending in the period.

For a comparative perspective on this aspect several works by Robert F. Smith are essential: *The United States and Revolutionary Nationalism in Mexico, 1916–1932* (1972), 'The Formation and Development of the International Bankers' Committee on Mexico' *Journal of Economic History* 23 (December 1963), 'The Morrow Mission and the International Committee of Bankers on Mexico' *Journal of Latin American Studies* 1 (November 1969).

There is a wealth of general information on international finance and trade in L.V. Chandler *Benjamin Strong: Central Banker* (1958) and *American Monetary Policy, 1928–1941* (1971), Milton Friedman and Anna Schwartz *A Monetary History of the United States, 1867–1960* (1963), Clay Anderson *A Half-Century of Federal Reserve Policy-Making, 1914–1964* (1965), C.W. Phelps *The Foreign Expansion of American Banks* (1927), D. Joslin, *A Century of Banking In Latin America* (1963), Frank Costigliola 'Anglo-American Rivalry in the 1920's' (paper presented to the Organization of American Historians, Denver, Colorado 1974),

'The Other Side of Isolationism: The Establishment of the First World Bank' *Journal of American History* 59 (December 1972) and Henry Wallich *Monetary Problems of An Export Economy: The Cuban Experience* (1950).

The establishment of the Foreign Bondholders' Protective Council and the effort to stabilize inter-American financial relations receive attention in: Herbert Feis, 1933: *Characters in Crisis* (1966), J.M. Blum, ed. *From the Morgenthau Diaries 1: Years of Urgency, 1938-1940* (1965), I. Mintz *Deterioration of the Quality of Foreign Bonds Issued in the United States, 1920-1930* (1951), J. Nichols 'Roosevelt's Monetary Diplomacy in 1933' *American Historical Review* 56 (January 1951), U.S. Securities and Exchange Commission *Report on the ... Protective and Reorganization Committees Pursuant to Section 211 of the Securities Exchange Act of 1934* part 5: *Protective Committees and Agencies for Holders of Defaulted Bonds* (1937), E.B. Nixon, ed. *Franklin D. Roosevelt and Foreign Affairs* (3 vols. 1969), the annual reports of the FBPC and the bulletin of the Institute of International Finance contain useful data. Ellis Hawley provides an insightful analysis of business-government relations in *The New Deal and the Problem of Monopoly* (1966).

There is a growing body of literature on direct foreign investment in Latin America. Raymond Mikesell, ed. *Foreign Investments in Latin America* (1955) and M. Bernstein, ed. *Foreign Investment in Latin America* (1968) deal with the broader context.

Studies which examine the growth of the multinational corporation are Raymond Vernon *Sovereignty at Bay* (1971) and C.P. Kindleberger, ed. *The International Corporation* (1970). S. Hymer 'Direct Foreign Investment and the National Economic Interest' in Peter Russell, ed. *Nationalism in Canada* (1966) is a leftist critique with particular attention to Canada. Mira Wilkins *The Emergence of Multinational Enterprise* (1970) provides a fine examination of the pre-1914 period. The essays in Mikesell, ed. *Foreign Investment in the Petroleum and Mineral Industries* (1971) are suggestive of areas for further research. S. Wurfel *Foreign Enterprise in Colombia* (1965) is an examination of potential areas for foreign investment.

Several studies deal with the petroleum industry in a historical perspective. The official history of Standard Oil, New Jersey, especially the volume by George Gibb and Evelyn Knowlton, *A History of Standard Oil: The Resurgent Years, 1911-1927* (1956) and the sequel by H.M. Larson et al., *New Horizons, 1927-1950* (1971), is an excellent example of business history. Harold F. Williamson et al. *The American Petroleum Industry: The Age of Energy, 1899-1959* (1963) provides background material. Karl Gabriel 'The Gains to the Local Economy from the Foreign-Owned Primary Export Industry; The Case of Oil in Venezuela' (PHD dissertation, Harvard Graduate School of Business Administration 1967) discusses a dimension which warrants additional research. Gerald Nash *United States Oil Policy* (1968) and Edward A. Shaffer *The Oil Import Program of the United States* (1968) provide the domestic perspective for the petroleum industry's problems between the wars.

One of the most recent analyses of petroleum diplomacy is Michael Hogan 'Informal Entente: Public Policy and Private Management in Anglo-American Petroleum Affairs' *Business History Review* 48 (Summer 1974). Hogan's thesis of voluntarism and business-government cooperation is perceptive but not new. He also tends in my view to overstate the degree of international cooperation in Latin America, although the Colombian instance indicates that there was often more rivalry between foreign offices than between corporations. For the Colombian case see my 'International Corporation and American Foreign Policy: The United States and Colombian Petroleum, 1920–1940' *The Canadian Journal of History* 9 (August 1974) and 'The Barco Concession in Colombian-American Relations' (paper presented to the Organization of American Historians, Chicago 1973), subsequently published in *The Americas* 33 (July 1976).

Early statements of international rivalry are E.H. Davenport and Sidney Cook *The Oil Trusts and Anglo-American Relations* (1924), Louis Fischer *Oil Imperialism: The International Struggle for Petroleum* (1926), and Harvey O'Connor *World Crisis in Oil* (1962), who overstates the conspiratorial nature of the business-government relationship, as does Camilo Barcía Trelles *El Imperialismo del petróleo y la paz mundial* (1925). The best treatment of this question for the period immediately following the first world war is Joseph Tulchin *Aftermath of War*. Herbert Feis *Petroleum and American Foreign Policy* (1944) is an account by an historian and State Department official.

H.S. Klein 'American Oil Companies in Latin America: The Bolivian Experience' *Inter-American Economic Affairs* 18 (Autumn 1964), David Green *The Containment of Latin America*, R.F. Smith *The United States and Revolutionary Nationalism in Mexico*, E. David Cronon *Josephus Daniels in Mexico* (1960), and A. Pinelo *The Multinational Corporation as a Force in Latin American Politics* (1973) all provide comparative perspective on the petroleum question.

There is as yet no history of the Colombian petroleum industry, although some of the material in the Standard Oil history is useful. Félix Mendoza and Benjamín Alvarado *La Industria del petróleo en Colombia* (1939) is superficial. Eduardo Ospina-Racines *La economía del petróleo en Colombia* (2nd ed. 1947) is more valuable. J. Fred Rippy provides some early background in 'Colombia's Petroleum Laws' *Southwest Political and Social Science Quarterly* (Summer 1928) and 'The United States and Colombian Oil' *Foreign Policy Association Information Bulletin* 5 (3 April 1929). Jorge Villegas *Petróleo, oligárquico, e império* (1969) is polemical. Alfonso Ordóñez *Historical Resumé of the Tropical Oil*

Company's Concession (ESSO Inter-America records 1928), is useful as a supplement to the history of the parent company, as are several articles in the *Imperial Oil Review*. The Andian National Corporation defends its interests in an *Informe rendido ... al Ministro de Industrias* (1930); the result of the lengthy debate over Gulf Oil's Barco concession is Colombia, Ministerio de Industrias *Contrato Chaus-Folsom y documentos relacionados con ésta negociación* (1931); Gonzalo Buenahora *Huelga en Barranca* (1938) is a leftist account of strike action against Tropical Oil in the mid-1930s. Isaac Gutiérrez Navarro *La Luz de una vida* (1949) is the account of a participant in a 1927 Tropical Oil strike. Eugene Havens and M. Romieux *Barrancabermeja, conflictos sociales en torno a un centro petrolero* (1966) is a sociological analysis of life in the petroleum workers' town. Miguel Urrutia *The Development of the Colombian Labor Movement* provides a broader context for labor relations in the petroleum industry.

There is no history of the United Fruit Company in Colombia, although some of the general histories provide materials on the pre-1940 period. Stacy May and Galo Plaza The *United Fruit Company in Latin America* (1958) is an apology for the company. Charles Wilson *Empire in Green and Gold: The Story of the American Banana Trade* (1947) is very general. Critical analyses are to be found in Charles Kepner and J. Soothill *The Banana Empire* (1935) and *Social Aspects of the Banana Industry* (1936). Watt Stewart *Keith and Costa Rica* (1963) provides a biography of Minor C. Keith, one of the key figures in the development of railroads in Central America. The company's annual reports also provide information, largely of a statistical nature. Luis C. Ortiz 'El Ferrocarril de Santa Marta y las compañías imperialistas: La United Fruit Company y the Santa Marta Railway Co., Ltd.' *Acción Liberal* (December 1937) is a critical account of the monopoly held by the railroad in the banana zone. Further comment on the López administration is contained in J.V. Garcés Navas 'La Administración López y la industria bananera del Magdalena' *Acción Liberal* (August 1938).

Miguel Urrutia presents the most careful account of the 1928 strike against the company in *The Development of the Colombian Labor Movement*. Contemporary accounts are less reliable. Alberto Castrillón *120 Días bajo el terror militar* ... (1929) is an account by one of the strike leaders; equally unreliable is Carlos Cortés Vargas *Los sucesos de las bananeras* (1929), written by the head of the military government which took control of Magdalena when President Abadía declared martial law. More valuable is the report of the congressional commission sent to investigate conflicts between United Fruit and domestic growers: *Informe de la comisión* ... (1930). There is some discussion of the role of Jorge Gaitán in Antonio García *Gaitán y el problema de la revolución Colombiana* (1955).

Matthew Josephson *Empire of the Air: Juan Trippe and the Struggle for World Airways* (1944) is still a good account of the expansion of Pan American Airways.

Pan American currently has under way a history project which will be more satisfying. W.P. Newton 'International Aviation Rivalry in Latin America, 1919-1927' *Journal of Inter-American Studies* 7 (July 1965) and his forthcoming *The Perilous Skies* provide useful background on the development of SCADTA in Colombia and the diplomacy surrounding its competition with Pan American. Older, but still valuable, are O.J. Lissitzyn *International Air Transport and National Policy* (1942), W.A. Burden *The Struggle for Airways in Latin America* (1943), and 'Pan American Airways' *Fortune* 13 (April 1936). Herbert Boy, one of SCADTA's chief pilots, provides an interesting perspective in *Una Historia con alas* (1963). F.D. McCann Jr 'Aviation Diplomacy: The United States and Brazil, 1939-1941' *Inter-American Economic Affairs* 21 (Spring 1968) and his *The Brazilian-American Alliance in World War II, 1937-1945* (1973) provide a comparative perspective for the effort of the United States to eliminate the threat of SCADTA. Stetson Conn and Byron Fairchild *The Framework of Hemisphere Defense* (1960) is also useful in this regard. My own analysis of the Colombian context now tends to place greater emphasis on the strategic dimension than was the case with an earlier version, 'Inter-American Aviation Rivalry: The United States and Colombia, 1927-1940' *Journal of Inter-American Studies and World Affairs* (August 1972).

Index